MMEDIA 2019

The Eleventh International Conferences on Advances in Multimedia

March 24 - 28, 2019

Valencia, Spain

MMEDIA 2019 Editors

Ishikawa Hiroshi, Tokyo Metropolitan University, Japan

Printed from e-media with permission by:

Curran Associates, Inc.
57 Morehouse Lane
Red Hook, NY 12571

Printed by Curran Associates, Inc. (2019)

International Academy, Research, and Industry Association (IARIA)
412 Derby Way
Wilmington, DE 19810

Phone: (408) 893-6407
Fax: (408) 527-6351

petre@iaria.org

Additional copies of this publication are available from:

Curran Associates, Inc.
57 Morehouse Lane
Red Hook, NY 12571 USA
Phone: 845-758-0400
Fax: 845-758-2633
Email: curran@proceedings.com
Web: www.proceedings.com

Table of Contents

MMEDIA 2019

Forward

The Eleventh International Conference on Advances in Multimedia (MMEDIA 2019), held between March 24, 2019 and March 28, 2019 in Valencia, Spain, continued a series of events presenting recent research results on advances in multimedia, mobile and ubiquitous multimedia and to bring together experts from both academia and industry for the exchange of ideas and discussion on future challenges in multimedia fundamentals, mobile and ubiquitous multimedia, multimedia ontology, multimedia user-centered perception, multimedia services and applications, and mobile multimedia.

The rapid growth of information on the Web, its ubiquity and pervasiveness makes the www the biggest repository. While the volume of information may be useful, it creates new challenges for information retrieval, identification, understanding, selection, etc. Investigating new forms of platforms, tools, principles offered by Semantic Web opens another door to enable humans programs, or agents to understand what records are about, and allows integration between domain-dependent and media-dependent knowledge. Multimedia information has always been part of the Semantic Web paradigm, but requires substantial effort to integrate both.

The new technological achievements in terms of speed and the quality of expanding and creating a vast variety of multimedia services like voice, email, short messages, Internet access, m-commerce, to mobile video conferencing, streaming video and audio.

Large and specialized databases together with these technological achievements have brought true mobile multimedia experiences to mobile customers. Multimedia imply adoption of new technologies and challenges to operators and infrastructure builders in terms of ensuring fast and reliable services for improving the quality of web information retrieval.

Huge amounts of multimedia data are increasingly available. The knowledge of spatial and/or temporal phenomena becomes critical for many applications, which requires techniques for the processing, analysis, search, mining, and management of multimedia data.

We welcomed academic, research and industry contributions. The conference had the following tracks:

- Multimedia content-based retrieval and analysis
- Multimedia applications
- Social Big Data in Multimedia

We take here the opportunity to warmly thank all the members of the MMEDIA 2019 technical program committee, as well as all the reviewers. The creation of such a high quality conference program would not have been possible without their involvement. We also kindly thank all the authors who dedicated much of their time and effort to contribute to MMEDIA 2019. We truly believe that, thanks to all these efforts, the final conference program consisted of top quality contributions.

We also thank the members of the MMEDIA 2019 organizing committee for their help in handling the logistics and for their work that made this professional meeting a success.

We hope that MMEDIA 2019 was a successful international forum for the exchange of ideas and results between academia and industry and to promote further progress in the field of multimedia. We also hope that Valencia, Spain provided a pleasant environment during the conference and everyone saved some time to enjoy the historic charm of the city.

MMEDIA 2019 Chairs

MMEDIA Steering Committee
Jean-Claude Moissinac, TELECOM ParisTech, France
Daniel Thalmann, Nanyang Technological University, Singapore

MMEDIA Industry/Research Advisory Committee
Trista Chen, Trista Chen Consulting, USA
Alexander C. Loui, Kodak Alaris Inc., USA
Dimitrios Liparas, Information Technologies Institute (ITI) - Centre for Research & Technology Hellas (CERTH), Greece
Giuseppe Amato, CNR-ISTI, Italy

MMEDIA 2019 Special Tracks Chair
Jose Miguel Jimenez, University of Haute-Alsace, France // Universitat Politecnica de Valencia, Spain

MMEDIA 2019
Committee

MMEDIA Steering Committee

Jean-Claude Moissinac, TELECOM ParisTech, France
Daniel Thalmann, Nanyang Technological University, Singapore

MMEDIA Industry/Research Advisory Committee

Trista Chen, Trista Chen Consulting, USA
Alexander C. Loui, Kodak Alaris Inc., USA
Dimitrios Liparas, Information Technologies Institute (ITI) - Centre for Research & Technology Hellas (CERTH), Greece
Giuseppe Amato, CNR-ISTI, Italy

MMEDIA 2019 Special Tracks Chair

Jose Miguel Jimenez, University of Haute-Alsace, France // Universitat Politecnica de Valencia, Spain

MMEDIA 2019 Technical Program Committee

Vladimir Alexiev, Ontotext AD, Bulgaria
Giuseppe Amato, CNR-ISTI, Italy
Ramazan S. Aygun, University of Alabama in Huntsville, USA
Jenny Benois-Pineau, University of Bordeaux, France
Fernando Boronat Seguí, Universitat Politecnica de Valencia, Spain
Pierre Boulanger, University of Alberta, Canada
Dumitru Dan Burdescu, University of Craiova, Romania
Nicola Capuano, University of Salerno, Italy
Shannon Chen, Facebook, USA
Trista Chen, Trista Chen Consulting, USA
Luis A. da Silva Cruz, University of Coimbra, Portugal
Maaike de Boer, TNO, Netherlands
Jana Dittmann, Otto-von-Guericke-University Magdeburg, Germany
Vlastislav Dohnal, Masaryk University, Czech Republic
Magda El Zarki, UC Irvine, USA
Marcio Ferreira Moreno, IBM Research, Brazil
Daniela Giorgi, Institute of Information Science and Technology - National Research Council of Italy, Italy
Nikolaos Gkalelis, Information Technologies Institute - Centre for Research and Technology Hellas, Greece
William Grosky, University of Michigan-Dearborn, USA
Jung Hyun Han, Korea University, Korea
Masaharu Hirota, Okayama University of Science, Japan

Shigang Yue, University of Lincoln, UK
Sherali Zeadally, University of Kentucky, USA
Pavel Zemcik, Brno University of Technology, Czech Republic
Ligang Zhang, Centre for Intelligent Systems - Central Queensland University, Brisbane, Australia

Regional Analysis Based on Location Information and Time Series Change Using Geotagged Tweets

Masaki Endo, Shigeyoshi Ohno
Division of Core Manufacturing
Polytechnic University
Kodaira-shi, Tokyo
e-mail: endou@uitec.ac.jp, ohno@uitec.ac.jp

Masaharu Hirota
Faculty of Informatics
Okayama University of Science
Okayama-shi, Tokyo
e-mail: hirota@mis.ous.ac.jp

Tetsuya Araki, Hiroshi Ishikawa
Graduate School of Systems Design
Tokyo Metropolitan University
Hino-shi, Tokyo
e-mail: araki@tmu.ac.jp, ishikawa-hiroshi@tmu.ac.jp

***Abstract*—Because of the popularization of Social Networking Services (SNSs), it is possible to acquire large amounts of data in real time. For this reason, various studies are being conducted to analyze social media data and to extract real-world events. Among them, a salient advantage of analysis using positional information is that one can accurately extract events from target areas of interest. However, data having position information in social media data remain few: the data amount might be insufficient for analysis. Therefore, we are assessing a method for real-time analysis using data with location information that has been accumulated over a certain period of time. In this research, we are studying a method of regional analysis by position information and time series change using tweets with Twitter position information. Herein, we explain the results obtained from area analysis using the proposed method.**

Keywords-location information; time series; Twitter.

I. INTRODUCTION

In our everyday life, because of the wide dissemination and rapid performance improvement of various devices such as smartphones and tablets, diverse and vast data are generated on the web. SNSs have become especially popular because users can post data and various messages easily. Twitter [1], an SNS that provides a micro-blogging service, is used as a real-time communication tool. Numerous tweets have been posted daily by vast numbers of users. Twitter is therefore a useful medium to obtain, from a large amount of information posted by many users, real-time information corresponding to the real world.

By analyzing the information sent by these SNSs, the possibility exists of obtaining useful information in real time. We are conducting research related to providing tourist information to travelers. Therefore, this study specifically examines the provision of real-time sightseeing information.

Herein, we describe the provision of information to tourists using web contents. Such information is useful for tourists, but providing timely and topical travel information entails high costs for information providers because they must update the information continually. Today, providing reliable information related to local travel is not only strongly demanded by tourists, but also by local governments, tourism organizations, and travel companies, which bear high costs of providing such information.

For that reason, providing current, useful, real-world information for travelers by ascertaining changes of information according to seasons and time zones of the tourism region is important for the travel industry. It is possible to disseminate information using the popular SNS, but organizations that can actually do the work are limited by human resources and cost. Therefore, analysis using an SNS that can provide useful data leading to real-time information provision is one means of overcoming this difficulty.

To solve this problem, much research to analyze SNS data is currently being conducted. Research using Twitter is one branch of investigation. Because tweets comprise short sentences, a location can be estimated if a tweet includes the place name and the facility name, but if such information is not included, identifying the location from a tweet might be difficult. For this reason, research using tweets with location information or tweets which give location information in the tweet itself is being conducted. Because geotagged tweets can identify places, they are effective for analysis. Nevertheless, few geo-tagged tweets exist among the total information content of tweets. It is therefore not possible to analyze all regions. For that reason, we also use geotagged tweets to conduct research using information interpolation to estimate the position around the area that is not specified by the position information [2].

Currently, we are considering a method for real-time analysis by collecting temporal and spatial information for a certain period of time using only geotagged tweets, which are said to have a small amount of information. This report presents an experimental approach.

The remainder of the paper is organized as follows. Section II presents earlier research related to this topic. In Section III, we propose a method for real-time analysis using data collected for a certain period. Section IV describes experimentally obtained results for our proposed method and a discussion of the results. Section V presents a summary of the contributions and expectations for future work.

II. RELATED WORK

Various studies are being conducted using SNS position information. Omori et al. [3] proposed a method to extract geographical features such as coastlines using tags of photo sharing sites with geotags. Sakaki et al. [4] proposed a method to detect events, such as earthquakes and typhoons based on a study estimating real-time events from Twitter. By analyzing the Twitter text stream, Pratap et al. [5] proposed a solution to optimize traffic control by considering previous traffic analysis methodology and social data in real time. Various analytical methods have been proposed for analyzing SNS using position information and time series information. However, analysis of data in which large amounts of position information and time series information exist is mainly addressed. Few research efforts examine information using only a few data.

Some research has examined visualization. Nakaji et al. [6] proposed using a geotagged and visual feature of a photograph and suggested a way to select photographs related to a given real event from geotagged tweets. They developed a system that can visualize real-world events on online maps. In the GeoNLP Project [7], we are developing a geotagging system that extracts location descriptions such as place names and addresses contained in natural language sentences. The system provides metadata about where the sentences are descriptions. It is also offered as open source software. These studies are very useful for extraction of specific designated events and for analysis of preregistered places. However, another discussion must be held about automatically extracting events and identifying new places.

As described above, conducting research using geotagged tweets for places with small information amounts and new events and places represents a new approach. Therefore, this research was conducted to identify events and places in real time using accumulation of information and differences in space-time space.

III. OUR PROPOSED METHOD

This section presents a description of a method for target data collection using our method of real-time analysis with position information and time series information.

A. Data collection

Here, we explain the data collection target for this research. Geotagged tweets sent from Twitter are the collection target. The range of geotagged tweets includes the Japanese archipelago (120.0° E ≤ longitude ≤ 154.0° E and 20.0° N ≤ latitude ≤ 47.0° N) as the collection target. Collection of these data was done using a streaming Application Programming Interface (API) [8] provided by Twitter Inc.

Next, we describe the number of collected data. According to a report by Hashimoto et al. [9], among all tweets originating in Japan, only about 0.18% are geotagged tweets: they are rare among all data. However, the collected geotagged tweets number about 70,000, even on weekdays. On some weekend days, more than 100,000 such messages are posted. We use about 423 million geotagged tweets from 2015/2/17 through 2018/12/26. Therefore, we examined 19 million geotagged tweets in Tokyo for these analyses.

B. Preprocessing

This section presents preprocessing after data collection. Preprocessing includes reverse geocoding and morphological analysis, with database storage for data collected using the process.

Reverse geocoding identified prefectures and municipalities by town name using latitude and longitude information from the individually collected tweets. We use a simple reverse geocoding service [10] available from the National Agriculture and Food Research Organization in this process: e.g., (latitude, longitude) = (35.7384446N, 139.460910W) by reverse geocoding becomes (Tokyo, Kodaira-Shi, Ogawanishi-machi 2-chome). In addition, based on latitude and longitude information of the collected tweets, data are accumulated by the same place. As data accumulate, the data are saved in mesh form as time elapses.

Morphological analysis divides the collected geo-tagged tweet morphemes. We use the “Mecab” morphological analyzer [11]. As an example, “桜は美しいです” (“Cherry blossoms are beautiful.” in English) is divisible into "(桜 / noun), (は / particle), (美しい / adjective), (です / auxiliary verb), (。 / symbol)".

Preprocessing performs the necessary data storage from the result of data collection, reverse geocoding, and morphological analysis processing. Data used for this study are the tweet ID, tweet posting time, tweet text, morpheme analysis result, latitude, and longitude.

C. Analysis method

This section presents a description of the method of real-time analysis using position information and time series information.

The analytical method we proposed has the following three stages.

1. Extraction of places by fixed point observation
2. Analysis considering the time series based on 1
3. Analysis using co-occurring words of 2

Therein, 1 is an estimate of the location derived from stationary observation. At such spots, even in places with few tweets, one can discover the location through long-term observation. This method does spot extraction by adding geotagged tweets including specific keywords for long periods at every latitude and longitude.

As presented above, 2 is a method of extracting new spots using spot information accumulated over a long period as a baseline, by consideration of the time series and finding differences.

As shown above, 3, time series analysis including co-occurrence words in 2 and for keywords used in 1 is performed using the results of morphological analysis of tweets. It is a method used because differences in latitude, longitude, and time series alone might be insufficient to extract differences in data.

Through analyses using these proposed methods, we aim to capture real-time changes in specific areas.

IV. EXPERIMENTS

This section presents a description of a real-time analysis experiment using the method proposed in Section III.

A. Dataset

Datasets used for this experiment were collected using streaming API, as described for data collection in Section III-A. Data are geo-tagged tweets from Tokyo during 2015/2/17 – 2018/12/26. The data include about 19 million items. We use these datasets for experiments to conduct the three methods proposed in Section III.

B. Experimental method

In this section, experiments using the proposed method shown in Section III are described in 1 to 3.

1. Extraction of places by fixed point observation

   This experiment was conducted for Takao-machi, Hachioji, Tokyo: an area of about 4 km east–west and about 2.5 km north–south, as shown in Figure 1. Experimentally obtained results described later are included within the thick frame depicted in Figure 1. For this area, we conducted an extraction experiment with the target word as "cherry blossom" in Japanese as "桜", "さくら", or "サクラ". In all, 65 tweets were found to include a target word.

2. Analysis in considering of time series based on 1

   This experiment was conducted for 4-chome, Myojin-cho, Hachioji city, Tokyo: an area of about 700 m east–west, and about 600 m north–south, as shown in Figure 2. Experimentally obtained results described later are included within the thick frame in Figure 2. For this area, we conduct an extraction experiment with the target word as "ramen" in Japanese as "ラーメン", "らーめん", or "拉麺". In all, 301 tweets were found to include a target word.

3. Analysis using co-occurring words of 2

   This experiment was conducted for Marunouchi 1-chome, Chiyoda-ku, Tokyo: an area of about 1 km east–west and about 1 km north–south, as shown in Figure 3. Experimentally obtained results described later are included within the thick frame in Figure 3. For this area, we set the target word as "ramen", as in the second experiment, in Japanese as "ラーメン", "らーめん", or "拉麺". In all, 6,979 tweets included a target word. As words co-

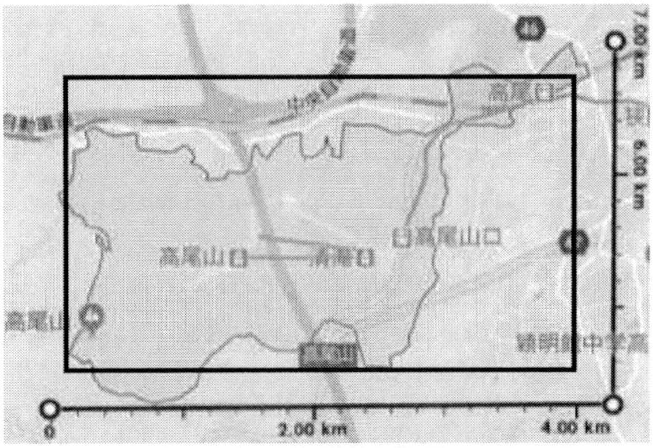

Figure 1. Target of Takao-machi, Hachioji City.

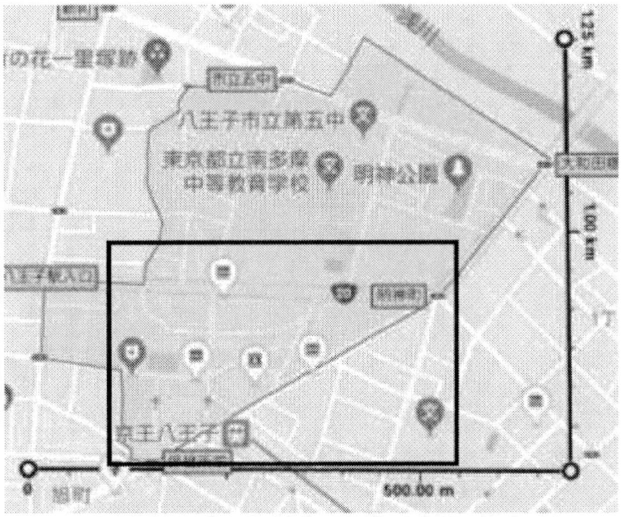

Figure 2. Target of Myojin-cho 4-chome, Hachioji City.

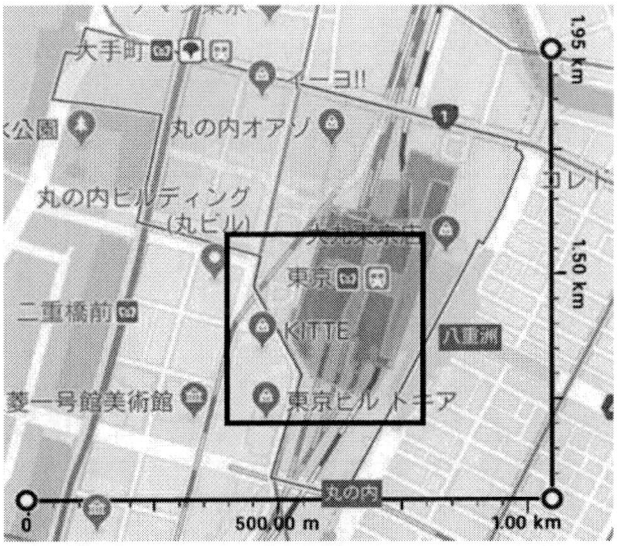

Figure 3. Target area of Marunouchi 1-chome, Chiyoda-ku.

occurring after the object, we target tweets including "㐂蔵" and "玉", which represents the ramen shop name; the respective numbers of tweets were 273 and 31.

C. Experimental result

In this section, the results of 1–3 experiments explained in the previous section are presented.

1. Extraction of places by fixed point observation

   The distributions of geotagged tweets in Takao-machi, Hachioji City including cherry blossoms obtained in the experiment are shown in Figure 4 in 2017 and in Figure 5 in 2018. The interior are of the bold frame in Figure 1 is shown in the table. It is about 265 m measured east–west and about 85 m measured north–south. The closer the color of the cell is to black, the more data are shown.

   Data extracted for this experiment were very few: 65 for the entire collection period. However, in 2017 and 2018, we confirmed tweets to JR Takao Station, Takao Yamaguchi Station, Takao Station of Ropeway, and Takao Mountain. The correlation coefficient between the extracted spots in 2017 and 2018 was 0.769: high positive correlation was found. Extraction of spots is possible even with few data. Moreover, various spots can be extracted when using longer periods. Therefore, fixed point extraction of sightseeing spots is regarded as possible through continuing observation of geotagged tweets.

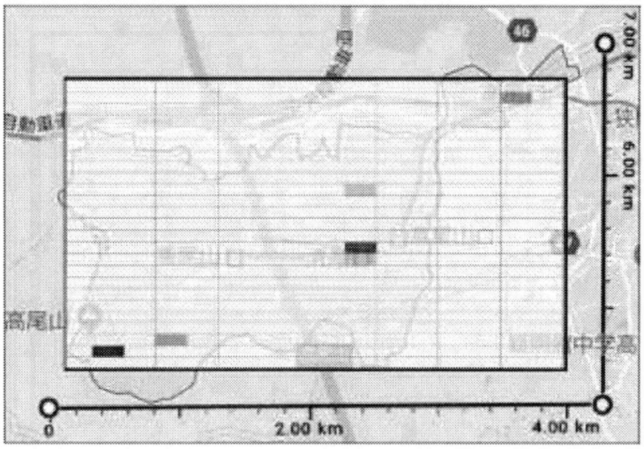

Figure 4. Number of Tweets including Target Words in Takao-machi in 2017.

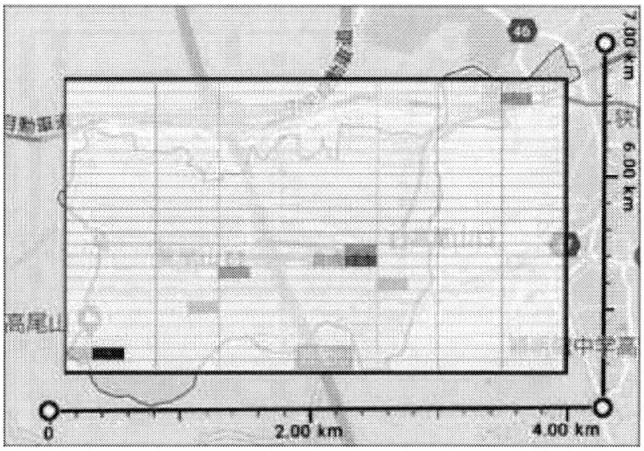

Figure 5. Number of Tweets including Target Words in Takao-machi in 2018.

2. Analysis in considering of time series based on 1

   The results for distribution of the geotagged tweets of Myojin-cho 4-chome, Hachioji City including the ramen obtained in the experiment are shown in Figure 6 in 2016, Figure 7 in 2017, and Figure 8 in 2018. The area inside of the bold frame in Figure 2 is shown in the table. It is about 102 m measured east–west and about 39 m north–south. The closer the color of the cell is to black, the more data are shown.

   In this experiment, 301 data were extracted in all collection periods. The target area has three ramen shops, which can be extracted from the table of each year. Furthermore, in 2018, a new ramen shop opened at one point; in 2018 we extracted a new spot (latitude, longitude) = (35.69540009399, 139.345001221). For this reason, the correlation coefficient between data of 2016 and 2017 was 0.991, a high positive correlation was obtained. Nevertheless, the correlation coefficient between 2017 and 2018 was only a weak positive correlation of 0.161. These results demonstrated the possibility of extracting new spots by fixed point observation.

3. Analysis using co-occurring words of 2

   Distributions of geotagged tweets of Chiyoda-ku including Ramen obtained in the experiment are shown in Figure 9 for 2017 and Figure 10 for 2018. The interior area of the bold frame in Figure 3 is shown in the table. It is about 80 m measured east–west and about 25 m north–south. The closer the color of the cell is to black, the more data are shown.

   The data extracted in this experiment were 6,979 in all collection periods. The area of about 540 m east–west and about 540 m north–south in the frame of the heavy line in Figure 3 is a spot called Tokyo Ramen Street, with eight ramen shops. Therefore, as an analytical example using words co-occurring in the target word, Figure 9 and Figure 10 are experimentally obtained results including A="㐂蔵" co-occurring in the target word and B = "玉".

   The ramen shop including A opened in September 2013 and closed in September 2018. The ramen shop including B opened on October 30, 2018.

   Therefore, although a difference exists in the number of data, it can be extracted as a spot. However, the closed A information is unsuitable for use as real-time information. The results of analysis considering the time series information are shown in Figure 11. From these results, tweets containing A are not extracted after 2018/9. However, tweets containing B have been extracted since 2018/10. Therefore, by considering the time series in addition to latitude and longitude information, one can omit the old information in addition to extracting new spots. This result confirmed the possibility of realizing real-time information extraction.

Figure 6. Number of Tweets including Target Words in Myojin-cho in 2016.

Figure 7. Number of Tweets including Target Words in Myojin-cho in 2017.

Figure 8. Number of Tweets including Target Words in Myojin-cho in 2018.

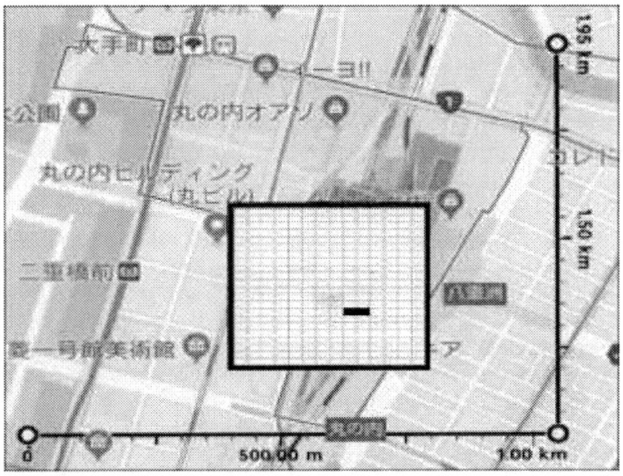

Figure 9. Number of Tweets including "A" Co-occurring in Target Words in Marunouchi 1-chome.

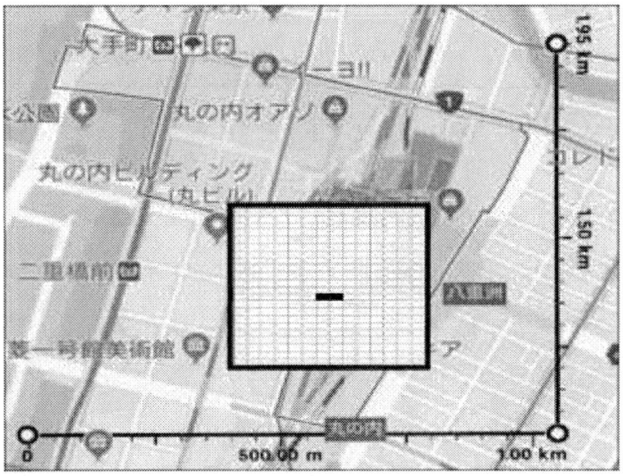

Figure 10. Number of Tweets including "B" Co-occurring in Target Words in Marunouchi 1-chome.

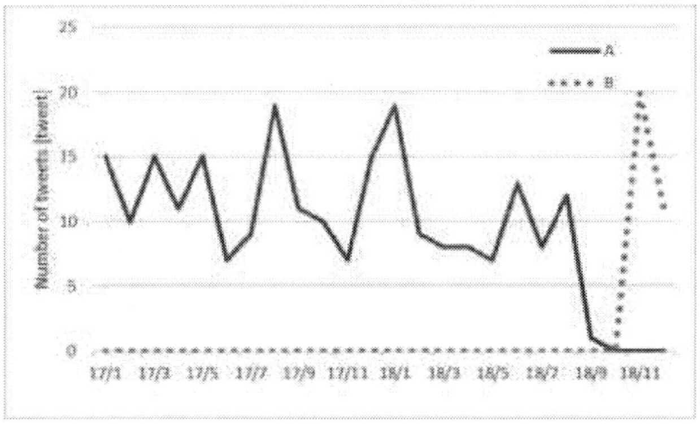

Figure 11. Trends in number of tweets including target words.

V. Conclusion

As described in this paper, we evaluated a regional analysis method based on positional information and time series change using tweets with Twitter location information to provide real-time information.

To conduct real-time regional analysis, after proposing a method using geotagged tweets' position information and time series information, we showed experimentally obtained results obtained using that method. Experiment results demonstrated that, even when geotagged tweets were few, spots could be extracted using position information with long-term accumulation. We also confirmed that new spots can be extracted by conducting time series analysis of spot information of position information. Furthermore, using morphological analysis results of tweets, we demonstrated the possibility of analyzing spots, even in densely populated areas with a large amount of information.

Results show that we demonstrated the usefulness of SNS for providing real-time information. Future studies will examine other methods using machine learning to establish even more effective methods.

Acknowledgment

This work was supported by JSPS KAKENHI Grants No. 18K13254, 16K00157, and 16K16158, and a Tokyo Metropolitan University Grant-in-Aid for Research on Priority Areas "Research on social big data."

References

[1] Twitter. *It's what's happening.* [Online]. Available from: https://Twitter.com/ 2015.02.15

[2] M. Endo, S. Ohno, M. Hirota, D. Kato, and H. Ishikawa, "Examination of Best-time Estimation for Each Tourist Spots by Interlinking using Geotagged Tweets," International Journal on Advanced in Systems and Measurements (IARIA), vol. 10, No 3&4, pp. 163-173, 2018.

[3] M. Omori, M. Hirota, H. Ishikawa, and S. Yokoyama, "Can geo-tags on flickr draw coastlines?," In Proceedings of the 22nd ACM SIGSPATIAL International Conference on Advances in Geographic Information Systems (SIGSPATIAL '14). ACM, pp. 425-428, 2014.

[4] T. Sakaki, M. Okazaki, and Y. Matsuo, "Earthquake shakes Twitter users: real-time event detection by social sensors," WW W 2010, pp. 851–860, 2010.

[5] A. R. Pratap, J. V. D. Prasad, K. P. Kumar, and S. Babu, "An investigation on optimizing traffic flow based on Twitter Data Analysis," 2018 Second International Conference on Inventive Communication and Computational Technologies (ICICCT), pp. 320-325, 2018.

[6] Y. Nakaji and K. Yanai, "Visualization of Real-World Events with Geotagged Tweet Photos," 2012 IEEE International Conference on Multimedia and Expo Workshops, pp. 272-277, 2012.

[7] GeoNLP Project. *A place name information processing system which maps sentences automatically.* [Online] Available from: https://geonlp.ex.nii.ac.jp/ 2019.02.14

[8] Twitter Developers. *Twitter Developer official site.* [Online] Available from: https://dev.twitter.com/ 2015.02.15

[9] Y. Hashimoto and M. Oka, "Statistics of Geo-Tagged Tweets in Urban Areas (<Special Issue>Synthesis and Analysis of Massive Data Flow)," JSAI, vol. 27, No. 4, pp. 424–431, 2012 (in Japanese).

[10] National Agriculture and Food Research Organization. *Simple reverse geocoding service.* [Online]. Available from: http://www.finds.jp/wsdocs/rgeocode/index.html.ja 2015.04.10

[11] MeCab. *Yet Another Part-of-Speech and Morphological Analyzer.* [Online]. Available from: http://mecab.googlecode.com/svn/trunk/mecab/doc/index.htm l 2015.04.15

Identifying Obscure Venues Using Classification of User Reviews

Masaharu Hirota
Department of Information Science
Faculty of Informatics
Okayama University of Science
Okayama-shi, Okayama
Email: hirota@mis.ous.ac.jp

Masaki Endo
Division of Core Manufacturing
Polytechnic University
Kodaira-shi, Tokyo
Email: endou@uitec.ac.jp

Hiroshi Ishikawa
Graduate School of Systems Design
Faculty of System Design
Tokyo Metropolitan University
Hino-shi, Tokyo
Email: ishikawa-hiroshi@tmu.ac.jp

Abstract—**Today, tourism occupies an essential position in many countries as a critical industry. When sightseeing, many people visit different places such as restaurants, hotels, and tourist spots. Some of these venues, while worthwhile, are considered obscure, secret, not well-known, or having little popularity. Their extraction and recommendation are vital to improving the satisfaction of tourists. Although some studies have been proposed on extracting obscure venues based on their degree of popularity, the interest in such venues varies from person to person. In addition, these studies have defined what constitutes an obscure venue and use such criteria for venue extraction. This study proposes a method for discovering obscure venues using classifiers for identifying reviews, including obscure impressions. To achieve this goal, in this study, a model was developed to classify venues as obscure or not obscure using reviews with language indicating their obscurity. This study also analyzes the differences among venues perceived by reviewers as being obscure. We demonstrate the performance of the proposed approach by indicating that the posting destination of obscure reviews differs for each user.**

Keywords–Tourism information; Text classification; Support Vector Machine;Review Analysis.

I. Introduction

In recent years, it has become commonplace for many people to give their opinions and impressions regarding several types of venues, such as tourist spots, hotels, and restaurants, on review websites such as Yelp [1], Expedia [2], and TripAdvisor [3]. In this paper, we call such spots venues. Reviews written about venues describe information regarding the venues themselves and the impressions and behaviors of the users. Such reviews are useful for travel planning, obtaining information on travel destinations, tourist behavior, and visitor impressions of popular tourist spots. Therefore, some studies have extracted tourism information from user-provided reviews [4][5].

Some venues are obscure, secret, or not well-known. Despite not being popular, such venues may be well-regarded by visitors. Because some obscure venues can lead to improved tourist satisfaction and the acquisition of repeat visitors, some methods for describing obscure venues and recommending them to tourists have been proposed [6][7]. Definitions regarding obscure venues have been proposed in such studies. Studies on this subject commonly define an obscure venue as one in which the visibility for tourists is low but the value is high. For example, the authors in [6] defined obscure spots as less known, but still worth visiting, and extracted such spots. Also, [8] extracted hidden tourist spots with low popularity but a high level of satisfaction. However, precisely identifying obscure venues is difficult because the places that people feel are obscure depends on their own personality.

In this research, we identify obscure venues from review sites, and the proposed approach focuses on words in the text of the venue reviews. This study then extracts obscure reviews without directly giving a definition of obscure to accommodate the fact that the impression of a venue differs among different people. For this study, we regard a venue with many reviews written about the impression of its obscurity as an obscure venue (hereinafter referred to as "obscure review").

This study extracted such reviews from all reviews on a particular venue. In this paper, a review is defined as an obscure review if its text contains terms related to "obscure" (hereinafter referred to as "obscure words"). If the ratio of reviews of a venue that includes obscure words accounts for the majority, the venue is defined as obscure.

Although the aim of this research is the identification of obscure venues using user-provided reviews that include obscure words, in most cases the number of reviews on a venue is small, and customers might frequently visit there. Because an obscure venue might be less well-known by people even if worthwhile, there will be few reviews for such venues. In addition, few reviews obtain obscure words. As a result, the number of reviews to be classified as obscure is insufficient for identification of obscure venues. Moreover, it is unrealistic to define all expressions related to the word obscure. Therefore, to extract obscure reviews that do not include obscure words but rather the description of an obscure venue, this study applies the development of a classification model of the representation of contents of a review as obscure or not, regardless of whether a review contains an obscure word. Reviews that do not contain obscure words were classified using the model, and the classifier was evaluated using a dataset of reviews submitted by users.

Moreover, different reviewers have posted various reviews on different venues, and the criteria by which a venue is considered obscure differs according to the reviewer. Therefore, this research revealed that the reviewer who posts an obscure review for each venue is different. As a result, this study examined the efficiency of the proposed approach in identifying obscure venues using the obscure-word based classifier without a direct definition of the term obscure.

A summary of contributions from this study is as follows.

- We design a new approach for identifying obscure venues using user-provided venues.
- We propose a classifier for identifying obscure reviews without the word review or obscure words.
- We analyze the posting destination of obscure review differently for each user.

The remainder of this paper is organized as follows. Section

II presents previous studies related to this topic. Section III describes our proposed method for the development of a classifier for discovering obscure reviews by using obscure words and the identification of obscure venues. Section IV describes the experiments evaluating our proposed method using the Yelp dataset and an analysis of the hypothesis that an obscure venue is perceived differently for each user. Section V provides some concluding remarks along with a discussion of results and areas of future work.

II. Related Works

The main aim of our research was to find obscure venues for tourism analysis using user-provided reviews posted to social media sites. This section introduces the related studies published in the area of analysis of tourism information using reviews and extracting obscure venues.

A. *Analysis for tourism using reviews*

Research has been conducted on the extraction of tourism information through user-generated content on social media sites. In addition, extracting helpful or useful information from text data like reviews and blogs is one of the research tools used to analyze reviews. Our proposed research on extracting obscure venues from reviews is related to the analysis of reviews for recommendation and the analysis of tourism information.

[9] analyzed factors affecting the perceived usefulness of reviews to findings contributing to tourism marketers. [10] predicted where memorable is the travel destination using the user-generated photographs in blogs. [11] proposed a method for identifying dimensions of satisfaction using an unsupervised learning algorithm with numerical and textual information from user-generated online reviews, and analyzed the multiple factors contributing to consumer satisfaction. [12] predicted how helpful a review is and presented a list of ranked reviews based on an evaluation. [13] proposed a method for detecting reviews that reliably predict foodborne illnesses using review classification. [14] proposed a method for detecting the topic of phrases in helpful recommending reviews. [15] proposed a method for aspect-based opinion mining of tourism reviews to classify them into negative or positive aspects. [16] proposed an approach for sentiment classification of online hotel booking opinions using a dependency tree structure.

These studies analyzed user-provided reviews on social media sites for improving sightseeing satisfaction. This paper tackles the analysis of user perception of obscure venues based on reviews.

B. *Extracting obscure venues from social media sites*

Studies have been conducted on extracting obscure venues and tourist spots from social media sites. Because obscure spots are expected to spread tourists to other tourist spots and improve the satisfaction of the tourism experience, some studies extracting posts on such spots have been conducted.

[6] proposed a method for evaluating sightseeing spots that are less well-known but are worth visiting. [7] defined the term obscure to indicate spots that are not famous but have high evaluations, and extracted such spots based on name recognition and user evaluations. [8] proposed a method for providing tourism information of hidden spots for increasing tourism satisfaction. [17] extracted hot and cold spots based on a spatial analysis of user-generated content to extract knowledge of tourist behaviors.

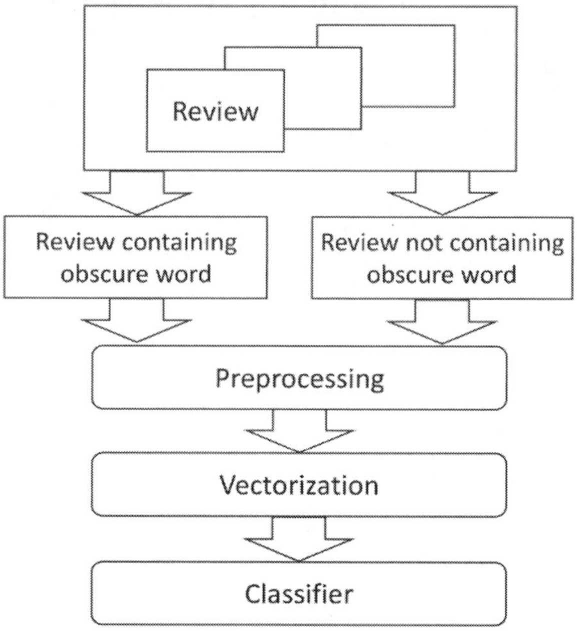

Figure 1. Overview of classifier for extracting obscure reviews using obscure words.

TABLE I. OBSCURE WORDS.

secret grate spot	secret grate place
kept secret place	kept secret spot
little known hot	spot secret spot
little known hot place	best kept secret
secret place	

This research used a classifier to extract obscure venues using reviews that include the word obscure to comprehensively deal with familiarity and user interest. The main characteristic of this research is the extraction of sightseeing spots recognized by reviewers as obscure venues.

III. Proposed Method

In this section, we describe our proposed method for discovering obscure venues based on user reviews.

This study extracted reviews including obscure words from the Yelp website and generated a classifier for both obscure and non-obscure reviews. We demonstrate an overview of our proposed classifier in Figure 1. First, we extract obscure and non-obscure reviews from the training dataset. Next, we apply preprocessing and a vectorization method. Finally, we create a model of the classifier using a vector to classify a review as obscure or not.

After this process, the classifier is applied to all reviews on a venue, and the venue is classified as obscure or non-obscure based on the reviews classified as obscure.

A. *Obscure words*

This section explains obscure words for extracting obscure reviews. In this research, obscure words are used to identify obscure venues from all reviews in a venue. This study defined nine obscure words, as shown in Table I. The criterion for selecting obscure words is to select an English phrase manually that seems to represent a word indicating obscurity, and not an expression that has no meaning other than obscurity. Because these words do not cover all words expressing user perceptions of obscurity, we conduct supervised learning using reviews including these words.

B. Preprocessing

This section describes the preprocessing applied to vectorize the reviews for machine learning. First, reviews written in English were extracted from all reviews. The texts from the extracted reviews were converted into lower-case texts. Next, we apply stop-word elimination and stemming to each word. This study defined 319 stop words, such as "the" and "and," which are commonly used in sentences.

C. Vectorization

Next, the preprocessed reviews were vectorized. First, Term Frequency (TF) and Inverse Document Frequency (IDF) were applied to the texts for determining what words in reviews might be more efficient for extracting obscure reviews. In this paper, we calculated the TFIDF of each word t in review r. The term frequency $tf(t, d)$ and inverse document frequency $idf(t, D)$ are calculated using the follow equations:

$$tf(t, r) = \frac{f_{t,r}}{\sum_{t \in r} f_{t,r}} \tag{1}$$

$$idf(t, R) = \log \frac{|R|}{|\{r \in R : t \in r\}|} \tag{2}$$

where the number of reviews is $|R|$, and $f_{t,r}$ is the number of occurrences of word t in review r.

Then, the TFIDF of each word t in review r in reviews R is calculated through the following equation:

$$tfidf(t, r, R) = tf(t, r) \times idf(t, r) \tag{3}$$

Next, to decrease the number of dimensions, a Principal Component Analysis (PCA) was conducted [18]. This process resulted in a feature vector of each review.

D. Classification of obscure reviews

In this section, we describe the procedure for generating a classification model of reviews regardless of whether they are obscure reviews. Our method proposed in this study identifies obscure venues using obscure reviews even if the review does not include obscure words. Therefore, our proposed method creates a classifier for identifying such reviews that do not include obscure words but when their content represents an obscure venue.

A method is proposed to classify the reviews into obscure or non-obscure reviews. In this research, we apply a binary classification method using vectors generated as described in Section III-C. The first class is thus obscure reviews, which consists of reviews that contain an obscure word. The other class is non-obscure reviews, which consists of reviews that do not contain an obscure word. This study used a binary classification Support Vector Machine (SVM) [19] to classify reviews as obscure or not obscure.

E. Identification of obscure venue

Herein, we describe how to find obscure venues using a classifier. Figure 2 shows an overview of the procedure for identification of an obscure venue. We collect all review texts of a venue and apply the classifier described in Section III-D to the reviews. Finally, we count the reviews classified as obscure or non-obscure reviews of a venue. As a result, this study regards an obscure venue as one in which the percentage of obscure venues is greater than the threshold. In this paper, when the ratio of reviews classified as obscure among all reviews on a venue is larger than half, the venue is considered obscure, otherwise it is non-obscure.

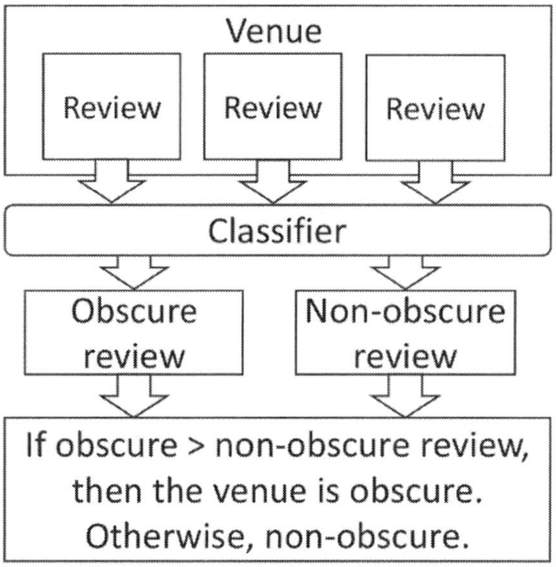

Figure 2. Overview of procedure for identification of obscure venues using obscure and non-obscure reviews.

IV. EXPERIMENTS

In this paper, we evaluate the performance of our proposed method through an evaluation experiment based on classification. First, we describe the experimental conditions of the dataset and the evaluation criteria. Next, we describe our experiments conducted for an evaluation of obscure review discovery. Finally, we evaluate and discuss the differences in which each reviewer evaluates a venue as obscure or not. In addition, we used the Python software scikit-learn [20] for implementation of the SVM, PCA, TFIDF, and evaluation criteria in the following experiments.

A. Dataset

Herein, we describe the dataset used for this experiment, namely, the Yelp Dataset Challenge (round 9) [21], which includes 144,072 venues and 4,153,150 reviews. This study comprises 1,978 reviews that mention an obscure word at least once.

B. Experimental conditions

This section describes the procedure used for the creation of classifiers for obscure reviews. The training data for the SVM includes 140 reviews that present an obscure word and are proven to be about an obscure venue, and 1,000 reviews that do not include an obscure word.

This experiment used a Gaussian kernel for the SVM kernel function. In addition, the hyperparameters of the SVM were searched through a grid search with five cross-validations, using parameters with the highest F-values measured through this experiment. The number of dimensions found through the PCA was 100.

TABLE II. CLASSIFICATION RESULTS OF OBSCURE REVIEWS.

	Precision	Recall	F-value	Accuracy
Obscure review	0.92	0.73	0.81	0.98
Non-obscure review	0.96	0.99	0.98	
Average	0.95	0.96	0.95	

TABLE III. TOP-10 OF VENUE WITH A HIGH PERCENTAGE OF OBSCURE REVIEWS.

Venue	Obscure reviews	All reviews	Percentage
Fashion 1	4	5	0.80
Restaurants 1	4	5	0.80
Fitness & Instruction1	4	5	0.80
Health & Medical 1	4	5	0.80
Shopping 1	4	5	0.80
Restaurants 2	4	5	0.80
Home Services 1	3	4	0.75
Shopping 2	3	4	0.75
Beauty & Spas 1	3	4	0.75
Restaurants 3	3	4	0.75

In this paper, four evaluation criteria were used for the classification performance: accuracy, precision, recall, and F-value.

C. Classification result of obscure reviews

In this section, we describe and discuss the evaluation results of classifying reviews into obscure or non-obscure reviews. Table II shows the evaluation results of the classification of obscure reviews through the procedure described above. In Table II, "Obscure review" shows the reviews that include an obscure word, whereas "Non-obscure review" shows reviews that do not include an obscure word. Comparing the results shown in Table II for obscure and non-obscure reviews, the evaluation scores of the non-obscure reviews are lower than those of the obscure reviews. In particular, there is a vast difference between both scores regarding the recall rate. The evaluation score is achieved because reviews with an obscure word are misclassified as non-obscure in certain cases because the number of reviews in the training dataset is unbalanced. However, the purpose of this research is to identify obscure venues using extracted obscure reviews. As shown in Table II, the precision of the obscure reviews was 0.92, which shows that it is rare for a classifier to misclassify the content of reviews unrelated to obscurity. With the following, we worked on finding obscure venues through this classifier.

D. Classification results of obscure venue

This section describes and discusses the evaluation results of discovering an obscure venue using a classifier. In this experiment, we apply the classifier to all reviews of a venue and calculate the percentage of reviews classified as obscure.

Table III shows the results of the top-10 venues with a high percentage of reviews classified as obscure. The terms "Obscure reviews" and "All reviews" present the number of obscure reviews and all reviews of a venue. In addition, the name of the venue is anonymous, and is represented by the category name in Yelp and a serial number.

In Table III, we confirm the reviews posted on each venue manually. As a result, those reviews include many phrases of "I knew for the first time," "It was hard to access, but the service was good," and so. These phrases seem to be related to obscurity. Therefore, we believe that our method discovers venues that people have evaluated as obscure.

TABLE IV. PERCENTAGE OF DIFFERENCES IN REVIEWERS FEELING A VENUE AS BEING OBSCURE.

Pattern ①	50
Pattern ②	883
① / (① + ②)	0.053

E. Analysis of obscurity in each category

In this section, we analyze the obscure venues in each category. We denote the venue where the percentage of obscure reviews is 50% or more, according to the description in Section III-E, and find the proportion of venues classified as obscure within the same category.

We calculate the proportion of venues classified as obscure within a category. Here, we used 27 categories whose number of reviews in a category is 1,000 or more. We show the percentage of obscure venues in each category, as indicated in Figure 3. In this figure, the vertical axis shows the proportion of venues classified as obscure within the same category, and the horizontal axis shows the category names in Yelp. The highest percentage of obscure venues is for "Local Services" at approximately 14%. Subcategories of this category include junk removal & hauling, bike repair / maintenance, and mobile phone repair. In addition, according to Figure 3, the top categories with a high percentage of obscure venues contain many categories used in daily life. In contrast, the categories "restaurants" and "nightlife" where many people go to popular venues ranked the lowest. In these categories, popular venues are sometimes a type of sightseeing spot. In addition, it seems that a large number of shops related to food services (such as Mexican restaurants and bars) affects the percentage of obscure venues.

F. Differences between venues evaluated as obscure for each reviewer

This section analyzes the differences among venues considered by reviewers as obscure.

Herein, we show the difficulty of providing a unique definition for obscure venues using our proposed method for obscure venue extraction. Using the classifier described in Section III-D, we classify whether a user review on a venue is obscure or not. Then, if the types of reviews on the venue are different, the venue that the user feels is obscure is different.

This research focused on cases in which two different reviewers posted similar reviews on two venue pairs. Two patterns of venues whose reviews refer to obscurity were considered, as shown in Figure 4. Pattern ① is a case in which two reviewers posted an obscure review and a non-obscure review to different venues. This pattern represents a case in which the reviewer felt that the referred venue was different. Pattern ② is a case in which the reviews posted by two different reviewers are the same for the referred venues. This pattern is one in which the venues the reviewers felt as obscure are the same. Therefore, if there is a certain number of reviews considered as pattern ①, it can be said that the venue perceived as obscure is different for each reviewer; the classification of obscure reviews reveals the contribution of the identification of obscure venues.

The procedure of this experiment is as follows. First, obscure venues to which two users posted similar reviews were extracted. During this experiment, 1,278 obscure venues that had obscure reviews were extracted, comprising more than

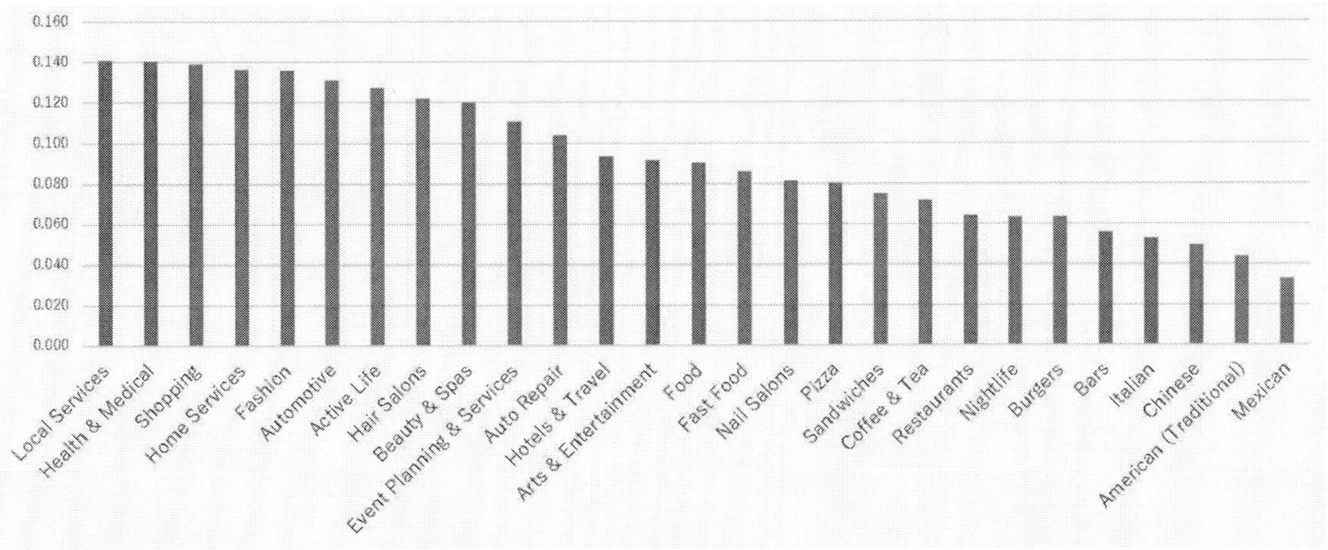

Figure 3. The percentage of obscure venues in each category

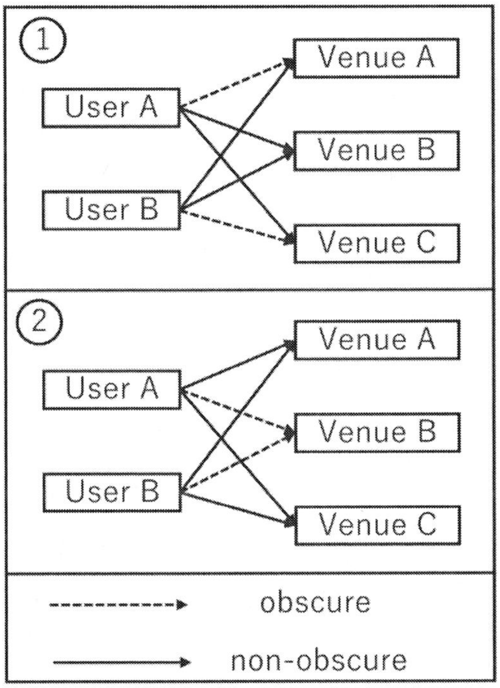

Figure 4. Pattern in which two reviewers evaluate venues as obscure.

50% of all reviews; there were 696 reviewers. The classifier was then applied to the written reviews as described in Section 4.2. The numbers of the two patterns were calculated based on the classification results.

Table IV shows the experimental results. From Table IV, pattern ① comprised approximately 5.3% of the total. In other words, the combination of 5.3% of reviewers differs from the venue that was perceived as obscure. This result shows that the venues perceived as an obscure venue are not necessarily the same for all reviewers. Therefore, the approach of abstractly treating as obscure a review that includes an obscure word without criteria on the obscure venue used to extract the venue has the potential to be effective.

V. Conclusion

In this research, we proposed a method for identifying obscure venues by extracting reviews that include descriptions regarding obscure posts on Yelp. Through reviews that include obscure words, a classifier was created to differentiate the reviews describing obscurity from those that do not, based on reviews in which the reviewers recognize the venues as being obscure. Experimental results showed that the classifier is useful for extracting obscure reviews. Furthermore, this study formulated and verified the hypothesis that venues perceived as obscure by reviewers are different. As a result, the venues perceived as being obscure are not necessarily the same for all reviewers.

Future studies will include a more detailed experiment and analyze the number of obscure venues and the various categories present in each city. This paper is limited to analyzing obscure venues extracted using our proposed method in a qualitative manner. For a discovered venue, it is necessary to analyze whether it is obscure or not and to evaluate how useful the information is. For this purpose, we will conduct questionnaires by evaluators on the obscure venues by our proposed method. Further studies may apply our classifier to other cities to discover unique, obscure venues.

Acknowledgment

This work was supported by JSPS KAKENHI Grant Numbers 16K00157 and 16K16158, and Tokyo Metropolitan University Grant-in-Aid for Research on Priority Areas "Research on social big data."

References

[1] "Yelp," URL: https://www.yelp.com/ [accessed: 2019-02-27].

[2] "Expedia," URL: https://www.expedia.com/ [accessed: 2019-02-27].

[3] "Tripadvisor," URL: https://www.tripadvisor.com/ [accessed: 2019-02-27].

[4] D. Ukpabi, S. Olaleye, E. Mogaji, and H. Karjaluoto, "Insights into online reviews of hotel service attributes: A cross-national study of selected countries in africa," in Information and Communication Technologies in Tourism 2018, B. Stangl and J. Pesonen, Eds. Cham: Springer International Publishing, 2018, pp. 243–256.

[5] V. Browning, K. K. F. So, and B. Sparks, "The influence of online reviews on consumers' attributions of service quality and control for service standards in hotels," Journal of Travel & Tourism Marketing, vol. 30, no. 1-2, 2013, pp. 23–40.

[6] C. Zhuang, Q. Ma, X. Liang, and M. Yoshikawa, "Anaba: An obscure sightseeing spots discovering system," in 2014 IEEE International Conference on Multimedia and Expo, vol. 00, 2014, pp. 1–6.

[7] D. Kitayama, "Extraction method for anaba spots based on name recognition and user's evaluation," in Proceedings of the 18th International Conference on Information Integration and Web-based Applications and Services, ser. iiWAS '16. ACM, 2016, pp. 12–15.

[8] S. Katayama, M. Obuchi, T. Okoshi, and J. Nakazawa, "Providing information of hidden spot for tourists to increase tourism satisfaction," in Proceedings of the 2018 ACM International Joint Conference and 2018 International Symposium on Pervasive and Ubiquitous Computing and Wearable Computers, ser. UbiComp '18. ACM, 2018, pp. 377–380.

[9] Z. Liu and S. Park, "What makes a useful online review? implication for travel product websites," Tourism Management, vol. 47, 2015, pp. 140 – 151.

[10] M. Toyoshima, M. Hirota, D. Kato, T. Araki, and H. Ishikawa, "Where is the memorable travel destinations?" in Social Informatics. Cham: Springer International Publishing, 2018, pp. 291–298.

[11] Y. Guo, S. J. Barnes, and Q. Jia, "Mining meaning from online ratings and reviews: Tourist satisfaction analysis using latent dirichlet allocation," Tourism Management, vol. 59, 2017, pp. 467 – 483.

[12] C. Vo, D. Duong, D. Nguyen, and T. Cao, "From helpfulness prediction to helpful review retrieval for online product reviews," in Proceedings of the Ninth International Symposium on Information and Communication Technology, ser. SoICT 2018. ACM, 2018, pp. 38–45.

[13] Z. Wang, B. S. Balasubramani, and I. F. Cruz, "Predictive analytics using text classification for restaurant inspections," in Proceedings of the 3rd ACM SIGSPATIAL Workshop on Smart Cities and Urban Analytics, ser. UrbanGIS'17. ACM, 2017, pp. 14:1–14:4.

[14] R. Dong, M. Schaal, M. P. O'Mahony, and B. Smyth, "Topic extraction from online reviews for classification and recommendation," in Proceedings of the Twenty-Third International Joint Conference on Artificial Intelligence, ser. IJCAI '13. AAAI Press, 2013, pp. 1310–1316. [Online]. Available: http://dl.acm.org/citation.cfm?id=2540128.2540317

[15] M. Afzaal, M. Usman, A. C. M. Fong, S. Fong, and Y. Zhuang, "Fuzzy aspect based opinion classification system for mining tourist reviews," Adv. Fuzzy Sys., vol. 2016, Oct. 2016, pp. 2–.

[16] T. S. Bang and V. Sornlertlamvanich, "Sentiment classification for hotel booking review based on sentence dependency structure and sub-opinion analysis," IEICE Transactions on Information and Systems, vol. E101.D, no. 4, 2018, pp. 909–916.

[17] E. van der Zee, D. Bertocchi, and D. Vanneste, "Distribution of tourists within urban heritage destinations: a hot spot/cold spot analysis of tripadvisor data as support for destination management," Current Issues in Tourism, vol. 0, no. 0, 2018, pp. 1–22.

[18] S. Wold, K. Esbensen, and P. Geladi, "Principal component analysis," Chemometrics and Intelligent Laboratory Systems, vol. 2, no. 1, 1987, pp. 37 – 52, proceedings of the Multivariate Statistical Workshop for Geologists and Geochemists.

[19] C. Cortes and V. Vapnik, "Support-vector networks," Machine Learning, vol. 20, no. 3, 1995, pp. 273–297.

[20] F. Pedregosa, G. Varoquaux, A. Gramfort, V. Michel, B. Thirion, O. Grisel, M. Blondel, P. Prettenhofer, R. Weiss, V. Dubourg, J. Vanderplas, A. Passos, D. Cournapeau, M. Brucher, M. Perrot, and E. Duchesnay, "Scikit-learn: Machine learning in Python," Journal of Machine Learning Research, vol. 12, 2011, pp. 2825–2830.

[21] "Yelp dataset challenge (round 9)," URL: https://www.yelp.com/dataset/challenge [accessed: 2019-02-27].

Analysis of Rarely Known Tourist Attractions by Geo-tagged Photographs

Jhih-Yu Lin
Graduate School of Systems Design
Tokyo Metropolitan University
Tokyo, Japan
lin-jhihyu@ed.tmu.ac.jp

Shu-Mei Wen
Department of Statistics and Information Science in Applied Statistics
Fu Jen Catholic University
Taipei, Taiwan
126531@mail.fju.edu.tw

Masaharu Hirota
Department of Information Science
Faculty of Informatics
Okayama University of Science
Okayama, Japan
hirota@mis.ous.ac.jp

Tetsuya Araki
Graduate School of Systems Design
Tokyo Metropolitan University
Tokyo, Japan
araki@tmu.ac.jp

Hiroshi Ishikawa
Graduate School of Systems Design
Tokyo Metropolitan University
Tokyo, Japan
ishikawa-hiroshi@tmu.ac.jp

***Abstract*—Today, with the advancement of the Internet and transportation, we can readily travel around the world using diverse modes of travel. On these journeys, many people use various mobile devices to obtain the latest tourist information from the Internet. However, most of the information focuses on popular tourist attractions and leads to crowds flocking there. Unlike existing studies, which concentrate on analyzing popular tourist attractions, we attempt to disperse crowds from popular tourist attractions and provide more spots for travelers to choose by analyzing rarely known tourist attractions. For this study, we propose a formula for ranking tourist attractions by analyzing geo-tagged photographs on Flickr. The results of our questionnaire survey successfully revealed tourist locations that were unfamiliar to the majority of respondents, but which were attractive to them.**

Keywords-Flickr; geo-tagged photograph; rarely known tourist attractions.

I. INTRODUCTION

In this era of the Internet and smartphones, most people can readily share and record their touristic experiences on Social Networking Services (SNSs) such as Facebook and Flickr. Numerous studies have analyzed user records of tours on SNS to elucidate user hobbies and preferences. It is possible to discover popular tourist attractions and recommend some tour plans for a user according to their preferences [1]–[4]. Using SNSs, we can immediately obtain the newest status of our friends, particularly using well-known functions check-ins and "geo-tagged" photographs, which are useful when one wants to share a location with friends.

Aside from geolocation, diverse information is available from different people using SNSs. That information includes many important and useful data for research. For instance, Hausmann et al. [5] pointed out that social media contents might provide a swift and cost-efficient substitute for traditional surveys. Furthermore, Liu et al. [6] proposed an approach for the discovery of Areas of Interest (AoIs) by analyzing "geo-tagged" photographs and "check-in" information to supply popular scenic locations and popular spots with travelers. Another study with similar aims to our own used SNS users' information and "geo-tagged" photographs to discover obscure sightseeing spots [7].

Most tourists have received sightseeing information through travel websites. However, these websites only present well-known tourist attractions. Consequently, although the attractions are crowded and congested, visitors will be led there. We conducted a preliminary investigation which showed that the great majority of tourists do not like crowded spots that make them feel uncomfortable.

As the number of tourists continue to increase, they will bring huge revenues for tourism-related industries. Nevertheless, benefits from tourists are accompanied by latent crises as well, which we should face. Kakamu et al. [8] discovered that when the number of foreigners and the police force increase, the rate of crime will also increase. However, if criminal rates increase, it will reduce visiting willingness and tourism income will be lost [9].

Most earlier studies have specifically addressed analyses of popular tourism attractions or AoIs and neglected other unnoticed places. Therefore, for the present study, through dispersing crowds from more popular tourist attractions, our goal is to improve several aspects: (1) crowded popular tourist attractions make visitors feel uncomfortable; (2) foreigners are too numerous at popular tourist attractions, engendering higher rates of crime; and (3) supporting tourist industries of regions apart from popular regions.

To accomplish our aim, we analyzed scenic "geo-tagged" photographs taken in Japan from Flickr. Thereby, we discovered worthwhile and rarely known tourist attractions. We studied this topic based on scenic photographs to assess tourism in many categories such as human landscape, ecotourism, and natural landscape. For this study, we specifically examine natural landscapes. Therefore, we used scenic photographs to reach our aim of making travelers realize natural landscape intuitively. In addition, it is clearer to define the research scope. Moreover, we can provide more tourist attractions options for tourists and reduce crowding at well-known tourist attractions.

The rest of the paper is organized as follows: Section II presents an overview of the method. Section III explains the method used for scenic photograph evaluation. In Section IV, we present rarely known tourist attraction estimation and explain our questionnaire results. In Section V, we discuss improvements to the survey questionnaire and present conclusions and future works.

II. OVERVIEW OF THE METHOD

This section introduces an overview of our method, as shown in Figure 1. Our method comprises two components: definition of rarely known tourist attractions and data construction.

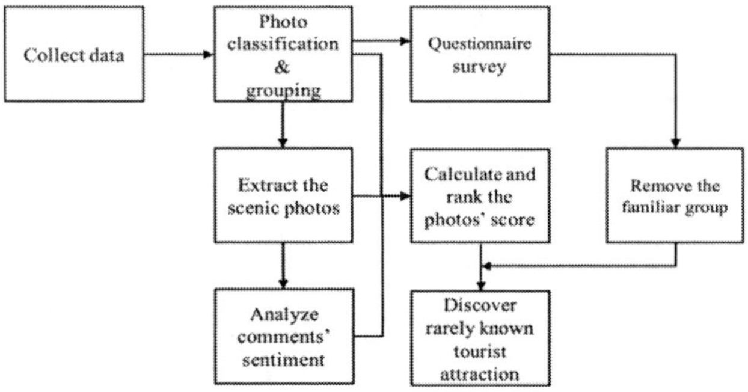

Figure 1. Overview of the method.

A. *Definition of Rarely Known Tourist Attractions*

To differentiate well-known and rarely known tourist attractions, we adopt two definitions of rarely known tourist attractions.

Definition 1: Only some people know about this tourist attraction.

Definition 2: That tourist attraction deserves to be visited and it is attractive for tourists.

B. *Data Construction*

Using Flickr API, we collected 769,749 photographs shot in 2017 with geolocation in Japan. After extracting the photographs' latitude and longitude to gather details of addresses through Google geocoding API, we sorted the 47 prefectures and 1,159 cities by the number of photo-counts in descending order. Finally, we used a grouping method of unequal class interval to divide prefectures and cities into eight groups, as shown in Table I. This grouping method is presented in the next section. However, 309 photographs had no details of addresses because these photographs were shot in the sky or on the ocean.

TABLE I. GROUP OF PREFECTURE

Group	***Prefectures***
Group 1	Tokyo, Kyoto, Chiba, Kanagawa, Aichi
Group 2	Osaka, Hiroshima, Hokkaido, Saitama
Group 3	Gunma, Nara, Nagano, Okinawa
Group 4	Hyogo, Fukuoka, Mie, Tochigi, Shizuoka
Group 5	Yamanashi, Oita, Okayama
Group 6	Ibaraki, Aomori, Miyagi, Gifu, Ishikawa, Wakayama, Kagawa, Niigata, Shiga, Ehime, Kumamoto, Akita, Toyama, Fukushima, Nagasaki
Group 7	Yamagata, Kagoshima, Tottori, Saga, Fukui
Group 8	Tokushima, Kochi, Yamaguchi, Iwate, Shimane, Miyazaki

We classified these photographs into different prefectures and cities according to the photographs' address details. We calculated the photo-counts in every prefecture and city. Figure 2 presents the Top 10 prefectures and cities for the photo-counts. Furthermore, we extracted 2,671 scenic photographs with tags which mean scenic in English and Japanese (e.g., "風景", "景色", "scenery"), and collected these photographs' comments and favorite counts.

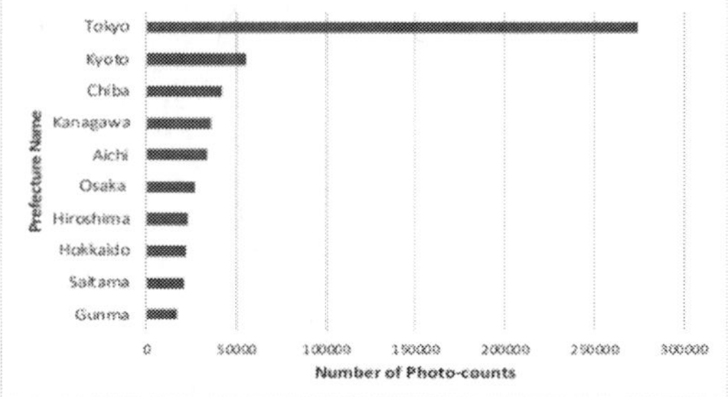

(a) Top10 Prefecture photo-counts

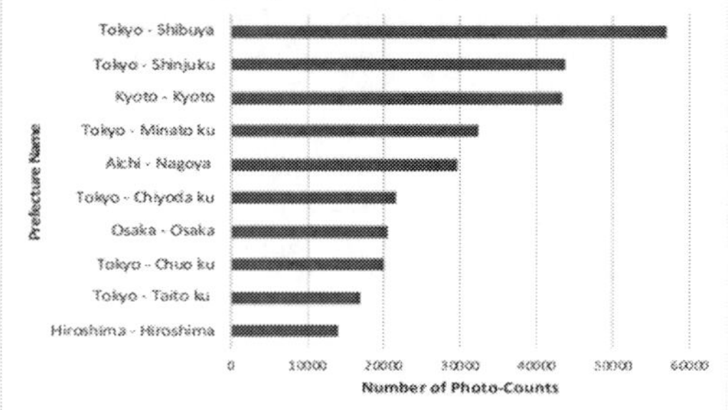

(b) Top10 City photo-counts

Figure 2. Numbers of photo-counts.

III. SCENIC PHOTOGRAPH EVALUATION

A. *Grouping Method of Unequal Class Interval*

In this subtask, we present that the unequal class interval is a kind of statistical grouping method. This method applies uneven index values and class intervals of group as dissimilar. We used a slightly modified method similar to the one reported by Arjunan et al. [10]. We used this method to divide the 47 prefectures and 1,159 cities into different groups according their respective photo-counts.

To complete this grouping method, we employed two methods.

1) Reduction rate: By calculating the rate of increase and reduction, we can observe the numerical change that is usually used to calculate the mortality rate, rainfall rate, unemployment rate, etc. [11]–[13]. For this study, we sorted the prefectures and cities in descending order. The reduction rate of prefectures and cities was calculated using equation (1) in the equation, x_i represents the count of photographs. Then, after dividing the data into different groups through observation of the reduction rate variation, the reduction rate variation needs to meet two conditions: first is that the reduction rate must be more than 10%; second is that the reduction rate must be decreased gradually, then the next reduction rate is increased. Figure 3 presents the reduction rates of the respective prefectures.

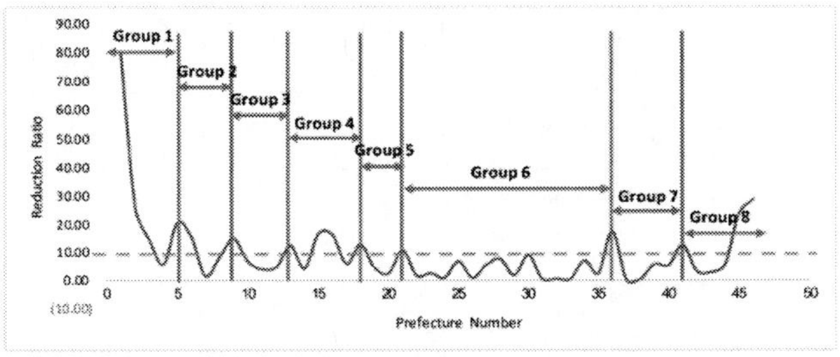

Figure 3. Photo-counts of reduction rate.

$$y = (x_i - x_{i+1})/x_i \times 100 \ ,(x_i > x_{i+1}) \qquad (1)$$

In Table II, we can use the conditions above to divide the data. Although the second reduction rate meets the conditions, we still allocate it into group 4 because the city count of every group must contain at least three cities. The third and fifth reduction rates of prefecture are gradually decreased. However, the sixth reduction rate is increased and it is greater than 10%. We determined the sixth row is the period with abrupt change and divided the second row to sixth row into the group 4.

TABLE II. PARTIAL PREFECTURE LIST

Prefecture name	Photo-count	Reduction rate	Group
Okinawa	14,823	12.29%	3
Hyogo	13,001	4.21%	4
Fukuoka	12,454	16.36%	4
Mie	10,416	16.13%	4
Tochigi	8,763	5.93%	4
Shizuoka	8,218	12.64%	4
Yamanashi	7,179	4.49%	5
Oita	6,857	2.42%	5
Okayama	6,691	10.69%	5

2) *Standard Deviation (STDEV):* In statistics, the standard deviation (s) is usually used to measure dispersion of a set of data values. A greater standard deviation and greater magnitude will indicate greater deviation of values. In the following equation, $\overline{x}$ represents the x sample average.

$$s = \sqrt{\frac{1}{n-1}\sum_{i=1}^{n}(x_i - \overline{x})^2} \qquad (2)$$

3) *Z-score:* z-scores are also called standard scores. In statistics, z-scores are used to compare an observation to a standard normal deviate. In the following equation (3), x, $\overline{x}$ and s represent the count of photographs, x sample average, and the standard deviation, respectively.

$$Z = \frac{x - \overline{x}}{s} \qquad (3)$$

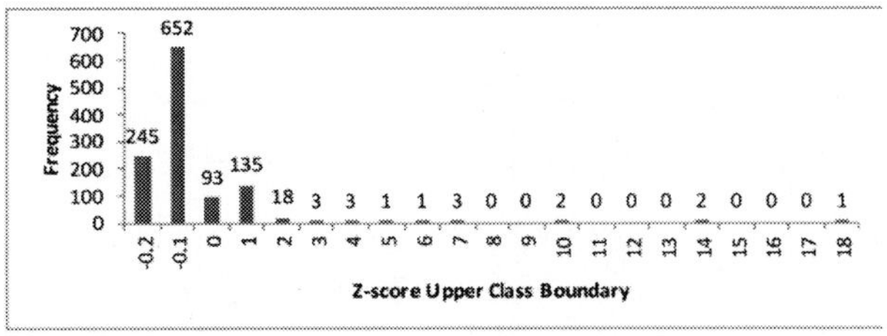

Figure 4. Z-score analysis of all city data.

4) *Application:* The change of the reduction rate might be readily apparent in the prefectures. Therefore, we only used the method of reduction to divide them into groups. For the group method of city data, in Figure 4, we can observe that about eighty percent cities' data center on -0.2 to 0, which means these photograph count of data less than the photograph count of average (656 photos). However, the data with z-score between 3 and 18 means that the data are excessively different and that many outliers exist. If we use only the z-score to group cities' data, that will show deviation, thereby we synthesized the methods above to group the cities' data. In the first to second group, the reduction rate of data might be readily apparent. We used the method of the reduction rate to group.

The reduction rate change might not be readily apparent (there is little discrepancy of photo-count in group 8). Groups 3–8 were grouped using their z-scores. Considering the class interval size of each group, we judged where z-scores are more than 4 that were divided into the same group, where z-scores are less than 4 and more than 3 as a group, where z-scores are less than 3 and more than 2 as a group , and so on (see Table III). Finally, we used these methods to divide prefectures and cities into eight groups. We also defined scores of the respective groups: group 1 can get 8 points, group 2 can get 7 points, and so on.

TABLE III. SCORE OF CITY GROUP

Group	Z-scores	Score	City counts
Group 1		8	17
Group 2		7	17
Group 3	$Z > 4$	6	20
Group 4	$4 > Z > 3$	5	16
Group 5	$3 > Z > 2$	4	23
Group 6	$2 > Z > 1$	3	50
Group 7	$1 > Z > 0$	2	162
Group 8	$Z < 0$	1	854

B. Comments' Sentiment

Only viewers' emotions need to be considered. Therefore, we collected the scenic photographs' comments; owner's replies are eliminated from the total comments. We analyzed the comments and extracted the positive comments, as shown in Table IV.

TABLE V. A PART OF RANKING RESULT

Address	Neighboring tourism attraction	Prefecture group	City group	Favorites	Positive comments	Total comments	Score
2871, Onna, Onna-son Kunigami-gun, Okinawa, 904-0411, Japan	Resort	3	3	1548	56	68	1297.63
Yunohama hotel, 1-2-30, Yunokawacho, Hakodate-shi, Hokkaido, 042-0932, Japan	Hot spring street	2	3	337	13	16	283.94
14-16, Suehirocho, Hakodate-shi, Hokkaido, 040-0053, Japan	Kanemori Red Brick Warehouse	2	3	306	5	10	257.67
510, Tangocho Takano, Kyotango-shi, Kyoto, 627-0221, Japan	---	1	7	187	4	7	157.72
Kendou 388sen, Inuma, Kawanehon-cho Haibara-gun, Shizuoka, 428-0402, Japan	---	4	8	126	46	56	106.66
Sinkawagensi 58, Fukuoka Yatsumiya, Shiroishi-shi, Miyagi, 989-0733, Japan	---	6	8	123	2	4	103.72
Ryuuanzi, Ryoanji Goryonoshitacho, Ukyo-ku Kyoto-shi, Kyoto, 616-8001, Japan	Temple of the Dragon at Peace	1	1	100	6	8	85.76
156, Fumoto, Fujinomiya-shi, Shizuoka, 418-0109, Japan	---	4	7	99	32	39	84.16

TABLE IV. COMMENT COUNTS

	Viewer comments	Owner comments	Sum
Positive comments	1,602	248	1,850
Total comments	2,417	572	2,989

We specifically examine English and Chinese comments by using TextBlob [14] and SnowNLP [15]. The scores of English comments' sentiments were -1 to 1. The Chinese sentiment scores were 0 to 1. The score represents the probability of positive meaning. Moreover, we discovered the English comments' sentiment score of more than 0.3 as best. It can get higher accuracy. Chinese sentiment scores should be greater than 0.4.

C. Formula of Evaluation

Considering the definitions of rarely known tourist attractions and data construction, we propose a formula to calculate and rank the photograph scores (S_i).

$$S_i = \sum_{p=1}^{3} F_{pi} W_p + \frac{R_i}{T_i}, 0 < W_p < 1 \ and \ \sum_{p=1}^{3} W_p = 1 \quad (4)$$

In equation (4), F_{1i} represents the prefecture group point; and W_1 is F_{1i} weight. F_{2i} represents a city group point; and W_2 is F_{2i} weight. F_{3i} represents the photographs' favorite counts and W_3 is the F_{3i} weight. R_i represents the positive comment count of the photographs. T_i represents the total comment count of the photographs. In this formula, R_i/T_i is regarded as an additional score because most photographs do not have comments. We supposed the photographs' favorite counts and positive comments as factors of attracting someone to visit. Therefore, we can rank all scenic photographs by this formula, as shown in Table V.

Table V presents some ranking results. The first column is the GPS address of the photograph from Google API. The second column is the neighboring popular tourist attraction. The third and fourth columns are photograph groups (not the group score). The fifth column is the favorite count of photographs. The sixth and seventh columns are counts of the photograph's comments. The last column is the photograph's score calculated using our formula. A high score means that the place deserves travelers to visit. In this table, the address of the first row is a famous resort in Okinawa. Additionally, the second row is a hotel on a famous hot spring street. The third row is a well-known tourist attraction in Hokkaido. The place of the seventh row is a renowned and historical temple in Kyoto. Others are obscure places.

D. Entropy Weight Method (EWM)

For this study, we used EWM to set the weights used for the formula. EWM is an objective set weight method because it depends only on the discreteness of data. Actually, EWM is used widely in the fields of engineering, socioeconomic studies, etc. [16]–[18].

In information theory, entropy is a kind of uncertainty measure. When information is larger, uncertainty and entropy will be smaller. Based on the properties of entropy information, we can estimate the randomness of an event and the degree of randomness through calculation of the entropy value. Furthermore, entropy values are used to gauge a sort of discreteness degree of index. When the degree of discreteness is larger, the index affecting the integrated assessment will be greater.

To complete the setting of the formula weights, we require some steps, as described below.

Calculate the ratio (P_{ij}) of the i-th index under the j-th index. Therein, x_{ij} means the j-th index of the i-th sample.

$$P_{ij} = \frac{x_{ij}}{\sum_{i=1}^{n} x_{ij}}, (i = 1, \dots, n;\ j = 1, \dots, m) \quad (5)$$

Calculate the entropy value (e_j) of the j-th index.

$$e_j = -k \sum_{i=1}^{n} P_{ij} \ln(P_{ij}), (j = 1, \dots, m;\ k = \frac{1}{\ln(n)} > 0) \quad (6)$$

Calculate the discrepancy of information entropy (d_j).

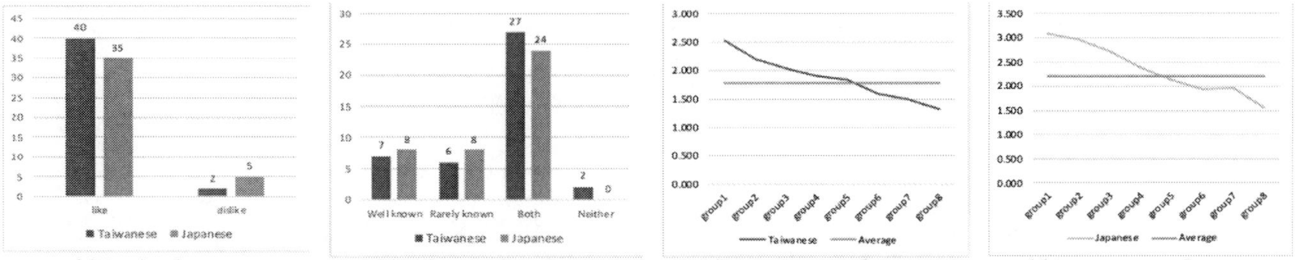

(a) Travel preference (b) Preference of travel spot (c)Taiwanese score of groups (d) Japanese score of groups

Figure 5. Result of Japanese city questionnaire.

$$d_j = 1 - e_j, (j = 1, \dots, m) \quad (7)$$

Calculate the weight (w_i) of each index.

$$w_i = \frac{d_j}{\sum_{j=1}^{m} d_j}, (j = 1, \dots, m) \quad (8)$$

We analyzed the prefecture group score (F_{1i}), the city group score (F_{2i}), and the favorite counts (F_{3i}) of 2,671 scenic photographs and determined the weight of formula in this research by EWM. In the equations, W_1 is equal to 0.0491; W_2 is equal to 0.1136 and W_3 is equal to 0.8371.

IV. Rarely Known Tourist Attraction Estimation

A. *Familiarity Level of Japanese City*

We designed a questionnaire and administered it to 42 Taiwanese and 40 Japanese participants to ascertain their level of familiarity with Japanese cities between different nationalities. Surveying levels of familiarity of cities from respondents is difficult. For that reason, we grouped the prefecture and city data. In this way, we were able to select a city's name randomly from each group to decrease the number of questions in the questionnaire. It is easier to investigate which city is unfamiliar to respondents. A rarely known tourist attraction might be included in unfamiliar groups.

According to the scale of each group, 23 cities' names were selected randomly in this questionnaire. In addition, a few background questions of travel were proposed for respondents (e.g., frequency of travel, age, occupation). We especially investigated respondents' preferences of tourist attractions (e.g., well-known, rarely known).

For these respondents, as shown in Figure 5(a), we observed that 75 respondents like to travel. More than half of the respondents like well-known tourist attractions and rarely known tourist attractions (Figure 5(b)). Respondents were provided with four choices to answer the city questions: (1) I have absolutely no idea; (2) I have heard of this city, but I do not know the relevant tourist attractions; (3) I have heard of this city and know the relevant tourist attractions; (4) I have been to this city. If a respondent chooses option (1) the respondent is assigned 1 point in this question; option (2) can get 2 points, and so on, with higher scores indicating greater familiarity with this city.

Finally, we calculated the average scores of respective groups, as shown in Table VI. The average represents the city question score (23 questions) average. When the score of a group is less than average, we categorize this group as the rarely known one. Figure 5(c) shows that group 6 – group 8 are unfamiliar to Taiwanese people. Figure 5(d) shows that Japanese people are unfamiliar with group 5 – group 8. We removed the familiar groups from the ranking of Section III as our aim.

TABLE VI. SCORE OF GROUP

Group	Taiwanese	Japanese
Group 1	2.536	3.075
Group 2	2.190	2.950
Group 3	2.204	2.725
Group 4	1.913	2.375
Group 5	1.841	2.125
Group 6	1.595	1.950
Group 7	1.488	1.975
Group 8	1.321	1.544
Average	1.733	2.214

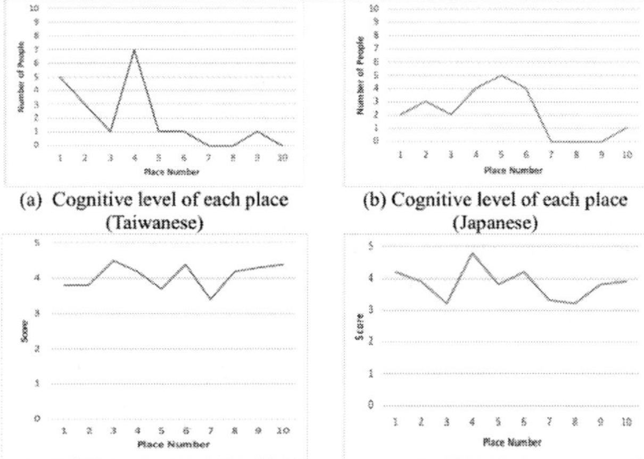

(a) Cognitive level of each place (Taiwanese) (b) Cognitive level of each place (Japanese)

(c) Average score of each place (Taiwanese) (d) Average score of each place (Japanese)

Figure 6. Result of verfication questionnaire.

B. *Verification Experiment*

Based on the discussion presented above, we can ascertain which group is unfamiliar to the Taiwanese (groups 6–8) and to the Japanese (groups 5–8). In this section, we use the questionnaire to verify these rarely known tourist attractions, which are obscure but attractive to respondents.

For the verification experiment, we extracted the top 10 rarely known tourist attractions (from Taiwanese and Japanese unfamiliar groups) to investigate 10 Taiwanese (who have touristic experience in Japan) and 10 Japanese. Two questions were asked for each attraction: "Do you know this place according to the address?" If respondents probably know this attraction, then the answer is "Yes". The second question is "According to this photograph, do you want to visit this place?" For the second question, respondents can score 1–5 for the attraction, with a higher score indicating greater attraction.

Figure 6 portrays the survey results. Figures 6(a) and 6(b) present how many people know this place. Figures 6(c) and 6(d) explain the level of attractiveness to respondents. In this questionnaire, we observed that each respondent knows two places out of ten on average. For Taiwanese participants, the average score of the places was 4.07. Furthermore, for Japanese participants, the average was 3.83. This result demonstrates that these places were known by a minority of respondents, but they still want to visit there. Results demonstrate that our research was successful.

V. Discussion and Conclusion

People from different countries have distinct familiarity with Japanese cities. We proposed a novel method to ascertain rarely known tourist attractions for people of different nationalities. By collecting and analyzing Flickr photograph information, we classified them into different prefectures and cities. Subsequently, we classified these prefectures and cities into eight groups.

Additionally, we used a questionnaire to survey Taiwanese participants and Japanese participants. We obtained the unfamiliar city groups of Taiwanese and Japanese participants. The scenic photographs were ranked using the formula for this research. We then removed the familiar city groups in the result of ranking for respondent. By a second questionnaire survey, we verified our results. Consequently, through this research, we were able to discover rarely known tourist attractions for travelers.

From the questionnaire survey, we obtained the surprising result that Taiwanese participants are more familiar with Japanese cities than Japanese participants are. The reason might be that Taiwan and Japan are neighboring countries. In addition, air travel from Taiwan to Japan is cheaper, which might lead to higher frequency of Taiwanese taking trips to Japan. We also discovered that most Taiwanese respondents prefer individual travel in Japan to travelling with groups. Furthermore, the questionnaire results demonstrated that income has little to do with travel frequency.

As future work, we expect to collect and analyze more photographs taken in distinct years. Then, we will try to use different methods of grouping and comparing them. Considering more factors of discovering rarely known tourist attractions, we expect to improve the formula used for this research. Rarely known tourist attractions will be classified into different seasons, weather, days, and nights according to photograph times and contents. We also want to provide a personal recommendation service using Collaborative Filtering (CF).

References

[1] K. H. Lim, J. Chan, C. Leckie, and S. Karunasekera, "Personalized Tour Recommendation Based on User Interests and Points of Interest Visit Durations," IJCAI, pp. 1778-1784, Jul. 2015.

[2] I. Memon, L. Chen, A. Majid, M. Lv, I. Hussain, and G. Chen, "Travel Recommendation Using Geo-tagged Photos in Social Media for Tourist," International Journal of Wireless Personal Communications, vol. 80, pp. 1347–1362, Feb. 2015.

[3] S. Jiang, Z. Qian, T. Mei, and Y. Fu, "Personalized Travel Sequence Recommendation on Multi-Source Big Social Media," *IEEE Trans. Big. Data,* vol. 2, no. 1, pp. 43–56, Mar. 2016.

[4] X. Peng and Z. Huang, "A Novel Popular Tourist Attraction Discovering Approach Based on Geo-Tagged Social Media Big Data," ISPRS International Journal of Geo-Information, vol. 6, no. 7, pp. 216, Jul. 2017.

[5] A. Hausmann et al. "Social Media Data Can be Used to understand Tourists' Preferences for Nature-Based Experiences in Protected Areas," Conservation Letters, vol. 11, no. 1, Jan. 2017.

[6] J. Liu, Z. Huang, L. Chen, H. T. Shen, and Z. Yan, "Discovering areas of interest with geo-tagged images and check-ins," ACM Multimedia, pp. 589–598, Nov. 2012, ISBN: 978-1-4503-1089-5

[7] C. Zhuang, Q. Ma, X. Liang, and M. Yoshikawa, "Discovering Obscure Sightseeing Spots by Analysis of Geo-tagged Social Images," ASONAM, pp. 590–595, Aug. 2015, ISBN: 978-1-4503-3854-7

[8] K. Kakamu, W. Polasek, and H. Wago, "Spatial interaction of crime incidents in Japan," Mathematics and Computers in Simulation, vol. 78, no. 2, pp. 276–282, Jul. 2008.

[9] D. Altindag, "Crime and International Tourism," Journal of Labor Research, vol. 35, no.1, pp. 1-14, Mar. 2014, doi: 10.1007/s12122-014-9174-8.

[10] S. Arjunan and P. Sujatha, "A survey on unequal clustering protocols in Wireless Sensor Networks," Journal of King Saud University-Computer and Information Sciences, 2017.

[11] J. C. Prentice, G. Marion, P. C. L. White, R. S. Davidson, and M. R. Hutchings, "Demographic processes drive increases in wildlife disease following population reduction," PLoS One, vol. 9, no. 5, May. 2014, doi: 10.1371/journal.pone.0086563.

[12] C. Hamashima et al. "Impact of endoscopic screeningon mortality reduction from gastric cancer," World J Gantroenterol, vol. 21, no. 8, pp. 2460–2466, Feb. 2015.

[13] A. Kayode, S. Arome, and S. F. Anyio, "The rising rate of unemployment in Nigeria the Socio-economic and political implications," Global Business and Economic Research Journal, vol. 3, no. 2, pp. 12–32, Jan. 2014.

[14] TextBlob.[Online]. Available from: https://pypi.org/project/textblob/ 2019.02.24

[15] SnowNLP.[Online].Available from: https://pypi.org/project/snownlp/ 2019.02.24

[16] Y. He, H. Guo, M. Jin, and P. Ren, "A linguistic entropy weight method and its application in linguistic multi-attribute group decision making," Nonlinear Dynamics, vol. 84, no. 1, pp. 399–404, Jan. 2016.

[17] Y. Ji, G. H. Huang, and W. Sun, "Risk assessment of hydropower stations through an integrated fuzzy entropy-weight multiple criteria decision making method: A case study of the Xiangxi River," Expert Systems with Applications, vol. 42, no. 12, pp. 5380–5389, Jul. 2015.

[18] A. Delgado and I. Romero, "Environmental conflict analysis using an integrated grey clustering and entropy-weight method: A case study of a mining project in Peru," Environmental Modelling & Software, vol. 77, pp. 108–121, Mar. 2016.

Tourist Behavior Analysis Using Instagram Hashtags

Daiju Kato
Nihon Knowledge Co. Ltd
Tokyo, Japan
d-kato@know-net.co.jp

Mitsuo Yoshida
Toyohashi University of Technology
Toyohashi, Japan
yoshida@cs.tut.ac.jp

Masaharu Hirota
Okayama University of Science
Okayama, Japan
hirota@mis.ous.ac.jp

Hiroshi Ishikawa
Tokyo Metropolitan University
Hino, Japan
ishikawa-hiroshi@tmu.ac.jp

Mitsuyoshi Nagao
Hokkaido Information University
Ebetsu, Japan
nagao@do-johodai.ac.jp

***Abstract*—Many people use Instagram to submit their experiences related to travel destinations with many hashtag related keywords for their feelings and experiences. Those hashtags describe not only their experience,s but also some values related to the destination. Therefore, Instagram users search locations with those hashtags to obtain information about experiences, meals and sightseeing. Hashtags entail much value for tourists. We have started to find seasonal trends and a tendency of tourists' experiences from Instagram data. We regard it as effective for distributing information to tourists. This paper describes the accuracy and analytical method of tourists' behavioral analysis using hashtags.**

Keywords- e-tourism; hashtag; Instagram; social media; tourist behavior.

I. INTRODUCTION

Today, many tourists use and enjoy social media as Social Network Services (SNSs) before travel, during travel, and after travel. They search for sightseeing information reviews of travel destinations and post various information related to sightseeing spots visited by social media. The media provide accumulated reviews of sightseeing information and review blog sites such as TripAdvisor [1].

In Japan, social media of many kinds exist. Each medium has characteristic contents, as presented in Table I. Many users use several media to accommodate their feelings to post their experiences. Already, Instagram users [2] are more numerous than Facebook users [3] in Japan [4]. Instagram not only has many active users; it has many young female users. This social media site continues to expand.

Many researchers use social media data for tourist behavior or to provide specific travel information to achieve tourists' satisfaction and to attract interested tourists. We analyzed tourist behavior at sightseeing spots in Japan using social media and thought about using it for behavior analysis. This paper describes analyses of tourist behavior and trends using Instagram hashtags.

TABLE I. TYPES OF SOCIAL MEDIA IN JAPAN

	Social Media			
	Facebook	***Instagram***	***Twitter***	***Line***
Registered Users (August, 2018)	28 million	29 million	45 million	78 million
Types of contents	• Text • Carousel • Link • Image • Movie • Streaming • Story (24 hr limit)	• Image • Carousel • Movie • Story • Story by streaming	• Text (maximum of 280 characters) • Link • Image • Move • Streaming	• Text • Image • Link • Streaming (Line Live)
Feature	• Rich of contents • Formal attitude • Target accuracy	• Photographs and movies are main • Importance of a world view • Many active users • Hashtag	• Realtime property • Expectation of expandability • Hashtag	• Rich stamp • Having two of messages and timeline • Many mobile users with using talk or call

https://gaiax-socialmedialb.jp/post-29375/

II. Proposed Analytical Method for Instagram Data

A. Target dataset

We analyze an example of tourists who visited Sapporo in Hokkaido, which, along with Kyoto, is famous as a Japan travel destination. We gather data about visiting Sapporo from Instagram. We search the tourist data in Instagram using the hashtag of '#札幌旅行 (Japanese, Sapporo Travel)'.

When browsing the data of the Sapporo travel hashtag, one can find posts for marketing use by restaurants, shops and so on in Sapporo city. These posts are not travelers. Therefore, we would like to raise the accuracy of tourist behavior analysis by suggesting a method of narrowing down travelers' submissions easily.

B. Proposed method specifically examining hashtag numbers

When extracting data with a hashtag of '#札幌旅行 (Japanese, Sapporo Travel)' from Instagram, we gather the following dataset.

- Period: 06/29/2013 – 12/19/2018
- Submission number: 8,229
- Number of unique submitting persons: 2,902

For these datasets, we ranked various factors and examined whether it was possible to conduct meaningful analyses. First, when ranking these datasets with users with many posts, as presented in Table II, the most frequent posts are those from owner id 4317813670, as shown in Figure 1. The post owner is a shop staff, posting information about handmade cookies to advertise them to Instagram users.

TABLE II. Ranking of posting users

Ranking	Owner Id	Submission number	Used hashtags number			
			total	*Min*	*Max*	*Avg*
1	4317813670	238	4,728	11	30	19.87
2	4027909537	198	5,902	23	31	29.81
3	2284144589	157	4,768	29	60	30.37
4	7583357588	138	2,918	8	29	21.14
5	5504659705	112	2,387	19	47	21.31
6	3839661803	99	1,544	8	25	15.60
7	4655960542	69	1,836	18	32	26.61
8	36184065	65	967	7	24	14.88
9	268071578	63	146	1	6	2.32
10	1958878171	58	1,282	14	30	22.10

TABLE III. Ranking of users who use many hashtags

Ranking	Owner Id	Submission number	Used hashtags number			
			total	*Min*	*Max*	*Avg*
1	2284144589	157	4,768	29	60	30.37
2	1981742792	16	482	30	31	30.13
3	6692218220	18	540	30	30	30.00
4	6231274057	11	330	30	30	30.00
5	229156278	5	150	30	30	30.00
6	290889411	5	150	30	30	30.00
7	280579655	10	299	29	31	29.90
8	1813842825	7	209	28	32	29.86
9	4027909537	198	5,902	23	31	29.81
10	1556307153	5	149	29	30	29.80

In addition, when ranking users with many hashtags used per post, as presented in Table III, one can find messages introducing stores, restaurants, and shops in the rankings. Owner Id 2284144589, which uses the greatest number of hashtags, is a lamb barbecue restaurant. The shop posts its time sales, as shown in Figure 2.

It is necessary to exclude users in marketing to improve the accuracy refinement of tourist-only datasets. However, because it is impossible to check and analyze large amounts of text data within the posts, we specifically examined the number of usage hashtags per post by one user and decided to see if it can choose whether to use marketing depending on the number of hashtags.

We have hypothesized that the similarity of sentences is high in postings by marketing users. We assume that persons who use Instagram for marketing use similar numbers of hashtags for their messages. To confirm that this hypothesis is correct, we choose to examine the similarity of sentences among posted users.

C. Investigation of sentence similarity

To obtain similarity of sentences by edit distance, the following are two methods for obtaining the edit distance.

- Levenshtein distance
- Jaro–Winkler Distance

The Levenshtein Distance is the distance represented by the minimum edit distance of a character string and another character string. Here we have a standardized Levenshtein distance. We calculate the similarity of sentences.

The Jaro–Winkler Distance calculates the distance from the number of characters that match in a character string different from a certain character string and the necessity of substitution. The Jaro–Winkler distance means that the possible values of the distance are 0 to 1. A larger distance value represents higher similarity between character strings.

The similarity between the previously submitted text and the next text was calculated on the posted sentence of the user who made two or more posts from the acquired dataset. We implemented these two editing distance algorithms and calculated the editing distance by posted users [5].

Using the edit distance, we graphed both the Levenshtein distance and the Jaro–Winker Distance similarity of the posted text. The texts submitted by users according to the number of posts never achieved higher similarity as the number of postings increased. Similarly, even if the number of uses of hashtags increases, the similarity of the submitted text will not increase, as shown in Figure 3. In other words, it turned out that the hypothesis that users who have many posts and hashtags described earlier are doing marketing activities is not applicable.

To find out if this hypothesis does not hold true, we examined whether it is specific to the dataset of '#札幌旅行 (Japanese, Sapporo Travel)', we calculated the same editing distance to the dataset of '#京都旅行 (Japanese, Kyoto Travel)'. The newly acquired dataset is the following.

- Period: 08/06/2011 – 01/08/2019
- Submits number: 303,013
- Unique number of submitted persons: 71,484

As in the case of Sapporo travel, the similarity of the posted text by post number and by hashtags was calculated, as shown in Figure 4.

For this dataset of Kyoto trips, even though the number of posts and hashtags usage increased, it was not apparent that the similarity of the text being posted would be high. Based on the number of hashtags of Instagram, it turned out that it can not readily exclude postings that are made as marketing tasks.

We speculated that shops and restaurants that use Instagram for marketing are repeatedly posting similar texts. However, a guess can not be formulated even if the editing distance is obtained. At present, we can not exclude posts by restaurants and shops using marketing unless full-text analysis is used.

III. Tourist Behavior Analysis

According to Section II, it is not possible to exclude marketing activities using the number of hashtags for post messages under Instagram. We use the acquired data as is and analyze the tourist behavior. The analytical method is applied as follows and analysis is made as to whether there is periodicity.

1. Quarterly ranking of hashtags included in posting messages at 2018
2. Quarterly classification tendency of posted photographs at 2-18
3. Quarterly hashtags ranking of posts containing food in posted photographs at 2018
4. Trend analysis for the "Shime Parfait"

First, we created quarterly rankings of hashtags in 2018 included in posting text and investigated whether the posting tendency differs depending on the time, as presented in Table IV. Many hash tags attached with hashtags of Sapporo travel indicate that Sapporo City is a city in Hokkaido; most post users use hashtags for location of Hokkaido, Sapporo and someplace of Sapporo area. Additionally, because the hashtags of "#札幌グルメ(Japanese, Sapporo gourmet)" are raised to the top, one can see that it is possible to enjoy a meal on a Sapporo trip.

When the data are acquired using Instagram, the JSON element data 'accessibility_caption' are included for each post. These data show what is included in the posted pictures by Instagram's own classification result as follows.

"accessibility_caption": "Image may contain: food"

It is possible to classify the posted photographs using this parameter. Therefore, we created a quarterly ranking of 'accessibility_caption' at 2018, as presented in Table V. By this ranking, one can see that the images are always on top with the food and the self-portraits.

Instagram does not disclose what technology is used for 'accessibility_caption' or how it analyzes information related to photos. Therefore, detailed analysis can not be performed using this parameter. However, because it can be understood simply whether the photograph is food, person, indoor or outdoor, it is thought that analysis by hash tag can be explored and developed further.

According to the ranking of hashtags attached to pictures of which food is taken, filter by accessibility_caption parameter, the top places of course have many hashtags of place names, but also include hashtags of specific foods such as sweets, Lamb meat barbecue called "Genghis Khan," and ice cream and gelato, as presented in Table VI. The rankings of sweets and cafés are nearly equal. Therefore, it is thought that they are eating sweets at a cafe.

Hashtag analysis can be used to check trends. For instance, magazines and web contents for Sapporo trips are written about "Sapporo Shime Parfait," a cold and sweet parfait that people can enjoy after a night of drinking. Since the Sapporo Parfait committee was established at September 1, 2015, it has advertised this item on its Web site [6].

Comparing "Shime Parfait" to the famous food of Sapporo, "Genghis Khan," tourists have gradually come to enjoy "Shime Parfait" as depicted in Figure 5 with a post and impressions. In addition, the extraction of the number of postings is done while considering synonyms.

By analyzing the use of hashtags, we can analyze the reasons for tourism given by visitors to Sapporo. Because these datasets are not limited to tourists, specific hashtags such as soup curry, lamb meat barbecue, and ice cream are assumed to be posted as a marketing strategy, so asking for seasonality by quarterly ranking can be regarded as difficult.

IV. Conclusion

The active use of Instagram is expanding. Many users enjoy posting pictures and videos to Instagram when they visit some place. Therefore, one can analyze the purpose of tourists visiting sightseeing spots by using the hashtags assigned to Instagram data. However, analysis of hashtags to analyze what meals tourists are enjoying in Sapporo, and what photographs tourists are taking when they are alone is impossible. Analyzing images of the posted photographs or analyzing the text body is necessary to conduct a detailed analysis.

Instagram can also post to Facebook and Twitter [7] simultaneously. Therefore, instead of conducting an analysis using Instagram data only, using methods such as analyzing the behavior of tourists in conjunction with analysis of tweets with location information can provide data for tourism behavior analysis without building a complicated system.

V. Future Work

As a method of finding similar posts, it is possible to calculate Jaccard coefficients by extracting hashtags from the contribution text in a regular expression. We would like to find a method of eliminating information posted by companies and shops to gather more accurate tourist data.

Because it is possible to post from Instagram to Twitter simultaneously, we conducted an analysis of places related to meals and places where seasonal variation occurs. By combining tweet data with positional information in Sapporo and hashtag analysis of Instagram, a more precise analysis of tourist behavior in Sapporo can be conducted.

REFERENCES

[1] https://www.tripadvisor.com

[2] https://www.instagram.com

[3] https://www.facebook.com

[4] https://blog.comnico.jp/we-love-social/sns-users, in japanese

[5] G. Dan. "Algorithms on strings, trees, and sequences." Cambridge University Press,1997, ISBN 0-521-58519-8.

[6] https://sapporo-parfait.com/en/

[7] https://www.twitter.com

[8] P. Del Vecchio, G. Mele, V. Ndou, and G. Secundo, "Creating value from Social Big Data: Implications for Smart Tourism Destinations," Information Processing & Management, vol. 54, issue 5, 2018, pp. 847-860.

[9] K. Wakayama, "Travel routes extraction from Tweets", "Journal of School of Foreign Languages, Nagoya University of Foreign Studies," vol. 50, 2016, pp. 167-177, in Japanese.

weddingクッキー大切な方の、結婚のお祝いにいかがでしょうかとってもかわいいリング幸せの鳩定番のハート型他にも種類ご用意しておりますので、是非お立ち寄りくださいお待ちしておりますクッキーオーダーはinfo@shonpy.jpまでお願いいたします♡オーダーが殺到しておりますので、お早めのご連絡をお願いいたします #shonpyサンデー#アイスクリーム#ジェラート#札幌カフェ#札幌アイス#札幌ジェラート#Shonpy#修学旅行#北海道旅行#札幌旅行#すすきの#アイシングクッキーオーダー#オーダーアイシングクッキー#オーダークッキー#アイシングクッキー#icingcookies #icingcookie

Figure 1. Submitted example by person ranked first (Contents are in Japanese).

生ラム本舗澄川店です！日曜は皆様ゆったり過ごされましたか？(^^)年末年始の長い休みまであと少し!!心待ちにして明日からも頑張っていきましょう(*^▽^*) 生ラム本舗澄川店は明日17(月)はお休みですが、18(火)~30(日)まで休まず営業致します(o´∀`o)道外の方も！道内の方も！ご近所さんも！2018年のジンギスカン納めは、ぜひ生ラム本舗澄川店にご来店下さいね ٩(*´︶`*)۶ ♡ 沢山の皆様のご来店お待ちしております♪↓↓↓↓↓↓↓↓↓↓↓↓↓↓↓↓↓↓↓↓↓後半は徐々にご予約も増えてきておりますので、お早目のご予約お願い致します♪https://s.tabelog.com/hokkaido/A0101/A010305/1050833/【忘年会・新年会のご予約承っております】当店は4種類の宴会プランをご用意してます♪食べ飲み放題 羊4300-ショルダー&ラムタン・野菜盛り・キムチ・カクテキ・ライスが食べ放題!!又は、ラムしゃぶ・野菜盛り・キムチ・カクテキ・ライスが食べ放題!!両方、計41種の飲み放題付き!! 飲んで満足宴会プラン 羊5000-生ラム盛り(肩ロース・ショルダー・ラムタン・ソルトラム・ラムボーン・マトンロース)野菜盛り・おつまみ3種盛り・キムチ・ライス!!日本酒&焼酎を多種類含む全92種の飲み放題!! 女子会プラン 羊3000-生ラム盛り(肩ロース・ショルダー・ラムタン・ソルトラム・ラムボーン)野菜盛り・サラダ・スープ・キムチ・ライス!!デザートにはロマン亭のケーキ!!計41種の飲み放題!!の4種類ご用意してます(*^^*) 飲み放題は全て90分(LO.10分前)となっております♪ぜひ忘年会・新年会はジンギスカンを皆で囲んで、ワイワイ1年間に思い出を語り合って下さい(^○^) 生ラム本舗澄川店011-598-0293札幌市南区澄川4条2丁目10-19 第5エイトビル 1F #北海道#札幌#澄川#南区澄川#ジンギスカン#成吉思汗 #生ラム本舗澄川店#生ラム本舗 #生ラム#ラム肉#ラム#ラムタン#ラムしゃぶ#羊#羊肉#日本酒#焼酎#芋焼酎#麦焼酎#北海道グルメ#北海道グルメ旅#札幌グルメ#札幌グルメ旅#北海道旅行#札幌旅行#北海道観光 #札幌観光#道産子#ソウルフード#フォトジェ肉

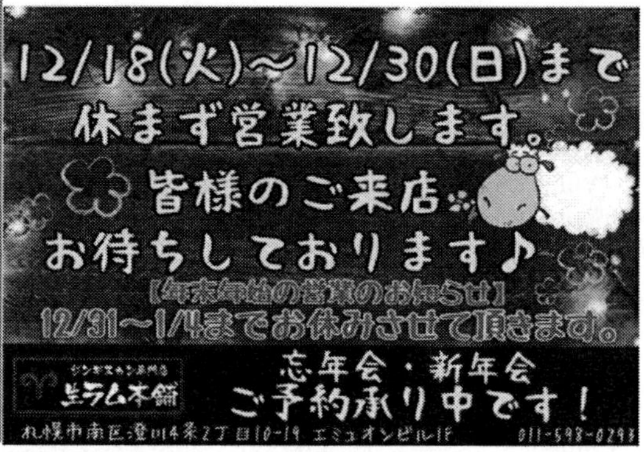

Figure 2. Submitted example by person who uses the most hashtags (Contents are in Japanese).

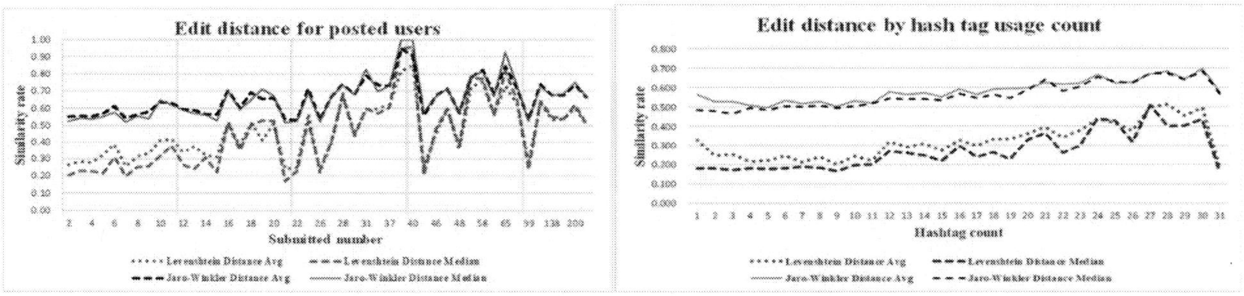

Figure 3. Edit distance for posted users and by hash tag usage count.

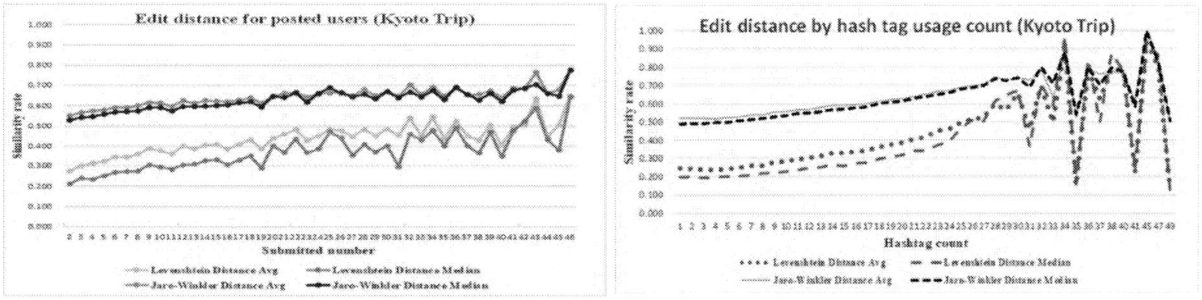

Figure 4. Edit distance for posted users and by hash tag usage count (Kyoto trip).

TABLE IV. QUARTERLY HASHTAGS RANKING AT 2018 (UPPER JAPANESE, LOWER TRANSLATION)

#	1Q		2Q		3Q		4Q	
	Submit No.	***Hashtag***	***Submit No.***	***Hashtag***	***Submit No***	***Hashtag***	***Submit No.***	***Hashtag***
1	782	#札幌 (#Sapporo)	1,076	#札幌 (#Sapporo)	1,528	#札幌 (#Sapporo)	2,154	#札幌 (#Sapporo)
2	484	#北海道 (#Hokkaido)	666	#rmet 北海道旅行 (#Hokkaido trip)	996	#北海道 (#Hokkaido)	1,676	#北海道 (#Hokkaido)
3	450	#sapporo	642	#北海道 (#hokkaido)	960	#北海道旅行 (#Hokkaido trip)	1,618	#北海道旅行 (#Hokkaido trip)
4	422	#北海道旅行 (#Hokkaido trip)	596	#札幌旅 (#Sapporo trip, abbreviation)	732	#札幌グルメ (#Sapporo gourmet)	1,108	#sapporo
5	388	#札幌旅 (#Sapporo trip, abbreviation)	578	#sapporo	696	#札幌旅 (#Sapporo trip, abbreviation)	1,050	#札幌観光 (#Sapporo sightseeing)
6	330	#札 (#Sappro abbreviation)	550	#札幌観光 (#Sapporo sightseeing)	680	#sapporo	942	#札幌グルメ (#Sappro gourmet)
7	316	#hokkaido	426	#札幌グルメ (#Sapporo Gourmet)	658	#札幌観光 (#Sapporo sightseeing)	706	#hokkaido
8	304	#北海 (#Hokkaido, abbreviation)	398	#札 (#Sapporo, abbreviation)	452	#札 (#Sapporo, abbreviation)	582	#北海道グルメ (#Hokkaido gourmet)
9	226	#札幌グルメ (#Sapporo gourmet)	344	#北海道旅 (#Hokkaido trip, abbreviation)	414	#北海道旅 (#Hokkaido trip, abbreviation)	538	#札幌旅 (#Sappro trip, abbreviation)
10	178	#北海道旅 (#sapporo trip, abbreviation)	320	#北海 (#Hokkaido, abbreviation)	384	#北海道グルメ (#Hokkaido gourmet)	490	#札 (#Sapporo, abbreviation)
11	154	#北海道グルメ	300	#札幌グル (#Sapporo gourmet,	368	#札幌スイーツ (#Sapporo sweets)	490	#札幌カフェ (#Sapporo café)

		(#hokkaido gourmet)		abbreviation)				
12	124	#北海道観光 (#Hokkaido sightseeing)	294	#北海道グル (#Hokkaido gurmet, abbreviation)	356	#札幌カフェ (#Sapporo café)	410	#すすきの (#Susukino)
13	122	#札幌グル (#Sapporo gourmet, abbreviation)	288	#すすきの (#Susukino)	338	#すすきの (#Susukino)	406	#旅行 (#Trip)
14	122	#trip	270	#hokkaido	338	#hokkaido	392	#北海 (#Hokkaido, abbreviation)
15	116	#japan	266	#札幌カフェ (#Sapporo café)	324	#北海 (#Hokkaido, abbreviation)	324	#trip

TABLE V. QUARTERLY RANKING USING BY ACCESSIBILITY_CAPTION PARAMETER AT 2018

#	1Q		2Q		3Q		4Q		Total	
	Submit No.	***Value***	***Submit No.***	***Value***	***Submit No.***	***Value***	***Submit No.***	***Value***	***Submit No.***	***Value***
1	344	food	576	food	672	food	1,056	food	2,648	food
2	50	outdoor	64	food and indoor	82	sky and outdoor	136	sky and outdoor	314	sky and outdoor
3	38	indoor	62	sky and outdoor	76	drink	114	outdoor	278	outdoor
4	34	sky and outdoor	62	drink	76	1 person	102	food and indoor	268	food and indoor
5	28	food and indoor	54	indoor	74	food and indoor	90	indoor	244	indoor
6	26	text	54	outdoor	62	indoor	68	text	222	drink
7	24	food and text	46	drink and indoor	60	outdoor	66	night and outdoor	196	1 person
8	22	drink	42	1 person	50	drink and indoor	64	dessert and food	164	text
9	20	night and outdoor	36	dessert and food	38	dessert and food	64	night, sky and outdoor	146	dessert and food
10	20	night, sky and outdoor	32	text	38	text	62	drink	136	drink and indoor
11	18	1 person	28	1 person, food	34	1 person, food	60	1 person	122	night, sky and outdoor
12	16	drink and indoor	28	sky, tree and outdoor	28	sky, cloud and outdoor	56	sky, cloud and outdoor	116	1 person, food
13	16	1 person, outdoor	26	2 people	24	food and text	48	sky, tree and outdoor	112	sky, cloud and outdoor
14	16	sky, cloud and outdoor	24	drink and food	22	one or more people	42	1 person, food	110	night and outdoor
15	12	1 person, night and outdoor	24	one or more people	22	sky, tree and outdoor	38	1 person, outdoor	106	sky, tree and outdoor
16	12	1 person, food	20	people sitting, table and indoor	22	night, sky and outdoor	34	one or more people	92	one or more people
17	12	2 people	20	food and text	20	2 people	28	tree, sky, plant, outdoor and nature	84	2 people
18	12	text and food	16	night, sky and outdoor	14	people sitting, table and indoor	28	tree, plant, sky, outdoor and nature	74	food and text
19	12	1 person, sky and outdoor	14	one or more people and indoor	14	people sitting and food	26	2 people	68	1 person, outdoor
20	12	one or more people	14	night and outdoor	14	sky, cloud, tree and outdoor	26	table and indoor	68	drink and food

TABLE VI. RANKING OF HASHTAGS CLASSIFIED BY ACCESSIBILITY_CAPTION PARAMETER AT 2018 (UPPER JAPANESE, LOWER TRANSLATION)

#	1Q		2Q		3Q		4Q	
	Submit No.	***Hashtag***	***Submit No.***	***Hashtag***	***Submit No***	***Hashtag***	***Submit No.***	***Hashtag***
1	58	#ジンギスカ (#Genghis Khan, abbreviation)	62	#プチギフト (#Smaill gift)	62	#グルメ (#Gurmet)	82	#スープカレー (#Soup curry)
2	54	#ラム	60	#ギフト	62	#ジェラート	76	#旅行

		(#Lamb)		(#Gift)		(#Gelato)		(#trip)
3	50	#ラ (#Lamb, abbreviation)	58	#candle	60	#アイスクリーム (#Icecream)	62	#寿 (#Bridal)
4	50	#道産 (#Hokkaido made)	58	#キャンドル教室 (#Candle class)	60	#Shonpy	62	#アイスクリーム (#Icecream)
5	50	#成吉思汗 (#Genghis Khan, displayed by Kanji-word)	58	#キャンドルトマト (#candle tomato)	60	#ハンドパフェ (#Hand parfait)	62	#ラーメン (#Ramen)
6	48	#ラムタ (#Ramta)	56	#candles	60	#修学旅行 (#School excursion)	60	#Shonpy
7	48	#生ラ (#Raw lamb, abbreviation)	56	#ハンドメイド (#handmade)	58	#八景島シーパラダイス (#Hakkeijima Sea Paradise)	60	#修学旅行 (#School excursion)
8	48	#生ラム本舗澄川 (#Raw lamb restrant Sumikawa)	52	#海鮮 (#Seafood)	58	#アイシングクッキー (#Icing cookie)	60	#大通 (#Oodori)
9	48	#ラムしゃ (#Ram Shabushabu, abbreviation)	46	#ブライダル (#Bridal)	52	#ジンギスカ (#Genghis Khan, abbreviation)	60	#ジェラート (#Gelato)
10	48	#芋焼 (#Roasting poteto)	44	#個室居酒屋 (#Private room tavern)	50	#icingcookies	60	#アイシングクッキー (#Icing cookie)

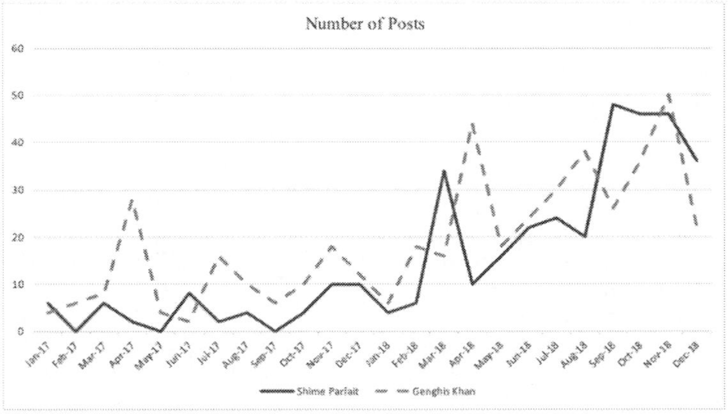

Figure 5. Number of posts about "Shime Parfait" and "Genghis Khan".

Towards Construction of an Explanation Framework for Whole Processes of Data Analysis Applications: Concepts and Use Cases

Hiroshi Ishikawa
Graduate School of Systems Design
Faculty of System Design
Tokyo Metropolitan University
Hino, Tokyo
E-mail: ishikawa-hiroshi@tmu.ac.jp

Yukio Yamamoto
Japan Aerospace Exploration Agency
Sagamihara, Kanagawa
E-mail: yamamoto.yukio@jaxa.jp

Masaharu Hirota
Department of Information Science
Faculty of Informatics
Okayama University of Science
Okayama, Okayama
E-mail: hirota@mis.ous.ac.jp

Masaki Endo
Division of Core Manufacturing
Polytechnic University
Kodaira, Tokyo
E-mail: endou@uitec.ac.jp

***Abstract*- The main contribution of the paper is to address the necessity of both macro and micro explanations for Social Big Data (SBD) applications and to propose an explanation framework integrating both of these, allowing SBD applications to be more widely accepted and used. The framework provides both a macro explanation of the whole procedure and a micro explanation of the constructed model, as well as an explanation of the decisions made by the model. For a macro explanation of the application, we introduce a data model for abstractly describing all processes from data acquisition to data analysis. We explain the processes based on the data model. For the micro explanation, we illustrate the basis of the interpretation of the analytical model and the decisions made when applying it. We describe some of the specific features of the explanation framework proposed through multiple use cases.**

Keywords*- *social big data; explanayion; data model; data management; data mining.

I. INTRODUCTION

We are surrounded by big data, which are waiting to be analyzed and used. Big data are real data, such as automobile driving data and space observation data, generated from real world measurement and observation, social data derived from social media, e.g., Twitter and Instagram, and open data published by highly public groups, e.g., weather data and evacuation location data. These are generally called social big data (SBD) [9] [11]. Furthermore, SBD are inherently represented by multimedia (MM). By integrating and analyzing social big data, new knowledge can be obtained, which is expected to bring new value to society.

Further, as the horizon of applications whose main task is data analysis has spread, the following problems have emerged:

- Application to science, e.g., lunar and planetary science

Analytical applications in this field require strictness as science. That is, explanation of the protocol (procedure) of analysis and explanation of the reason for decisions are required. In addition, as to the interpretation of the analytical model, it is necessary to explain the input data (for learning and test) and the data manipulation on the data, and the procedure (algorithm and program) for model construction. In order to interpret the individual results, it is necessary to explain the input data (actual data) and the reasons for the decisions.

- Application to Social Infrastructure, e.g., Mobility as a Service (MaaS)

Analytical applications in this field require consent of practitioners. That is, the analysis result must be consistent with the practitioners' own experiences, and especially in the case of applications such as ones related to human life, it is necessary to fulfill the accountability to the concerned parties. Interpretation of both a model and individual results is necessary as with science. In addition, especially if the data about the generic users are utilized in applications, interpretation of the model is also important in order to get rid of the general users' concerns.

In order for social big data to widely be used, it is necessary to explain to the user the application system. Both microscopic description, that is, interpretation of the analytical model and explanation of individual decisions and macroscopic description, that is, description of the whole process including the data manipulation and the model construction are required.

First of all, the reason why a macro explanation is necessary is described below. In order for social big data applications to be accepted by users, it is necessary to ensure at least their reliability. Since information science is one area of science, we should guarantee reproducibility as science. In other words, it is necessary to ensure that third parties can prepare and analyze data according to given explanation and can get the same results.

In addition, in order for the service to be operatable, it is necessary for the final user of the service to be convinced of how the service processes and uses the personal information. In addition, if the users can be convinced of the description of way of using the personal information, the progress of data portability can be advanced based on the EU's GDPR law on personal information protection [5] and Japan-based information bank to promote the use of personal information [18].

Next, a micro explanation is necessary for the following reasons. In order for analysts of social big data and field experts using the data to accept decisions made by the constructed model, it is assumed that they must understand the structure, actions and grounds of the model and are satisfied with them as well.

Up to now, the authors have been involved in the development of a wide range of social big data use cases ranging from tourism, disaster prevention to lunar and planetary science [12] [26]. In the course of these processes, from the users of the use cases, we have often received questions as to what kind of data are processed, what kind of model are created as the core of analysis, and furthermore, what are the grounds for the decisions. In other words, from the development experiences of multiple use cases, we have come to think that both the macro explanation proposed in this paper and the micro explanation emerging in AI are urgently needed.

To date, the authors created multiple seismic source classifiers of the lunar earthquakes (moonquakes) in the field of lunar and planetary science using the Balanced Random Forest [3], and the features, e.g., the distance between the moon and the earth, were calculated and studied for extracting features strongly related to cause of moonquakes as a micro explanation [12]. With regard to a macro explanation, the authors also showed that by observing many use cases, social big data applications should include different digital ecosystems such as data management (database operation) and data analysis (data mining, machine learning, artificial intelligence), we have noticed that it is necessary to have a method to generally describe the whole process of application consisting of such a hybrid digital ecosystem. Therefore, as a framework to describe processes in an abstraction level independent of a specific programming language, we have come to think of adopting a data model [8] developed in the field of database and proposed a framework for description using mathematical concept of set family [10]. As described in the subsequent section of the related works, the micro explanation research is being actively carried out, whereas as far as research on the framework for the macroscopic description is not known except our work.

The main contribution of the paper is to address the necessity of both macro and micro explanations for SBD applications and to propose an explanation framework integrating both of them. This will allow SBD applications to be more widely accepted and used. Although this paper describes our research-in-progress, we propose an integrated framework for explanation and introduce a part of its functions through case studies. In Section II, we introduce our explanation framework. Through use case examples of macroscopic description and microscopic description, we describe the features of the proposed approach in Sections III and IV, respectively.

II. OUR APPROACH

A. Explanation Framework

For a macro explanation of applications, the goal is to facilitate a data model for abstractly describing the entire processes from data acquisition to data analysis and to explain the processes based on the description. For the micro explanation, we aim to show the basis of the interpretation of the constructed model and the individual decisions made when applying it.

1) Construction of a theoretical foundation for integrated explanation

For that purpose, we build a theoretical framework of the technical foundation that integrates the following micro and macro explanatory methods.

a) Macro explanation function: The application system is a hybrid ecosystem consisting of data management and data mining (including machine learning and Artificial Intelligence, or AI), and the function must be able to describe the application seamlessly. Moreover, it must be able to describe the application in a high level not depending on individual environments or programming languages. Therefore, we first create a framework to unify the hybrid ecosystem based on the data model approach. In other words, we develop a method to provide macro explanations with the constituent elements (data structure and data manipulation) of the model based on the mathematical family of sets as a basic unit. The explanation mechanism provided by the proposed framework presents as a macro explanation a sequence of operations on databases to the user based on the model of SBD applications consisting of data management and data mining, as in a use case depicted in Section III.

b) Micro explanatory function: We develop an explanatory

method independent of analytical model by extending explanatory functions based on attributes or constituent elements, which is an emergent approach in AI, discussed in the related work subsection. In other words, in model categories for structured data consisting of attributes, such as Support Vector Machine (SVM) and decision trees, we develop a method for systematically discovering subsets of attributes with strong influence on analysis results based on multiple weak classifiers. Especially this function is used to interpret the model itself. In model categories like Deep Neural Network (DNN) suitable for non-structured data such as images, we develop a method of explaining the analysis result based on the constituent elements or decomposition of the image with the use of annotation or attention. Especially this function is used to show the basis of individual decisions. For the micro explanation of the reasons for decisions, if the analysis target is image data, a part of the image which leads to the conclusion is indicated by concepts or words as its annotations based on a heat map. If the object is structural data, that is, it consists of attributes, the micro explanation is presented in terms of the contribution ratios of the attributes as in a use case depicted in Section IV.

2) Collection of use cases and verification of basic technology

First, we collect several different kinds of use cases (tourism, mobility service, lunar exploration). We generate concrete explanations as targets for typical ones, using the integrated explanatory platform developed in items *a* and *b* and verify its feasibility

3) Implementation of Explanation generation and presentation method

Based on the theoretical framework of the integrated infrastructure, an automatic generation method of explanation and a presentation function of explanations are implemented. We evaluate their effectiveness by performing the experiments. We also incorporate InfoGraphics [23] as a method of presenting explanations to users since the users are not always analysis experts.

Basically, for micro explanation, we create explanations of individual decisions by solving partial problems that restrict information existing in original problems.

In this research, we aim to develop both the emerging microscopic-explanatory functions and macroscopic-explanatory functions and to build a framework for integrating two kinds of explanations.

B. Related Research

As a trend other than the authors' research, researches corresponding to micro explanatory functions have become active in AI, what is so called eXplainable AI (XAI) at present.

First, there is an attempt [14] to try to give a basic definition to the possibility of interpretation of a model in machine learning and a research [4] on the evaluation method of interpretability.

Next, individual studies on XAI are roughly classified into (1) description based on features, (2) interpretable model, and (3) derivation of explanation model. A research is done to create a classification rule for explanation by creating a subset of features in SVM as a category of (1) [15]. In addition, in the image classification using Convolutional Neural Network (CNN) and Long Short Term Memory (LSTM), there is a research to generate explanations based on both image features and class features [6]. Further there is a research introducing the explanation vector to make explicit the most important attributes [1]. In the category of (2), there is a research using a AND/OR tree to discover the components of the model [22] and a research to make models that can be interpreted by considering the generation process of features [13]. A research deriving description with reference of any classifier of the local approximation model falls into the category (3) [20].

While developing along the approaches of (1) and (3) as a micro explanatory technique, we aim to build a comprehensive explanation basis by conducting research on macroscopic explanation technology.

In addition, although there is an application of infographics to a tourism use case [25], our research aims at basic research that can be widely used for visualization of explanation of general analysis.

III. CASE STUDY: MACRO EXPLANATION OF TOURISM APPLICATION

We will describe a case that explains how our data is used in analysis application. For that purpose, an integrated data model is introduced as a macroscopic description of an analytical application which is a hybrid ecosystem. Then the application is described using the integrated model as a basis for macro explanation.

A. Integrated Model

We propose our SBD data model consisting of data structures and operations in the following subsections.

1)Data model for SBD

Our SBD model uses a mathematical concept of a *family* [24], a collection of sets, as a basis for data structures. Family can be used as an apparatus for bridging the gaps between data management operations and data analysis operations.

Basically, our database is a *Family*. A Family is divided into *Indexed family* and *Non-Indexed family*. A Non-Indexed family is a collection of sets.

An Indexed family is defined as follows:

- $\{Set\}$ is a Non-Indexed family with *Set* as its element.
- $\{Set_i\}$ is an Indexed family with Set_i as its *i-th* element. Here, *i: Index* is called *indexing set* and *i* is

an element of Index.

- Set is {<time space object>}.
- Set_i is {<*time space object*>}$_i$. Here, *object* is an identifier to arbitrary identifiable user-provided data, e.g., record, object, and multimedia data appearing in social big data. *Time* and *space* are universal keys across multiple sources of social big data.
- {*Indexed* $family_i$} is also an Indexed family with *Indexed* $family_i$ as its *i-th* element. In other words, Indexed family can constitute a hierarchy of sets.

Please note that the following concepts are interchangeably used in this paper.

- Singleton family ⇔ set
- Singleton set ⇔ element

As described later in this section, we can often observe that SBD applications contain families as well as sets and they involve both data mining and data management. Please note that a family is also suitable for representing hierarchical structures inherent in time and locations associated with social big data.

If operations constructing a family out of a collection of sets and those deconstructing a family into a collection of sets are provided in addition to both family-dedicated and set-dedicated operations, SBD applications will be described in an integrated fashion by our proposed model.

2) SBD Operations

SBD model constitutes an algebra with respect to Family, as follows.

SBD consists of Family data management operations and Family data mining operations. Further, Family data management operations are divided into Intra Family operations and Inter Family operations.

First, Intra Family Data Management Operations are described as follows:

a) Intra Indexed Intersect (*i:Index Db p*(*i*)) returns a singleton family (i.e., set) intersecting sets which satisfy the predicate *p*(*i*). Database *Db* is a Family, which will not be mentioned hereafter.

b) Intra Indexed Union (*i:Index Db p*(*i*)) returns a singleton family union-ing sets which satisfy *p*(*i*).

c) Intra Indexed Difference (*i:Index Db p*(*i*)) returns a singleton family, that is, the first set satisfying *p*(*i*) minus all the rest of sets satisfying *p*(*i*)

d) Indexed Select (*i:Index Db p1*(*i*) *p2*(*i*)) returns an Indexed family with respect to *i* (preserved) where the element sets satisfy the predicate *p1*(*i*) and the elements of the sets satisfy the predicate *p2*(*i*). As a special case of true as *p1*(*i*), this operation returns the whole indexed family. In a special case of a singleton family, Indexed Select is reduced to Select (a relational operation).

e) Indexed Project (*i:Index Db p*(*i*) *a*(*i*)) returns an Indexed family where the element sets satisfy *p*(*i*) and the elements of the sets are projected according to *a*(*i*), attribute specification. This also extends also relational Project.

f) Intra Indexed cross product (*i:Index Db p*(*i*)) returns a singleton family obtained by product-ing sets which satisfy *p*(*i*). This is extension of Cartesian product, one of relational operators.

g) Intra Indexed Join (*i:Index Db p1*(*i*) *p2*(*i*)) returns a singleton family obtained by joining sets which satisfy *p1*(*i*) based on the join predicate *p2*(*i*). This is extension of join, one of relational operators.

h) Select-Index (*i:Index Db p*(*i*)) returns *i:Index* of set_i which satisfy *p*(*i*). As a special case of true as *p*(*i*), it returns all index.

i) Make-indexed family (*Index Non-Indexed Family*) returns an indexed Family. This operator requires *order-compatibility*, that is, that *i* corresponds to *i-th set of Non-Indexed Family.*

j) Partition (*i:Index Db p*(*i*)) returns an Indexed family. Partition makes an Indexed family out of a given set (i.e. singleton family either w/ or w/o index) by grouping elements with respect to *p* (*i:Index*). This is extension of "groupby" as a relational operator.

k) ApplyFunction (*i:Index Db f*(*i*)) applies *f*(*i*) to *i-th* set of DB, where *f*(*i*) takes a set as a whole and gives another set including a singleton set (i.e., Aggregate function). This returns an indexed family. *f*(*i*) can be defined by users.

Second, Inter Family Data Management Operations are described as follows:

All are assumed to be Index-Compatible

a) Indexed Intersect (*i:Index Db1 Db2 p*(*i*)) union-compatible

b) Indexed Union (*i:Index Db1 Db2 p*(*i*)) union-compatible

c) Indexed Difference (*i:Index Db1 Db2 p*(*i*)) union-compatible

d) Indexed Join (i:Index Db1 Db2 p1(i) p2(i))

e) Indexed cross product (*i:Index Db1 Db2 p*(*i*))

Finally, Family Data Mining Operations are described as follows:

a) Cluster (*Family method similarity* {*par*}) returns a Family as default, where Index is automatically produced. This is an unsupervised learner.

b) Make-classifier (*i:Index set:Family learnMethod* {*par*}) returns a classifier (Classify) with its accuracy. This is a supervised learner.

c) Classify (*Index/class set*) returns an indexed family with class as its index.

d) Make-frequent itemset (*Db supportMin*) returns an Indexed Family as frequent itemsets, which satisfy *supportMin*.

e) Make-association-rule (*Db confidenceMin*) creates association rules based on frequent itemsets *Db*, which satisfy *confidenceMin*. This is out of range of our algebra, too.

Please note that the predicates and functions used in the above operations can be defined by the users in addition to the system-defined ones such as Count.

B. Tourist Applications

We describe a case study, finding candidate access spots for accessible Free Wi-Fi in Japan [16]. This case is classified as integrated analysis based on two kinds of social data.

This section describes our proposed method of detecting attractive tourist areas where users cannot connect to accessible Free Wi-Fi by using posts by foreign travelers on social media.

Our method uses differences in the characteristics of two types of social media:

Real-time: Immediate posts, e.g., Twitter

Batch-time: Data stored to devices for later posts, e.g., Flickr

Twitter users can only post tweets when they can connect devices to Wi-Fi or wired networks. Therefore, travelers can post tweets in areas with Free Wi-Fi for inbound tourism or when they have mobile communications. In other words, we can obtain only tweets with geo-tags posted by foreign travelers from such places. Therefore, areas where we can obtain huge numbers of tweets posted by foreign travelers are identified as places where they can connect to accessible Free Wi-Fi and /or that are attractive for them to sightsee.

Flickr users, on the other hand, take many photographs by using digital devices regardless of networks, but whether they can upload photographs on-site depends on the conditions of the network. As a result, almost all users can upload photographs after returning to their hotels or home countries. However, geo-tags annotated to photographs can indicate when they were taken. Therefore, although it is difficult to obtain detailed information (activities, destinations, or routes) on foreign travelers from Twitter, Flickr can be used to observe such information. In this study, we are based on our hypothesis of "A place that has a lot of Flickr posts, but few Twitter posts must have a critical lack of accessible Free Wi-Fi." We extracted areas that were tourist attractions for foreign travelers, but from which they could not connect to accessible Free Wi-Fi by using these characteristics of social media. What our method aims to find is places currently without accessible Free Wi-Fi.

Our method envisaged places that met the following two conditions as candidate access spots for accessible free Wi-Fi:

- Spots where there was no accessible Free Wi-Fi
- Spots that many foreign visitors visited

We use the number of photographs taken at locations to extract tourist spots. Many people might take photographs of subjects, such as landscapes based on their own interests. They might then upload those photographs to Flickr. As these were locations at which many photographs had been taken, these places might also be interesting places for many other people to sightsee or visit. We have defined such places as tourist spots. We specifically examined the number of photographic locations to identify tourist spots to find locations where photographs had been taken by a lot of people. We mapped photographs that had a photographic location onto a two-dimensional grid based on the location at which a photograph had been taken to achieve this. Here, we created individual cells in a grid that was 30 square meters. Consequently, all cells in the grid that was obtained included photographs taken in a range. We then counted the number of users in each cell. We regarded cells with greater numbers of users than the threshold as tourist spots.

[Integrated Hypothesis] Based on different data generated form Twitter and Flickr by using our generalized difference method, the fragment collects attractive tourist spots for foreign visitors but without accessible free Wi-Fi currently (See Figure 1):

$DB_{t/visitor}$ ← Tweet DB of foreign visitors obtained by mining based on durations of their stays in Japan;

$DB_{f/visitor}$ ← Flickr photo DB of foreign visitors obtained by mining based on their habitations;

T ← Partition (*i:Index grid* $DB_{t/visitor}$ *p*(*i*)); This partitions foreign visitors tweets into grids based on geo-tags; This operation returns a indexed family.

F ← Partition (*j:Index grid* $DB_{f/visitor}$ *p*(*j*)); This partitions foreign visitors photos into grids based on geo-tags; This operation returns a indexed family.

Index1 ← Select-Index (*i:Index T Density*(*i*) >= *th1*); *th1* is a threshold. This operation returns a singleton family.

Index2 ← Select-Index (*j:Index F Density*(*i*) >= *th2*); *th2* is a threshold. This operation returns a singleton family.

Index3 ← Difference (*Index2 Index1*); This operation returns a singleton family.

Plaese note that Partition and Select-Index are family data management operations while Difference is a relational (set) data management operation.

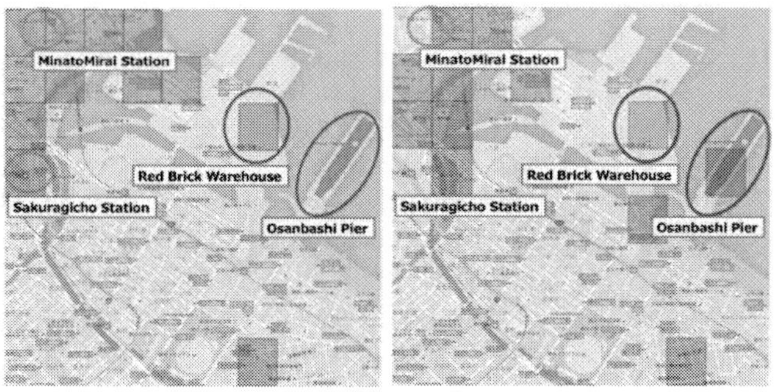

Figure 1. Differences of high-density areas of Tweets (left) and of Flickr photos (right).

We collected more than 4.7 million data items with geo-tags from July 1, 2014 to February 28, 2015 in Japan. We detected tweets tweeted by foreign visitors by using the method proposed by Saeki et al. [7]. The number of tweets that was tweeted by foreign visitors was more than 1.9 million. The number of tweets that was tweeted by foreign visitors in the Yokohama area was more than 7,500. We collected more than 5,600 photos with geo-tags from July 1, 2014 to February 28, 2015 in Japan. We detected photos that had been posted by foreign visitors to Yokohama by using our proposed method. Foreign visitors posted 2,132 photos. For example, grids indexed by *Index3* contain "Osanbashi Pier." Please note that the above description doesn't take unique users into consideration.

IV. CASE STUDY: MICRO EXPLANATION FOR SCIENCE APPLICATION

In this section, we present the case of determining features important for interpreting the constructed model by reducing features with small contribution ratios.

We apply Balanced Random Forest [3] which extends Random Forest [2], a popular supervised learning method in machine learning, to lunar and planetary science to verify the key features in analysis. Our verification method tries to confirm whether the known seismic source labels can be reproduced by Balanced Random Forest using the features described below based on the features constructed from the moonquakes with the seismic source label of the known moonquake as the correct label.

A. Features for Analysis

TABLE I shows the parameters in the coordinate systems used in this section. We use as seismic source of moonquakes the position on the planets of the moon, the sun, the earth, and Jupiter (X, y, z), velocity (vx, vy, vz), and distance (lt) . Based on the time of moonquake occurrence, we calculate and use features using SPICE [17]. Here, sun perturbation is the solar perturbation. The IAU MOON coordinate system is a fixed coordinate system centered on the moon. The z axis is the north pole direction of the moon, the x axis is the meridian direction of the moon, the y axis is the right direction with respect to the plane xz. The IAU EARTH coordinate system is a fixed coordinate system centered on the earth. Here, the z axis is the direction of the conventional international origin, the x axis is the direction of the prime meridian, and the y axis is the right direction with respect to the xz plane.

We also calculate the period of the perigee at the distance of earth from moon, the period based on the period of the perigee, the periods of the x coordinate and the y coordinate of the solar perturbation. *sin* and *cos* values are calculated from these periodic features and the phase angle based on them. In addition, at the positions moon from earth and sun from earth, we calculate the *cos* similarity as the features of the sidereal moon. As all possible combinations of these features, a total of 55 features are used in experiments described in this paper.

B. Balanced Random Forest

Random Forest is an ensemble learning that combines a large number of decision trees and is widely used in fields such as data mining and has a characteristic that the contribution ratio of features can be calculated. However, Random Forest has a problem such that when there is a large difference in the number of data to be learned depending on class labels, the classifier is learned biased towards classes with a large number of data. Generally, we address the problem of imbalanced data by weighting classes with a small number of data. However, if there is any large skew between the numbers of data, the weight of data belonging to classes with a small number will become large, which is considered to cause over fitting to classes with a small number of data. Since the deep moonquakes have a large difference in the number of events for each seismic source, it is necessary to apply a method considering imbalanced data.

As analysis considering imbalanced data, we apply Balanced Random Forest [3], which makes the number of samples even for each class when constructing each decision tree. Balanced Random Forest divides each decision tree based on the Gini coefficient. Gini coefficient is an index representing impurity degree, which takes a value between 0 and 1. The closer it is to 0, the higher the purity is, that is, the less variance the data have. The contribution ratio of the feature is calculated for each feature by calculating the reduction ratio by the Gini coefficient at the branch of the tree. The final contribution ratio is the average value of contribution ratios of each decision tree.

C. Experiment Setting

Here, we describe experiments for evaluating features effective for seismic source classification, together with the results and considerations. Based on the classification performance and the contribution ratio of the features by Balanced Random Forest, we analyze the relationship between the seismic sources in the features used in this paper.

The outline of feature analysis is shown below.

- Features are calculated based on the time of occurrence of moonquake.
- Balanced Random Forest is applied to each pair of all seismic sources.
- Classification performance and the contribution ratio of the features by Balanced Random Forest are calculated and analyzed.

In this paper, as one-vs-one method, by constructing the classifier for every pair of two seismic sources in the dataset, we perform analysis paying attention to characteristics of each seismic source and the relationship between seismic sources. 100 Random Forests are constructed for each classifier. The number of samples used to construct each decision tree are taken 50 by bootstrap method. Also, scikit-learn [19] was used to construct each decision tree in Random Forest.

In this paper, we perform the following analysis as feature selection.

• We create a classifier that learns all of the extracted 55 features.

TABLE I. PARAMETERS IN THE COORDINATE SYSTEMS COMPUTED USING SPICE.

Target	Observer	Coordinate system	Parameter
EARTH BARYCENTER	**MOON**	IAU MOON	**earth_from_moon**
SOLAR SYSTEM BARYCENTER	**MOON**	IAU MOON	**sun_from_moon**
JUPITER BARYCENTER	**MOON**	IAU MOON	**jupiter_from_moon**
SOLAR SYSTEM BARYCENTER	**EARTH BARYCENTER**	IAU EARTH	**sun_from_earth**
JUPITER BARYCENTER	**EARTHBARYCENTER**	IAU EARTH	**jupiter_from_earth**
SUN	**SOLAR SYSTEM BARYCENTER**	IAU EARTH	**sun_perturbation**

TABLE II. NUMBER OF DATA FOR EACH SEISMIC SOURCE.

Seismic source	A1	A5	A6	A7	A8	A9	A10	A14	A18	A20	A23	A25	A35	A44	A204	A218
Number of data	441	76	178	85	327	145	230	165	214	153	79	72	70	86	85	74

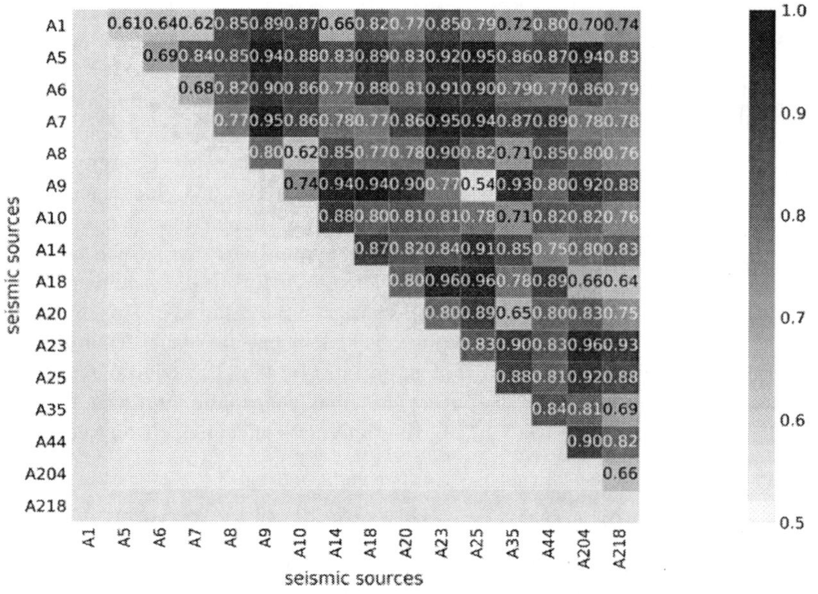

Figure 2. Averages of F-values for pairs of seismic sources.

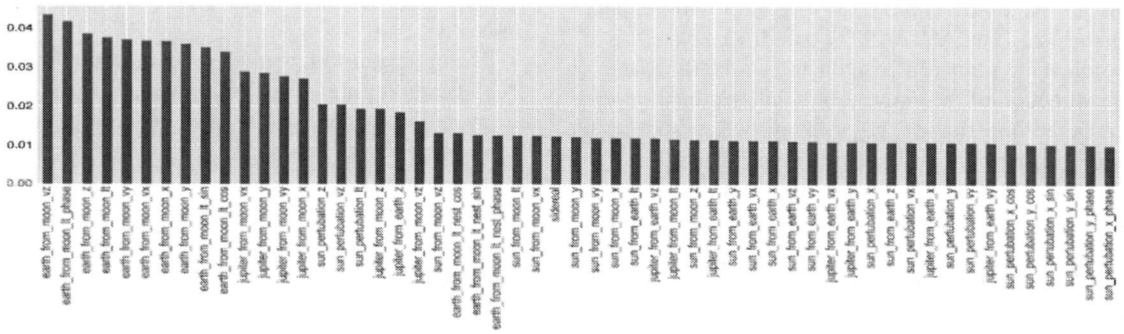

Figure 3. Averages of contribution ratios for each feature.

• Using the Variance Inflation Factor (VIF), we construct a classifier after reducing features.

Here, VIF is one of the indicators used to evaluate *multicollinearity*. In this paper, in order to make VIF of each feature 6 or less, experiments were conducted on a subset with reduced features. Based on the experimental results using all features, we calculate VIF and delete features with 6 or more VIF. To calculate VIF, statsmodel [21] was used.

TABLE II shows the dataset in this paper. We select events of 16 seismic sources whose observed number of moonquake events is 70 or more.

In this paper, the precision ratio, recall ratio, and F-value are used as indexes for evaluating the performance of classification of seismic sources.

The precision ratio is an index for measuring the accuracy of the classification, and the recall ratio is an index for measuring the coverage of the classification. F-value is the harmonic mean of recall and precision ratios and is an index in consideration of the balance of precision and recall. The score of the classifier in this paper is the average value of the F-values of the two classes targeted by the classifier.

D. Experiment Results

1) Experimental results using all features

a) Classification performance

Figure 2 is the average of the F-values of classifiers for each seismic source. The vertical axis and the horizontal axis show seismic sources, each value is a score of the average of F-value of classifier. In Figure 2, the highest classification performance is 0.96 and it is observed in multiple pairs of seismic sources. Also, the lowest classification performance is 0.54 as of classifier between A9 and A25. Figure 2 shows that some classification is difficult depending on combinations of seismic sources. Also, the number of classifiers with 0.9 or higher as classification performance is 20, about 17% of the total number of the classifiers. The number of classifiers with 0.8 or more and less than 0.9 is 60, 50% of the total. The number of classifiers with performance below 0.6 is only one. Most of the classifiers show high classification performance and show that the positional relationships of the planets are effective for the seismic source classification of the deep moonquakes.

b) Contribution ratio of features

Figure 3 shows the average value of contribution ratios for each feature. All features with the higher contribution ratios are those of the earth when they are calculated as the moon as the origin. In addition, it shows that the contribution ratios of Jupiter 's features are high when the moon is the origin while those of earth features is high when the moon is the origin. By comparing features when the moon is the origin and when the earth is the origin, the features with the moon as the origin has a higher contribution ratio than the features with the earth as the origin. Figure 3 indicates that relationships between the moon and the Earth affect the classification most strongly. However, there is a possibility that correlation between features, then it is necessary to further analyze each feature from view point of mutual independence. Therefore, in the following subsection, considering the correlations between features, we will describe the experimental results after feature reduction using VIF.

2) Experimental results of feature reduction using VIF.

a) Classification performance

Figure 4 shows the average of the F-values of the classifier when the features are reduced. Similarly, as in Figure 2, the vertical axis and the horizontal axis are seismic sources, respectively, and each value is the score of the F-value of the classifier in Figure 4. In addition, the number of classifiers whose classification performance is 0.9 or higher is 26, about 22% of the total. 54 classifiers with 0.8 or higher but less than 0.9 are 45% of the total. There is one classifier whose classification performance is less than 0.6. Compared with Figure 2, these show that the classification performance does not change significantly.

b) Contribution ratio of features

Figure 5 shows the average value of the contribution ratios of each seismic source after feature reduction. After reducing features, earth features when the origin is the moon are reduced to 4 features of the top 10 features which existed before feature reduction. The four features between top 11 and 14 positions of the features of Jupiter when the origin is the moon, as shown in Figure 3, are reduced to one feature. Other parameters of Jupiter are thought to have been affected by other features. The subset of the features after feature reduction is considered to have small influence of multicollinearity. Therefore, there is a possibility that the features of the Earth and some of the features of Jupiter are effective for classification when the moon is the origin,

E. Discussion of methods and features

By using Balanced Random Forest, contribution ratios of features can be easily calculated in addition to classification performance, so it is useful for feature analysis like the scientific research described in this section. However, in this method, there is room for consideration of parameters of classification techniques depending on the seismic sources as the classification targets. Moreover, in order to obtain higher classification performance, it is necessary to consider many classification methods. Furthermore, it is necessary to apply a method considering waveform information. In addition, since the findings obtained in this paper are only correlations, it is difficult to directly estimate the causal mechanism of the deep moonquakes. However, the results of this paper are shown to be useful for new analysis and knowledge creation of experts. If the knowledge of experts is available, the elucidation of the causal relationships between the seismic sources and the planetary bodies and ultimately that of the causal mechanism of the moonquakes can be expected.

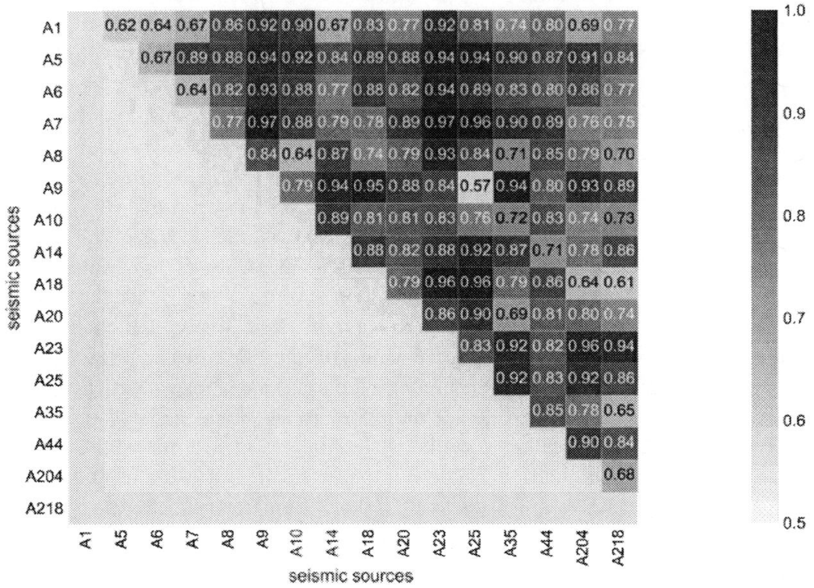

Figure 4. Averages of F-values for pairs of seismic sources after feature reduction.

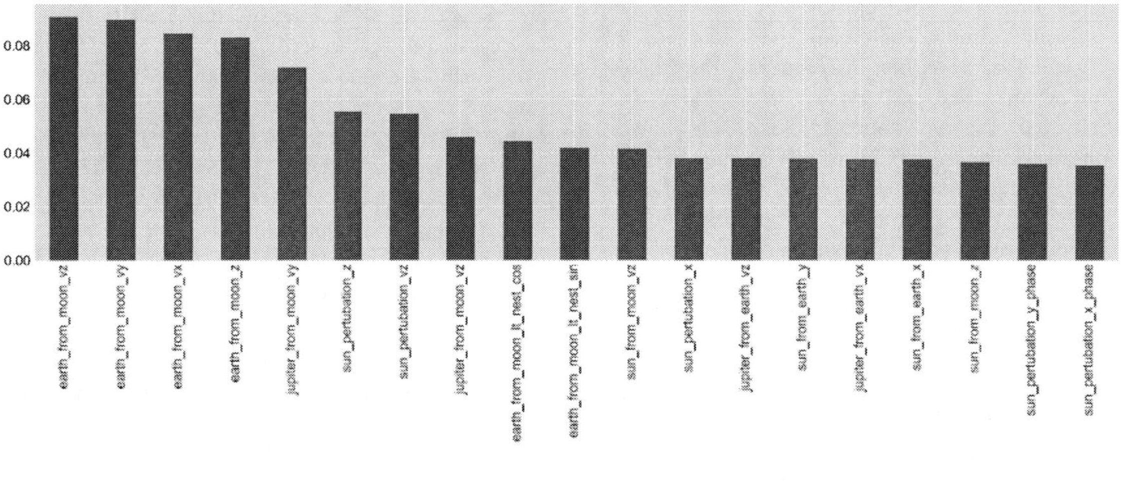

Figure 5. Averages of contribution ratios for each feature after feature reduction.

V. CONCLUSION

In this paper, we proposed a general framework of explanation necessary to widely promote implementation of analytical applications using social big data. The procedure of a tourism application based on integrated data model was described as an example of a macro explanatory function. In addition, we used Balanced Random Forest as a micro explanatory function to extract features effective for the seismic source classification of the deep moonquakes from the temporal and spatial features of the planets. We will develop a micro explanatory function showing the basis of individual decisions in analysis and complete the whole explanation framework and at the same time we will verify the versatility of the explanatory framework by applying it to a wider variety of use cases in the future.

ACKNOWLEDGMENT

This work was supported by JSPS KAKENHI Grant Number 16K00157, 16K16158, and Tokyo Metropolitan University Grant-in-Aid for Research on Priority Areas Research on social big data.

REFERENCES

[1] D. Baehrens et al., "How to explain individual classification decisions," The Journal of Machine Learning Research, vol.11, pp. 1803-1831, August 2010.

[2] L. Breiman, "Random forests," Machine learning, vol. 45, no. 1, pp. 5-32, 2001.

[3] C. Chen, A. Liaw, and L. Breiman, "Using random forest to learn imbalanced data," University of California, Berkeley, pp. 1-12, 2004.

[4] F. D. Velez and B. Kim, "A roadmap for a rigorous science of interpretability," pp. 1-13, 2017 (arXiv: 1702.08608, 2017).

[5] EU GDPR, https://eugdpr.org/ [retrieved: March, 2019].

[6] L. Hendricks et al., "Generating visual explanations," Proc. European Conference on Computer Vision, pp. 3-19, Springer, 2016.

[7] M. Hirota, K. Saeki, Y. Ehara, and H. Ishikawa, "Live or Stay ?: Classifying Twitter Users into Residents and Visitors," Proc. International Conference on Knowledge Engineering and Semantic Web (KESW 2016), pp. 1-2, 2016.

[8] H. Ishikawa, Database, Mori Kita Publishing, 2008 (in Japanese).

[9] H. Ishikawa, Social Big Data Mining, CRC Press, 2015.

[10] H. Ishikawa, D. Kato, M. Endo, and M. Hirota, "Generalized Difference Method for Generating Integrated Hypotheses in Social Big Data," Proc. ACM MEDES International Conference, pp. 13-22, 2018.

[11] H. Ishikawa and M. Hirota, S. Yokoyama, Social Big Data Practiced with Full Stack JavaScript and Python Machine Learning Library, Corona Publishing, 2019 (in Japanese).

[12] K. Kato, R. Yamada, Y. Yamamoto, M. Hirota, S. Yokoyama, and H. Ishikawa, "Investigation of Orbit Parameters to Classify the Deep Moonquake Sources," Journal of Space Science Informatics Japan, vol. 7, pp. 43-52, 2018 (in Japanese).

[13] B. M. Lake, R. Salakhutdinov, and J. B. Tenenbaum, "Human-level concept learning through probabilistic program induction," Science vol.350, issue 6266, pp. 1332-1338, 2015.

[14] Z. C. Lipton, "The Mythos of Model Interpretability," Communications of the ACM, vol. 61, no. 10, pp. 36-43, October 2018.

[15] D. Martens, B. Baesens, T. V. Gestel, and J. Vanthienen, "Comprehensible credit scoring models using rule extraction from support vector machines," Rule extraction from support vector machines, pp. 33-63, 2008.

[16] K. Mitomi, M. Endo, M. Hirota, S. Yokoyama, Y. Shoji, and H. Ishikawa, "How to Find Accessible Free Wi-Fi at Tourist Spots in Japan," Volume 10046 of Lecture Notes in Computer Science, pp. 389-403, 2016.

[17] NAIF, https://naif.jpl.nasa.gov/naif/ [retrieved: March, 2019].

[18] NRI, "information bank" acceptable to consumers?," NRI Journal [retrieved: March, 2019] (in Japanese).

[19] F. Pedregosa et al., "Scikit-learn: Machine learning in Python," Journal of Machine Learning Research, vol. 12, pp. 2825-2830, 2011.

[20] M. T. Ribeiro, S. Singh, and C. Guestrin, "Why Should I Trust You?: Explaining the Predictions of Any Classifier," Proc. CHI 2016 Workshop on Human Centered Machine Learning, pp. 1135-1144, 2016 (arXiv: 1602.04938v1 [cs.LG] 16 Feb 2016).

[21] S. Seabold and J. Perktold. "Statsmodels: Econometric and statistical modeling with python," Proc. 9th Python in Science Conference, pp. 57-61, 2010.

[22] Z. Si and S. C. Zhu., "Learning and-or templates for object recognition and detection," IEEE Trans. Pattern Anal. Mach. Intell., vol. 35, no. 9 pp. 2189-2205, 2013.

[23] W. V. Siricharoen, "Infographics: The New Communication Tools in Digital Age," Proc. International Conference on E-Technologies and Business on the Web, pp. 169-174, 2013.

[24] D. Smith, R. St. Andre, and M. Eggen, A Transition to Advanced Mathematics, Brooks/Cole Pub Co., 2014.

[25] K. W. Su, C. L. Liu, and Y. W. Wang, "A principle of designing infographic for visualization representation of tourism social big data." J Ambient Intell Human Comput, pp. 1-21, 2018, doi:10.1007/s12652-018-1104-9.

[26] T. Tsuchida, D. Kato, M. Endo, M. Hirota, T. Araki, and H. Ishikawa, "Analyzing Relationship of Words Using Biased LexRank from Geotagged Tweets," Proc. ACM MEDES International Conference, pp. 42-49, 2017.

Rapid Annotation Tool to Train Novel Concept Detectors with Active Learning

Maaike H. T. de Boer, Henri Bouma, Maarten Kruithof and Bart Joosten

Data Science & Intelligent Imaging
TNO
The Hague, The Netherlands
E-mails: {maaike.deboer, henri.bouma, maarten.kruithof, bart.joosten}@tno.nl

Abstract— **Annotating a large set of images, especially with bounding boxes, is a tedious task. In this paper, we propose an intuitive image annotation tool. This tool not only allows (non-expert) users to annotate images with novel concepts, but is also able to achieve acceptable performance with a smaller number of annotated images. The tool also proposes detections on unannotated images, to provide faster annotation and insight in the performance of the system. The tool is based on a Single Shot Multi-box Detector (SSD) neural network with active learning, by showing the images with high-confidence detections first, to have a fast verification and re-training. An experiment on simulated data shows that this active learning method can achieve higher performance in a shorter expected annotation time with a small number of images (less than 500). A small experiment on user annotated data shows that the annotation tool allows faster annotation compared to the case without the annotation tool.**

Keywords-image annotation; concept localization; deep learning; active learning.

I. INTRODUCTION

Concept detection is relevant to automatically detect and localize concepts in images and facilitate user query by keywords to find relevant images. Some generic concepts are publicly available (e.g., in YOLO9000 [1] or SSD [2]), but this is not sufficient for many applications in the security domain. For example, when looking for radicalization in online videos or when looking for products on illegal market places, specific concept detectors are required. For law-enforcement agencies, it is important to adapt a concept detector for their own specific concepts. Therefore, it is important to have an annotation tool that assists users to flexibly train novel concepts with minimal annotation effort.

Our main contribution is that we demonstrate an annotation tool that can use different active-learning strategies to train novel concepts with minimal effort. High-confidence detection has the advantage that minimal adjustments are needed [3]. Uncertain detections have the advantage that they are close to the decision boundary and that only a minimal amount of detections is needed [4]. In our experiments on the Nexar Challenge dataset [42], we show that the high-confidence detections minimize the annotation time and that both approaches perform better than random selection of the data. In our experiment on traffic images, we show that working with the annotation tool and active learning is faster compared to the case without the annotation tool.

The outline of this paper is as follows. Section 2 gives an overview of related work, Section 3 describes the annotation tool, Section 4 describes the experiments with the different annotation techniques, Section 5 shows the results and Section 6 summarizes conclusions.

II. RELATED WORK

In active learning, the results that are most informative for the system are displayed to a user to annotate and quickly learn a better model. We focus on active learning in which a large pool of unlabeled data is present and where the user may examine and select items from (pool-based sampling), as opposed to active learning based on streaming data (selective sampling) or synthesized data (query synthesis) [5][6]. Methods to measure informativeness include *uncertainty sampling* [7], *query-by-committee, expected gradient length, Fisher information* and *information density* [6]. Methods in uncertainty sampling include using the posterior probability or the entropy to measure the uncertainty and use the most uncertain items to learn from. Query-by-committee involves the Kullback-Leibler divergence [44] and voting of multiple classifiers to include items the classifiers disagree on. Expected gradient length uses the item that would create the largest change in the model if the label was known (largest expected gradient). Using the Fisher information [45], the item that minimizes the model variance is chosen. Information density weights the informativeness with the average similarity to all other items. While the other methods might favor outliers to select as most informative, this method does not.

In the computer-vision domain, active learning is typically used to train (or improve) concepts [8]. Active learning is distinguished from relevance feedback. In relevance feedback, the goal is to create a better model for a certain query by using positive and negative results, but not necessarily the most informative results. Typically in computer vision, the uncertainty sampling technique is used in which the items closest to the current boundary between the positive and negative items are perceived as the most uncertain items [9]-[13]. Zhao and Ding [14] use uncertainty sampling and use the top list as uncertain samples and the bottom list as fake negatives. Goh et al. [15] propose different sampling strategies for different semantic concepts based on scarcity, isolation and diversity, and Luan et al. [16] propose to start with items far from the boundary and move toward the items close to the boundary. Gavves et al. [17] propose to use zero-shot classifiers with priors to initialize and use a maximum conflict-label equality condition to select the most informative items. Holub et al. [18] and Kovashka et al. [19] use the entropy to determine the most informative items. Vondrick and Ramanan [20] use the Expected Gradient Length method. Dasgupta and Hsu [21] use hierarchical sampling and Zhu et al. [22] use a neighborhood graph on the unlabeled data.

With the current advances in Deep Learning, active learning has also been used. The activation of the softmax can be interpreted as the distance from the decision boundary [23]. Wang et al. [24] use the softmax response and pseudo-labelling of 'confident' samples in active learning with neural networks, and Zhou et al. [25] use the softmax response from Restricted Boltzmann machines. Stark et al. [26] use the highest output and divide this by the second highest to obtain an uncertainty. Geifman and El-Yaniv [23] and Sener and Savarese [27] propose to use coresets of the unlabeled data based on the activations in the neural network. Gal et al. [28] compare different informativeness measures, including maximum entropy, mutual information method named BALD by Houlsby et al. [29], and variation ratios, for Bayesian Neural Networks. Ducoffe et al. [30] use the query-by-committee strategy. They use a committee of partial Convolutional Neural Networks (CNNs) and batchwise dropout. The informativeness of an item is measured by the quantity of disagreement about the prediction of the label among the partial CNNs.

In concept localization, the goal is not only to correctly detect a concept, but to also localize this concept. There are several ways to handle concept localization [3] including drawing bounding boxes, segmentation, using point-click methods, using eye-tracking, using interactive annotation, using weakly-supervised object localization techniques and using active learning. In the weakly-supervised object localization techniques, Kolesnikov and Lampert [31] propose an annotation technique to improve object localization. This technique is based on the insight that objects and distractors form different clusters in the representation of a deep neural network. Cinbis et al. [32] use multi-fold multiple instance learning for the weakly supervised object localization. Konyushkova et al. [3] compare concept localization and annotation techniques such as weak and strong detectors, the difference between Drawing and Verification of the boxes, horizontal (re-training the whole detector) and vertical re-training (using a fixed detector and re-train with only the new part). The results show that horizontal training is better than vertical re-training. They used an annotation set of almost 5,000 images. Kao et al. [33] propose different evaluation metrics for localization: localization tightness (by estimating how tight the bounding box might enclose the true bounding box) and localization stability (by adding Gaussian noise) to select the items for active learning.

III. Annotation Tool

We developed an annotation tool where the user can annotate given concepts and train a deep neural network to detect and localize these concepts in an image. The user can select the concepts using a rectangle selection tool, as depicted in Figure 1. The user can upload images with the Graphical User Interface (GUI) to annotate or detect concepts. The user can also upload reference images for each concept. This will determine the concepts the tool is able to detect.

A. Deep Learning Network

The network we use for detecting the concepts is the Single Shot multi-box Detector (SSD) network [2]. We use the SSD300 network, which takes an image of 300 by 300 pixels as input and outputs the locations of detected concepts with a confidence score between 0 and 1. This confidence can be used to threshold the resulting detections. The number of output concepts is set to the number of concepts defined in the GUI. The network is pretrained on PASCAL VOC [34], MS-COCO [35], and ILSVRC [36].

B. (Re)Training for Concept Detection

After annotating a number of images, a neural network can be trained to detect the annotated concepts. We take all images that have a detection as an input to the training of the network. The images are converted to images of 300 by 300 pixels and the detections are converted using detection priors for input of the network. We freeze the first 3 layers to decrease the chance of overtraining on the current dataset. We train for 20 epochs and store the weights for each epoch. We use horizontal flipping and saturation variance for image augmentation. The batch size is set to 4 images. The weight file with the smallest loss is chosen as the weights to detect the concepts. Each time the network is trained the weights are reset to the pretrained weights on PASCAL VOC, MS-COCO, and ILSVRC. After the network is trained, the tool can run the network on an image and show the concepts the network detected. The slider controls the threshold of which detections are visible in the GUI, as shown in Figure 2.

The resulting detections can now be corrected by moving or resizing them or they can be accepted as they are. This process can be repeated multiple times resulting in increasing performance of the model.

C. Active Learning

As active learning technique, we choose the method by Konyushkova et al. [13] (*high-confidence*). The items will be sorted from highest to lowest, so the most confident items will be shown to the user first.

Figure 1. Overview of the GUI of the annotation tool; two concepts are annotated in this image.

Figure 2. Detected concepts by the network with a low threshold (0.4) on the left and a high threshold (0.6) on the right.

IV. EXPERIMENTS

In our experiments, we want to 1) verify our active learning choice and 2) validate that the annotation tool with active learning improves the annotation speed. In the first experiment, we use a vehicle dataset and calculate the anticipated performance and timing for each active learning method. In the second experiment, we use a street view dataset and ask the annotator to annotate the cars, bikes and persons.

A. *Simulation*

1) Dataset

We use the NEXET data from the Nexar Challenge 2 [42]. This open dataset contains 50,000 diverse images from the rear of vehicles from different locations. The bounding box annotations are included. We use the 5,000 images taken at daylight from New York City, with approximately 16,900 detections in total. All classes (car, vehicle, truck, pickup_truck, van) are renamed to 'vehicle' to focus on just one class. We randomly select 60% as train set (10,200 detections) and 40% as a held-out test set (6,700 detections). As evaluation, we use the evaluation script provided with the challenge, that calculates the mean Average Precision (mAP) with an Intersection over Union (IoU) of 0.75.

2) Conditions

In our experiments, we compare three conditions: 1. our chosen active learning technique based on Konyushkova et al. [13] (*high-confidence*), 2. the baseline (*random* selection of images) and 3. the uncertainty sampling technique (*uncertainty*).

In the *uncertainty* condition, the items closest to the current boundary between the positive and negative items are perceived as the most uncertain items. In this experiment, we select the items around the confidence value of 0.4 as most uncertain (based on experience):

$$u_i = |0.4 - c_i|,$$

where c_i is the confidence of item i and u_i is the uncertainty of item i.

Based on the uncertainty items, the images are sorted in the order of lowest to highest, so the images with the most uncertain items will be shown to the user first. The images are, thus, selected based on a single uncertain detection. All detections of this image, including the possibly more certain detection, are shown to the user. In the *random* selection, random images are selected and in *high-confidence* the values of c_i will be sorted from highest to lowest, so the most confident items will be shown to the user first.

3) Active Learning runs

For each of the three conditions explained in the previous section, we start with a model that is trained on 125 randomly selected images. We then apply the trained model on the trained images again to get the detections. We select 50 new images according to the condition and train a model on the 125 + 50 images. We thus train three new models, one based on each condition, with a different set of 175 images of which 50 are new. We apply this new model for this specific condition on the train images again and select 75 new images according to the condition. We train a model on the 125 + 50 + 75 images. We increase the number of images added, because a larger trainset requires a larger number of images being added to this set to make a difference. We keep on adding images with increasing step size until 2000 images.

4) Simulated Timing

In our experiments, we can automatically calculate the performance using the different active learning techniques, but we need an estimation of annotation time to simulate the timing. In the literature, different annotation times are mentioned [37]-[40], varying from 1.6 seconds to verify a bounding box to 25 second to draw a bounding box. An explanation for these differences in timing is the quality of the bounding box. Based on the results from these papers, we assume that it will take at least twice as long to draw a bounding box compared to verifying a bounding box. If the bounding box is, however, not correct, our tool allows users to adjust the bounding box. In previous experiments [41], we found that adjusting a bounding box takes on average twice as long as drawing a new bounding box. We use these proportions to indicate the timing.

Besides the timing to verify and modify a bounding box, we need a definition of when a bounding box is correct. We use the IoU for this purpose. If the IoU is higher than or equal to 0.9, the bounding box is perceived correct. If the IoU is between 0.5 and 0.9, the bounding box should be modified. In the cases that the IoU is lower than 0.5, no close enough match is found and a new bounding box should be drawn. Based on literature and our own previous experiment, we take the following annotation times (Table I).

TABLE I. TIMING ESTIMATES

	Definition	Time (seconds)
ValidateCorrectBBox	IoU => 0.9	0.5
ModifyBBox	0.5 <= IoU < 0.9	2.0
CreateBBox	IoU < 0.5	1.0

B. User Experiment

We use the vehicle dataset from the H2020 InDeV ("In-Depth understanding of accident causation for Vulnerable road users") project [43]. The dataset consists of 269 images and in total 1424 annotated vehicle bounding boxes. Of this dataset, 2%, 10% or 50% is used for training and 66 images (25%) are used for performance estimation. Four volunteers each annotated the same 66 images from this dataset four times. The first experiment is a manual mode and the other experiments are in assisted mode. The second experiment is based on a detector that is trained on a random selection of 2% of the data. In the third experiment, the detector is trained twice. The detector is first trained on 2% of the data, then the uncertainty-based active-learning approach is used to select the next 8% of data and the detector is trained again on the total 10%. In the fourth experiment, the detector is trained three times: first on random 2%, then on 10% and 50%, to allow reordering with active learning. To compensate for a learning effect, we use a Latin square.

The dataset is fully annotated. Therefore, it was possible to prepare all the data and perform training offline. So, the users only had to annotate the 66 images during the experiment.

V. Results

A. Simulation

1) mAP Performance

Figure 3 shows the mAP performance for different conditions (average over 10 runs). The plot shows that *high-confidence* stably increases with an increasing number of images. At 350 images, high-confidence reaches a mAP that is 22% higher than the mAP for random. However, this technique flattens out at the end. This is in agreement with the expectations, because high-confidence detections are becoming less and less informative. *Uncertainty* is closer to random with a smaller number of images, but improves with more images compared to *high-confidence.* At 2000 images, uncertainty reaches a mAP that is 3% higher than the mAP of high-confidence. This is also in agreement with the expectations, because initially the low-confidence detections can be confusing, but in the end the uncertain detections appear most informative.

2) Simulated Timing

Figure 4 shows the timing for the different performances (average over 10 runs). Random_baseline is without using the detections and Random is with using the detections.

Random_baseline is slower than *random* (including detections) with a smaller number of images. *High-confidence* is the techniqu that achieves a high performance in the least time. The high-confidence approach reaches an mAP of 0.2 70% faster than random. Because this technique uses the detections with the highest confidence, detections were more often validated as correct (with minimal annotation time) without necessity to modify the detections.

Uncertainty is not faster compared to random. The results are summarized in Table II. The table shows that high-confidence sampling reaches higher mAP in less time than the alternative methods.

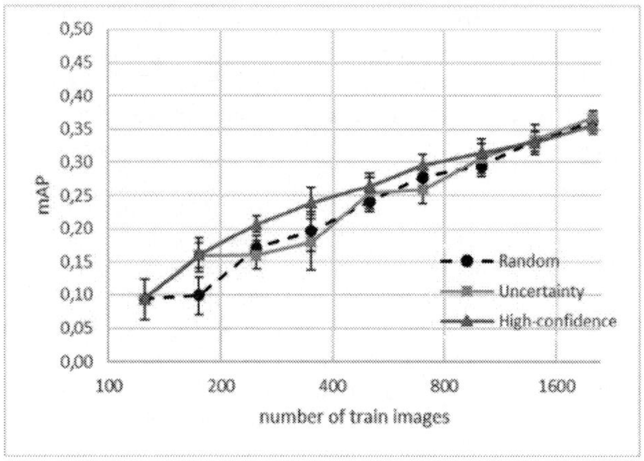

Figure 3. mAP performance for different number of train images, for all three conditions.

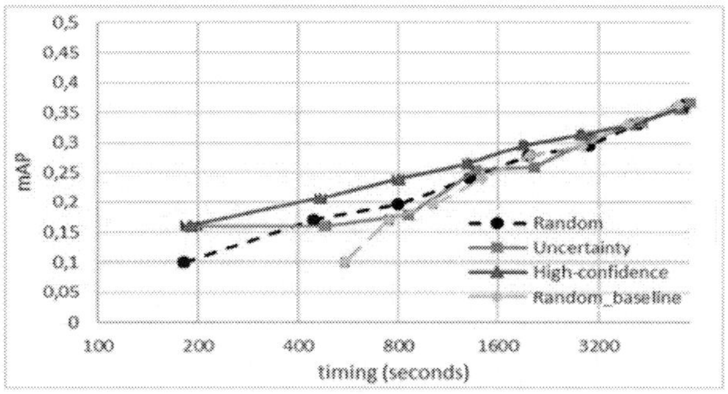

Figure 4. Estimated timing in seconds with respect to the mAP performance.

TABLE II. SUMMARY SIMULATION RESULTS

	mAP (%) at 250 im.	Time (min) at mAP=20%
Random sampling	17	13
Uncertainty sampling	16	16
High-confidence sampling	**21**	**7**

B. *User Experiment*

Tables III and IV show the results for the user experiment. Manual mode is significantly slower than assisted mode, and the 50% active learning approach is significantly faster than random 2%. Table IV shows that there is a learning effect: the first experiment is 25% slower than the average annotation time. This is expected, because the same 66 images are annotated in each condition. If we compensate for the learning effect by dividing the time by the effect (i.e. for first experiment divide by 1.25), the conclusion on manual vs. assisted is strengthened and the difference between random 2% and active 50% is also strengthened.

TABLE III. SUMMARY OF USER RESULTS

	Manual	Assisted Random 2%	Assisted Active 10%	Assisted Active 50%
Average Timing (sec)	1078 ± 182	634 ± 207	562 ± 246	443 ± 87

TABLE IV. TIMING PER EXPERIMENT (ORDER)

	Exp 1	Exp 2	Exp 3	Exp 4
Average Timing (sec)	807	637	646	629

VI. CONCLUSION

In this paper, we explained our annotation tool and compared active learning techniques in an experiment with a baseline of random image selection. The results of this experiment on a vehicle detection and localization dataset show that the High-confidence technique is faster than the uncertainty and random technique and performs better with a smaller number of images (<500).

In our second experiment, we tested our annotation tool with four annotators and we can conclude that the annotation tool in assisted mode with active learning is faster than an annotation tool in manual mode.

ACKNOWLEDGMENT

The ASGARD ("Analysis System for Gathered Raw Data") project has received funding from the EU H2020 Secure Societies program (FCT-01-2015) under grant agreement number 700381. The InDeV ("In-Depth understanding of accident causation for Vulnerable road users") project received funding from H2020-EU3.4 under grant agreement number 635895. Any opinions expressed in this paper do not necessarily reflect the views of the European Community. The Community is not liable for any use that may be made of the information contained herein.

REFERENCES

[1] J. Redmon and A. Farhadi, "YOLO9000: Better, Faster, Stronger," in *IEEE CVPR*, pp. 6517-6525, 2017.

[2] W. Liu et al., "SSD: Single Shot MultiBox Detector," ECCV, pp. 21-37, 2016.

[3] K. Konyushkova, J. Uijlings, C. H. Lampert and V. Ferrari, "Learning Intelligent Dialogs for Bounding Box Annotation," in *IEEE CVPR*, pp. 9175-9184, 2018.

[4] G. Burghouts, K. Schutte, H. Bouma and R. den Hollander, "Selection of negative samples and two-stage combination of multiple features for action detection in thousands of videos," *Machine Vision Applications*, vol. 25(1), pp. 85-98, 2014.

[5] T. S. Huang et al., "Active learning for interactive multimedia retrieval," *Proc. IEEE*, vol. 96, no. 4, pp. 648-667, 2008.

[6] B. Settles, "Curious machines: Active learning with structured instances," *Thesis Univ. Wisconsin*, 2008.

[7] D. Lewis and W. Gale, "Training text classifiers by uncertainty sampling," *ACM SIGIR, pp. 3-12*, 1994.

[8] C. Snoek and M. Worring , "Concept-based video retrieval," *Foundations and Trends in Information Retrieval*, 2(4), pp. 215-322, 2009.

[9] G. Schohn and D. Cohn, "Less is more: Active learning with support vector machines," in *ICML*, pp. 839-846, 2000.

[10] S. Tong and E. Chang, "Support vector machine active learning for image retrieval," in *ICML*, pp. 107-118, 2001.

[11] M. Chen, M. Christel, A. Hauptmann and H. Wactlar, "Putting active learning into multimedia applications: dynamic definition and refinement of concept classifiers," in *Proc. ACM Int. Conf. on Multimedia*, pp. 902-911, 2005.

[12] G. Nguyen, M. Worring and A. Smeulders, "Interactive search by direct manipulation of dissimilarity space," *IEEE Trans. Multimedia*, 9(7), 1404-1415, 2007.

[13] S. Vijayanarasimhan and K. Grauman, "Large-scale live active learning: Training object detectors with crawled data and crowds," *IJCV*, vol. 108, pp. 97-114, 2014.

[14] X. Zhao and G. Ding, "Query expansion for object retrieval with active learning using BoW and CNN feature," *Multimedia Tools and Appl.*, 76(9), pp. 12133-12147, 2017.

[15] K.-S. Goh, E. Y. Chang and W.-C. Lai, "Multimodal concept-dependent active learning for image retrieval," in *Proc. ACM Int. Conf. on Multimedia*, pp. 564-571, 2004.

[16] H. Luan et al., "Segregated feedback with performance-based adaptive sampling for interactive news video retrieval," in *ACM Int. Conf. MM*, pp. 293-296, 2007.

[17] E. Gavves, T. Mensink, T. Tommasi, C. Snoek and T. Tuytelaars, "Active transfer learning with zero-shot priors: Reusing past datasets for future tasks," in *IEEE ICCV*, pp. 2731-2739, 2015.

[18] A. Holub, P. Perona and M. C. Burl, "Entropy-based active learning for object recognition," in *IEEE CVPR*, 2008.

[19] A. Kovashka, S. Vijayanarasimhan and K. Grauman, "Actively selecting annotations among objects and attributes," in *ICCV*, 2011.

[20] C. Vondrick and D. Ramanan, "Video annotation and tracking with active learning," in *Advances in Neural Information Processing Systems*, pp 28-36, 2011.

[21] S. Dasgupta and D. Hsu, "Hierarchical sampling for active learning," in *ICML*, pp. 208-215, 2008.

[22] X. Zhu, J. Lafferty and Z. Ghahramani, "Combining active learning and semi-supervised learning using Gaussian fields and harmonic functions," in *ICML 2003 workshop*, 2003.

[23] Y. Geifman and R. El-Yaniv, *Deep Active Learning over the Long Tail.*, arXiv:1711.00941, 2017.

[24] K. Wang, D. Zhang, Y. Li, R. Zhang and L. Lin, "Cost-effective active learning for deep image classification," *IEEE Trans. Circuits and Systems for Video Technology*, vol. 27, no. 12, pp. 2591-2600, 2017.

[25] S. Zhou, Q. Chen and X. Wang, "Active deep learning method for semi-supervised sentiment classification," *Neurocomputing*, vol. 120, pp. 536-546, 2013.

[26] F. Stark, C. Hazrbas, R. Triebel and D. Cremers, "Captcha recognition with active deep learning," in *GCPR Workshop on New Challenges in Neural Computation*, 2015.

[27] O. Sener and S. Savarese, "Active learning for convolutional neural networks: A core-set approach," arXiv, 2018.

[28] Y. Gal, R. Islam and Z. Ghahramani, "Deep bayesian active learning with image data," *arXiv:1703.02910*, 2017.

[29] N. Houlsby, F. Huszár, Z. Ghahramani and M. Lengyel, "Bayesian active learning for classification and preference learning," *arXiv:1112.5745*, 2011.

[30] M. Ducoffe and F. Precioso, "Active learning strategy for CNN combining batch-wise Dropout and Query-By-Committee,," in *Proc. Europ. Symp. Artificial Neural Networks*, pp. 595-600, 2017.

[31] A. Kolesnikov and C. Lampert, "Improving weakly-supervised object localization by micro-annotation," *BMVC*, 2016.

[32] R. Cinbis, J. Verbeek and C. Schmid, "Weakly supervised object localization with multi-fold multiple instance learning," *IEEE Trans. PAMI*, vol. 39, no. 1, pp. 189-203, 2017.

[33] C. Kao, T.-Y. Lee, P. Sen and M. Liu, "Localization-aware active learning for object detection," *arXiv:1801.05124*, 2018.

[34] M. Everingham et al., "The Pascal visual object classes (voc) challenge," *Int. J. of Comp. Vision*, 88(2), pp. 303-338, 2010.

[35] T. Lin et al., "Microsoft COCO: Common objects in context.," in *ECCV*, pp. 740-755, 2014.

[36] A. Krizhevsky, I. Sutskever and G. Hinton, "Imagenet classification with deep convolutional neural networks," in *Adv. NIPS*, pp. 1097-1105, 2012.

[37] O. Russakovsky, L. Li and L. Fei-Fei, "Best of both worlds: Human-machine collaboration for object annotation", *IEEE CVPR*, pp. 2121-2131, 2015.

[38] D. P. Papadopoulos, J. R. R. Uijlings, F. Keller and V. Ferrari, "Extreme clicking for efficient object annotation," in *IEEE ICCV*, pp. 4940-4949, 2017.

[39] D. Papadopoulos, J. Uijlings, F. Keller and V. Ferrari, "We don't need no bounding-boxes: Training object class detectors using only human verification," in *IEEE CVPR*, 2016.

[40] H. Su, J. Deng and L. Fei, "Crowdsourcing annotations for visual object detection," in *AAAI Workshop*, 2012.

[41] H. Bouma et al., "Flexible image analysis for law enforcement agencies with deep neural networks to determine: where, who and what," in *Proc. SPIE*, vol. 10802, 2018.

[42] [Online]. Available: https://www.getnexar.com/challenge-2/. [Accessed 03, 2019].

[43] [Online]. [Accessed 03 2019] Available: https://www.indev-project.eu/InDeV/EN/Workpackages/WP_node.html.

[44] A. Nigam and K. McCallum, "Employing EM in pool-based active learning for text classification," *ICML*, pp. 359-367, 1998.

[45] M. Schervish, Theory of Statistics, Springer, 1995.

Automatic Analysis and Musicological Interpretation of Human Free Sorting of Musical Excerpts

Nicolas Dauban,
Christine Sénac,
Julien Pinquier

IRIT
University of Toulouse, UPS
Toulouse, France
nicolas.dauban@irit.fr
christine.senac@irit.fr
julien.pinquier@irit.fr

Pascal Gaillard,
Ludovic Florin

CLLE
University of Toulouse, UT2J
Toulouse, France
pascal.gaillard@univ-tlse2.fr
ludovic.florin@univ-tlse2.fr

Paul Albenge

IREMUS
University of Paris-Sorbonne
Paris, France
paul.albenge@gmail.com

***Abstract*—Most content-based music recommendation systems are relying on audio features which do not always match with musicological criteria. This paper describes the experimental protocol and the results of a sorting experiment, which leads to an 'average categorization' by volunteers. An automatic analysis afterward aims at identifying relevant acoustic parameters based on the obtained categories and sub-categories. A musicological analysis was also done in parallel.**

Keywords–Categorization; Music Information Retrieval; Recommendation.

I. INTRODUCTION

The role of music recommendation algorithms is to offer new songs to users of online music listening platforms. Research in Music Recommendation (MR) is very recent and underdeveloped in the academic world, because of the limitation -due to licensing issues- of access to the music signal on a large scale. Because basing a recommendation on simple metadata from collaborative filters is not always relevant, more and more works are based on the expertise acquired in Music Information Retrieval (MIR), which aims to extract information from the signal at different scales (notes, chords, sequence of notes, etc.) in order to characterize for example an instrument or to calculate descriptors, such as the tempo or the main melody. See [1] for a state of art on the MIR.

Thus, some authors have tried to rely on the measure of similarity between pieces of music [2]. While this approach is relevant for genre classification (the closest task to musical recommendations), it is quite disappointing for MR. Also, it was natural to introduce, in parallel to content-based approaches, information about user preferences [3] [4], or user behavior [5]. However, whatever the method, less known pieces (located in the 'long tail') are never (or rarely) proposed: some works aim to remedy this problem [6] [7].

One of the main difficulties raised by content-based methods is the selection of parameters. Indeed, among all the parameters we can extract from an audio signal, which of them can describe and explain the listeners' liking? How can we link these acoustic parameters to musicological and perceptive criteria? These problems are the major issues of the project in which this free categorization experience fits. The purpose of this experiment is to identify both acoustic parameters and musicological or 'non-expert' criteria according to which the subjects classify the pieces, starting from the assumption that the tastes of a listener are linked to a fixed combination of parameters or criteria.

Section II describes the constitution of the corpus and the experimental conditions. Section III presents the data generated by the experiment and the way we processed it automatically and how it was interpreted with a musicological point of view. Section IV describes a method based on audio features which aims at reconstruct the categorization made by volunteers.

II. EXPERIMENTAL PROTOCOL

A. *Corpus with musicological criteria*

One of the first steps of the project was to build a corpus, which had to meet several requirements: (1) wide range of musical genres; (2) good quality excerpts: Audio CD (stereo, 16 bits, 44.1 kHz); (3) long enought excerpts (at least 20s) and in sufficient numbers; (4) preferably with a copyright-free access database.

The corpus has been built with a musicological approach. First, we made a set of 15 criteria which can define the music in the most comprehensive way possible without using a commercial classification like genres. The concepts and lexicon used here rely mainly on the work of Pierre Boulez and Gilles Deleuze in [8] and [9].

- Recording Quality: perception of the support and mean of recording (noises, sound spectrum, intensity, etc.).
- Prevalence of an Instrument: salience of a special timbre.
- Voice: presence or absence of voice, type of voice (spoken, sung, declarative, repetitive, etc.).
- Space: feeling and representation of a diffusion space, deepness of the musical field.
- Memory Work: presence of one or several memorable elements, repetition of an element (stricte or similar), clear perception of a pattern or logic.
- Dynamic: change of quantity/density of events, contrast in the musical development.
- Narrative Development: evolution of musical elements, presence of different parts relatively distinct.

- Smooth/Striated time: according to Boulez [10], presence or absence of beat, diversity of elements, variation in quantity of elements in a short moment.
- Sensorimotor: instrumentalists' music, mostly animated by a desire of gesture and a research of the sensorial effect of the sound. As exemple, African music, percussion improvisations, jazz solos, or concrete pieces of music by Pierre Henry.
- Representation: what represents by a visible or hidden way the reality on the plastic plan, by trajectories, speeds, impacts or event realistic noises (Gregorien, occidental romanticism, many contemporary music).
- Rules: any written music, whether written as a classical counterpoint or transmitted orally as Pygmy polyphonies or M'Baka horns.
- Energy: intensity, body implication, involvement of the musician.
- Level of Technicity: there are two levels, instrumental and composition. Perception of the assurance of musician's intentions and/or presence of structural concepts.
- Cultural Elements: reference to a socio-cultural class.
- Chronological Situation: perception of elements specific to an era, such as type of recording, type of play, reference to a particular aesthetic.

For each of these criteria, we empirically selected three significant pieces which contain different musical characteristics in order to propose an eclectic ensemble. Although these would have been selected to initially correspond to a specific criterion, it is possible to find characteristics of other criteria. The goal here is not to recover this classification in the experimental results but to see which criteria were particularly relevant in the volunteer's sorting. For each selected track, we had to select a short excerpt in order to keep the experiment from being too long for the volunteers. Excerpts had to be still relevant regarding to the corresponding criterion. In the end, a corpus of 45 excerpts of 20 seconds was defined (see Figure 1).

Excerpt	Begining	Artist - Title
1	00:00	Les Doubles Six - Au Bout du Fil (Meet Benny Bailey)
2	00:02	Bill Bruford - One Of A Kind (Part 1)
3	00:00	Harry Burleigh - Go Down Moses
4	03:20	Rautavaara - Cantus Arcticus 2e mvt
5	00:50	Hector Berlioz - Symphonie Fantastique, Op. 14, Songe d'une nuit de sabbat
6	00:00	Corette - Concerto pour musette de cour 2 Adagio
7	00:00	Namibie Chant De Guerison - Nom Tzisi
8	00:00	Han Bennink & Willem Breuker - Mr. M.A. de R. in A.
9	00:00	Death Grips - Thru The Walls
10	00:00	Jazzoo - le pic et le moineau
11	00:24	Big Satan - Geeza
12	00:02	Lords Of The Underground - Here Come The Lords
13	00:02	Pygmées Aka
14	00:00	Deux Chants De Jeu Et De Danse - Polynésie Occ.
15	00:10	James Brown - Mother Popcorn
16	03:00	Suisse Yodel - Zauerli
17	00:13	Horace Silver - Capverdian Blues
18	03:10	Awa Poulo - Dimo Yaou Tata
19	00:00	Pharoah Sander - Love Will Find a Way
20	00:00	David Fiuczynski - Moonring Bacchanal
21	00:00	André Minvielle - L'Alambic
22	00:25	Edgard Varèse - Un Grand Someil Noir
23	00:30	The Residents - This Is Man's World
24	00:28	Theo Bleckmann & Ben Monder Late Green
25	03:40	Aphex Twin - Circlont14 [Shrymoming Mix]
26	00:00	Naked City - Une Correspondance
27	05:00	Bugge Wesseltoft - Dreaming
28	00:40	Ali Farka Touré - Sabu Yerkoy
29	00:46	A Ram Sam Sam
30	00:05	Sleepytime Gorilla Musuem - The Putrid Refrain
31	08:20	John Zorn - Through The Night
32	00:20	Liadov : Baba Yaga
33	00:28	Don Ellis - Strawberry Soup
34	00:30	Ligeti - Quatuor à cordes n°2 - come un meccanismo di precisione
35	00:27	Arvo Pärt "Ludus" du Tabula Rasa
36	00:20	John Zorn, Filmworks - Cynical Hysterie Hour Through the
37	01:50	Jaco Pastorius - Come On, Come Over
38	00:00	Bach/ Glenn Gould - The Art of the Fugue, BWV 1080- Contrapunctus III
39	02:30	Julien Loureau - Conrod
40	00:25	Dayton - Krackity Krack
41	00:43	Aka Moon - For Drummers Only
42	00:15	Sec - Run Away
43	00:23	Tool - Lateralus
44	00:00	Bruckner - scherzo 9e symphonie
45	00:30	Naked City - Speedball

Figure 1. List of 20 seconds excerpts and their beginning time.

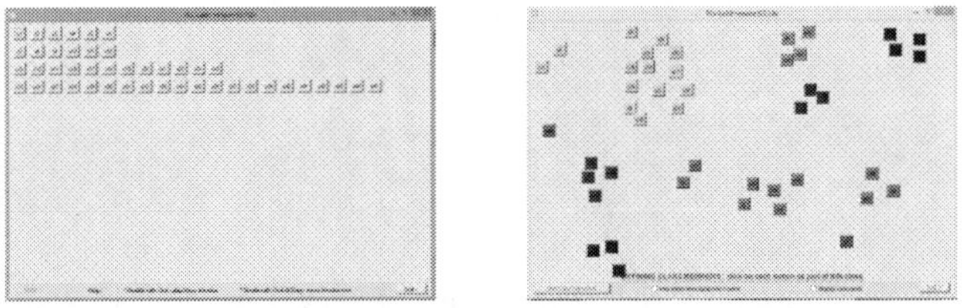

Figure 2. Interface presented at the beginning of the experiment (each excerpt is represented by a numbered icon), and after the free sorting (excerpts are grouped by volunteer).

B. Experimental conditions

In order to limit the impact of the age of the participants on the results, we used participants/volunteers from 20 to 25 years old (30 in number). For the experiment, we used the TCL-labX tool [11] [12].

The interface (see Figure 2) was presented in an identical way to all volunteers who were asked to freely sort excerpts and thus form as many categories as they wished, based on the similarities between the pieces. To do so, the users could listen as many times as necessary excerpts and could move and group them freely on the interface.

III. FREE SORTING AND INTERPRETATION

A. MetaData

For each volunteer, the program generates a file in which is indicated the distribution of the excerpts in the different classes. The software also generates a "cookie" file containing the history of the operations performed by the user: moving icons and listening to excerpts. We can replay all actions performed by the volunteer. In addition, the software carries out an automatic analysis of these files in order to extract several statistics on the participants. The average duration of the experiment was 37 minutes, the maximum duration exceeded one hour (1h 2min) and the minimum duration was 15 minutes. The standard deviation over the duration of the experiment is 10 minutes. On average, participants formed 15.5 classes, the minimum being 8 classes and the maximum 20. The standard deviation on the number of classes is 3.2.

B. Automatic Results Analysis

1) Matrices of co-occurrence and dissimilarity: to accomplish this task, we based ourselves on the work of [13]. First, we built a co-occurrence matrix C^i for each participant i. A co-occurence matrix is square and symmetrical, of dimension $N \times N$ with N equal to the number of sorted excerpts. In each cell, we indicate the distance between two excerpts: if these two excerpts are in the same category, the distance is considered as zero, otherwise we assign a unit distance.

Then, we calculate an average co-occurrence matrix of all participants, called the D dissimilarity matrix. This dissimilarity matrix gives us a distance measurement for each pair of musical excerpts, this distance being based on the classification by the n participants.

We have also computed a matrix of variance M_{var} from the matrices of co-occurrence C^i and the dissimilarity matrix D (see equation 1). For a pair of excerpts, this variance is null if the set of n participants sorted these two excerpts identically. Conversely, this variance is maximal ($var_{max} = 1$) if half of the participants put these excerpts together, and the other half separately.

$$M_{var}^{j,k} = \frac{1}{n} \sum_{i=1}^{n} (C^{i,j,k} - D^{j,k})^2 \quad (1)$$

with $M_{var}^{j,k}$ the cell of the line j and column k of the matrix M_{var}, $C^{i,j,k}$ the cell (j,k) of the matrix C^i and $D^{j,k}$ the cell (j,k) of the matrix D.

Since the C^i matrices contain only binary values, for a pair of excerpts, a null variance necessarily corresponds to a dissimilarity of 1 or 0, and a unit variance necessarily corresponds to a dissimilarity of 0.5. The closer the dissimilarity is to an extreme value (1 or 0), the more these two excerpts will be 'unanimously' put in their class by volunteers. The closer the dissimilarity is to 0.5, the more these two extracts will have 'divided the opinion' of the volunteers.

2) Dendrogram: from the dissimilarity matrix, we were able to perform an ascending hierarchical classification. We have chosen to use the *Ward's method* [14], which consists in grouping the classes so that the increase of the inertia interclasses, given by (2) is maximized. This, according to the *Huygens theorem*, is equivalent to minimize the increase of the intraclass inertia (see (3)) [15].

$$I_e = \frac{1}{n} \sum_{i=1}^{k} n_i \times d^2(g_i, g) \quad (2)$$

$$I_a = \frac{1}{n} \sum_{i=1}^{k} \sum_{j=1}^{n_i} d^2(e_j, g_i) \quad (3)$$

We obtained the dendrogram of Figure 3. It tells us about the links between excerpts put by users. The vertical axis represents the distance between excerpts or groups of excerpts. Thus, two excerpts that have been very often placed together by the volunteers have a low link on the figure, such as on the numbers 11 and 17 or the numbers 15 and 37.

C. Musicological Interpretation

The dendrogram obtained previously was interpreted from a musicological point of view in order to understand how the volunteers had made their classification. The dendrogram has been annotated with the criteria common to excerpts belonging to the same branch, see Figure 3.

The name indicated under each node corresponds to a presumed musicological criterion common to all the excerpts which are below it. This name was choosen analysing the content of each category. The four main categories are described as follows.

1) Audio-Tactile: Pieces of music in this category are all very rhythmic and belong to the genre jazz or funk and more generally to Africo-American. "Audio-tactility" refers to a particular relationship with the body. Within this category, the excerpts have been distinguished by the predominant instrument.

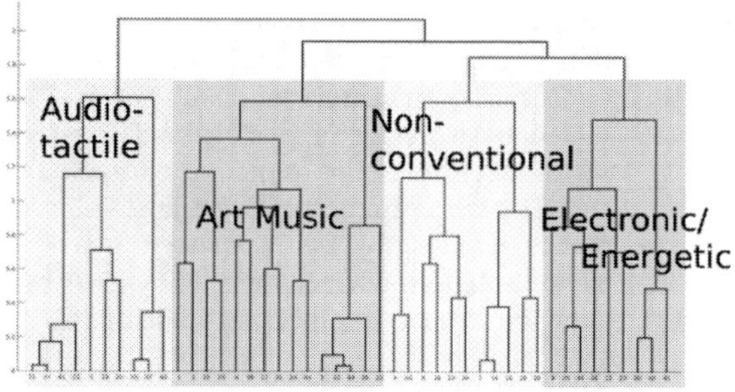

Figure 3. Dendrogram annotated by musicologists. y axis corresponds to the distance between two excerpts or clusters of excerpts; excerpts to the x axis.

2) Art Music: this category is a hybrid grouping of academic Western Music, of music evoking a sacred or spiritual aspect and finally of the excerpts where the voice is predominant.

3) Non-conventional: this category includes music built outside the conventional rules governing Western music, particularly based on melody and harmony. Therefore, we find music without pitch of precise notes and the non-Western music. Any music that does not follow the hierarchies present in Western codes is necessarily perceived as a group apart.

4) Electronic/Energetic: most of the excerpts in this category were produced from electronic instruments. This category also includes pieces with contrasts in terms of energy. However, the distance remains particularly high between these two sub-categories.

The objective was not to recover, via the results of the experiment, the free classification created but to see which dimensions are the most important while listening to music. We can notice that the musicological criteria used to establish the corpus are not found through the free classification of non-expert participants. This shows that there are different types of musical analysis and valuation. The musicological criteria allowed us to obtain a very varied corpus and the categories identified by the participants reveal other more accessible criteria for non-experts.

IV. Towards an Automatic Classification

The aim here was to verify whether an automatic classification of musical extracts based on acoustic parameters could approach the free classification made by humans and based not only on the signal, but also on knowledge. As music (in term of production) commonly refers to a series of sound events (notes, percussive sounds, voiced or unvoiced sounds) defined by their rythm, timbre, dynamics, and pitch, we have extracted some of these parameters. So, we calculated 31 audio parameters on each excerpt of the corpus using the MIR Toolbox [16]. The extraction of these parameters is described in detail in the following subsection.

A. Extraction of Acoustic Parameters

1) Rhythm: it describes the temporal location of sound events and their duration. Generaly, in conventional western music, a regular pulse determines the beat, a measure being composed of several beats. In a score, the rhythm (inside the beat) is described by the different shapes of notes (crotchet, quaver, semiquaver, etc.) and of silences (pause, minim, etc.) as well as by the time signature.

- Event Detection and Density: all the rhythmic parameters are based initially on the temporal location of each event. For this, we use a peak detection algorithm on the signal envelope. Once the peaks are detected, we can then calculate the number of events per second. These features are extracted on 10 seconds window without overlapping.
- Tempo: the tempo calculation, which is based on a detection of the periodicity of events, selects the highest peak. Periodicity detection is performed using the autocorrelation function [16]. This feature is extracted on a 3 second window with and overlap of 0.3 seconds.
- Pulse Clarity: the pulse clarity can be calculated according to the method detailed in [17]. This parameter describes how much the beat is dominant in the rhythm, or in other words, how much emphasis is placed on the beats: for example, the clarity of the beat is strong for disco rhythms, and is often low for complex rhythms, like those of jazz. This feature is extracted on a 5 second window with and overlap of 0.5 seconds.

2) Timbre: it describes the spectral composition of a note, that is to say the amplitude of the harmonics and the variation in time of these harmonics. This distinguishes, for example, two notes played at the same pitch by a piano and a guitar. These features (excepted the attack) are extracted on a 50ms window with and overlap of 25ms.

- Attack: the attack of a note describes the variation of amplitude at the moment when it is played. It is measured by its duration, its amplitude or by its slope [18]. For example, struck strings of the piano have a stronger attack than violin strings played with a bow. When a note is detected, the beginning and the end of the attack are marked, then the difference of amplitude or the duration between the two points is calculated (the slope is obtained using these two informations).
- Zero Crossing Rate: it is calculated on the original signal by multiplying all successive pairs of samples, and iterating a variable when the product is negative (signal change). This variable is then divided by the duration to obtain the rate [19].
- Rolloff Frequency: it informs us about the amount of energy present in the low frequencies. On a spectrum, we calculate the frequency below which 85% of the energy is contained. The lower the frequency, the more energy is concentrated in the low frequencies.
- Brightness: it informs us about the amount of energy present in the high frequencies [20]. On a spectrum, we calculate the amount of energy present beyond a fixed frequency (usually 1500 Hz).
- Statistical Parameters of Spectral Distribution: it is possible to calculate statistics as well as moments of different orders on the spectrum, such as Centroid, Spread, Skewness, Kurtosis, Flatness, as well as the Entropy.
- MFCC (Mel Frequency Cepstral Coefficients): MFCCs are cepstral coefficients calculated by a discrete cosine transform applied to the power spectrum of a signal [21]. The different frequency bands are determined according to the perceptive logarithmic scale Mel, which is modeled on the human hearing system.
- Roughness: it describes the phenomenon of audible beat in the presence of two near frequencies [22]. Two notes spaced half tone apart (or less) will generate strong roughness, which decreases as spacing increases. Roughness is almost zero from 5 half tones.
- Irregularity of a Spectrum: this is the degree of amplitude variation of two successive peaks (harmonics or not) of the spectrum [16].

3) Dynamics: it describes the relative amplitude of different sounds, which results in shades of intensity. On a score, the dynamics is indicated by terms, such as 'pianissimo' or 'forte' that tell the musician to play relatively more or less loudly. In signal processing and generally, dynamics describes the range of variation of the different values taken by a signal. In music, dynamics describes the ratio of sounds of strong and weak amplitudes. These features are extracted on a 50ms window with and overlap of 25ms.

- RMS (Root Mean Square) level: the effective value of an ergodic random signal over a time interval is the square root of the square signal mean, or the square root of its mean power. In practice, for a discrete time signal, the RMS level is calculated on a finite number of samples.
- Low Energy Rate: it is the number of points whose value is less than the RMS value of the signal. For a signal with peaks at the high RMS level, this rate will be high whereas for a signal at the RMS level rather constant, this rate will be low.

4) Pitch: it describes the fundamental frequency of a sound played by an instrument, which defines the note.

- Note detection: the default method for detecting notes is to decompose the signal into several frequency bands, then calculate the auto-correlation and finally detect the peaks in order to obtain an estimate of the notes. This feature is extracted on a 46.4ms window with and overlap of 10ms.
- Harmonies Detection: from the detection of notes, it is then possible to detect harmonies, that is to say combinations of different notes. It is also possible to calculate the key of an extract, as well as the temporal evolution of all these parameters. This feature is extracted on a 743ms window with and overlap of 74ms.

B. Selection of Acoustic Parameters

We averaged each parameter to obtain a matrix of the form $N \times P$ with $N = 45$ (excerpts) and $P = 31$ (parameters). Note that by keeping only the mean, we lose the temporal evolution, but this allows us to have only one scalar per excerpt and per parameter. For each parameter, we computed the distance for each pair of excerpts and thus form a dissimilarity matrix P^i for each parameter i. Then, we established a model of the matrix of dissimilarity of the human free sorting from a linear combination of the matrices of the parameters.

$$M_{model} = \sum_{i=1}^{31} a_i P^i \qquad (4)$$

The values contained in each dissimilarity matrix were normalized between 0 and 1 in order to remain consistent with the matrix values of the free sorting.

Rather than using all P^i matrices, we selected the most relevant matrices by computing the correlation coefficient of each matrix of parameters with the matrix of the volunteers and we selected the m more correlated. Indeed, the matrices the most correlated with the matrix of dissimilarity established during the free sorting are by definition the most 'similar'.

C. Regression

1) Complete matrix: with these first m matrices, we used a gradient descent algorithm to find the best linear combination, the criterion to be optimized being the quadratic error between this linear combination and the dissimilarity matrix of the free sorting. This algorithm therefore returns the coefficients a_i by which the matrices of dissimilarity are multiplied in order to obtain the matrix most resembling the dissimilarity matrix formed by the set of results of the volunteers. These coefficients inform us of the importance of each parameter: if a coefficient is low then it is not influential for the volunteers to sort the pieces, and vice versa.

To simplify the calculations, the dissimilarity matrices have been transformed into V_p and V_d vectors of length $L = 45 \times 45 = 2025$.

For m used dissimilarity matrices of parameters, the quadratic error equation is defined by:

$$J = \sum_{j=1}^{L} \left[\left(\sum_{i=1}^{m} a_i V_p^{i,j} \right) - V_d^j \right]^2 \tag{5}$$

The gradient of this error is:

$$\overrightarrow{\text{grad}}\ J = \begin{bmatrix} \frac{\partial J}{\partial a_1} \\ \cdots \\ \frac{\partial J}{\partial a_k} \\ \cdots \\ \frac{\partial J}{\partial a_M} \end{bmatrix} \tag{6}$$

where:

$$\begin{aligned} \frac{\partial J}{\partial a_k} &= \sum_{j=1}^{L} \frac{\partial \left[\left(\sum_{i=1}^{m} a_i V_p^{i,j} \right) - V_d^j \right]^2}{\partial a_k} \\ &= 2 \sum_{j=1}^{L} \left[\left[\left(\sum_{i=1}^{m} a_i V_p^{i,j} \right) - V_d^j \right] V_p^{k,j} \right] \end{aligned} \tag{7}$$

We successively tested the algorithm with the m 'best' parameters, in the sense of the correlation. By successively increasing the number of parameters, the total squared error decreases to 2.20. From 7 parameters, the error increases again. The 6 first parameters are: *Irregularity, Brightness, Rolloff, Harmony Change Detection, Spectrum Entropy, Attack.*

From the matrix estimated with 6 parameters, we generated a new dendrogram (see Figure 4) in order to visually compare the result of this estimation with the dendrogram obtained at the end of the free sorting (see Figure 3). We can see these two dendograms do not resemble a lot one another. This can be explained by the fact that the participants did not use the same 'rule' to classify all the excerpts. For example, some excerpts have been grouped with respect to rhythmic similarities, and others with respect to their melody. It is difficult to establish a general rule on the parameters to estimate with good precision the overall classification. This is probably due to the fact that the excerpts were highly variable. If we consider dendrogram sub-parts, the excerpts belonging to each of them are more similar to each other, and we can therefore suppose that it will be easier to isolate discriminant parameters.

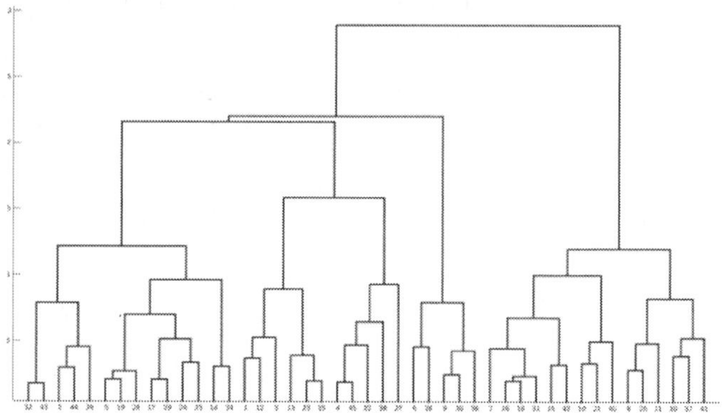

Figure 4. Dendrogram estimated from 6 parameters.

2) Sub-Matrices/Parts: we used the same method as above on each of the four sub-parts, named by the musicologists: Audio-Tactile, Art Music, Non-conventional and Electronic/Energetic. We calculated the most correlated criteria, and used them again to form linear combinations.

3) Audio-Tactile: the most correlated parameters are: *Brightness, Irregularity, MFCC10, Attack, MFCC4, Spectrum Entropy, Pulsation Clarity, Zero Crossing Rate, Low Energy, Spectrum Kurtosis, MFCC3, Rolloff, Tempo, MFCC8.*

At the end of the gradient descent, the total squared error is 5.5. We note that several MFCCs were involved in the classification. We can explain this by the fact that for this category, the volunteers distinguished the excerpts according to the predominant instruments. The dendrogram was well reconstructed, except for excerpts 5 and 6 which were exchanged.

4) Art Music: For this category, the results were rather mitigated, even using all the parameters. Indeed, at the end of the gradient descent, the total squared error is 9.5. These weaker results can be explained by the fact that this category contains more excerpts, which are ill-matched making it more difficult to generalize a categorization rule.

5) Non-conventional: We obtained good results with 18 parameters. At the end of the gradient descent, the total squared error is 3.8. The most correlated parameters are: *Sensory Dissonance, Attack, Number of Events Per Second, Zero Pass Rate, Spectrum Kurtosis, Key Clarity, Entropy, MFCC8.*

Figure 5. Dendrogram obtained for the Electronic/Energetic category.

6) Electronic/Energetic: The method has been the most efficient for this group (see Figure 5). Except for the first excerpt, the dendrogram was well reconstituted. For each sub-group i of size N_i, the initial indices of the excerpts were replaced by indices ranging from 1 to N_i. If the dendrogram of a sub-group has been reconstituted, the excerpts are placed in ascending order. We obtained a total squared error of 2.8. We used the following 9 parameters: *Attack, MFCC3, MFCC8, MFCC11, Rolloff, Brightness, MFCC4, Zero Crossing Rate, MFCC0 (i.e. Energy).*

Overall, the results are quite satisfactory because we were able to reconstruct the dendrogram of each category with a limited number of errors.

D. Classification of new excerpts

The objective of this part was to find a method to assign to a 'new' excerpt the right category. In all the methods that follow, we successively considered each excerpt as a new individual, taking care to remove it from the learning base (leave-one-out cross-validation). The score for each method is therefore between 0 and 45 (where all the excerpts were assigned to the right categories). In addition, the parameters were centered and reduced in order to eliminate the influence of the unit of measure used for each of them.

The first method consisted in calculating the center of gravity of each category according to the 31 parameters, and then assigning the new extract to the class with its nearest barycenter: we thus obtained 30 correct assignments (67%).

In the second method, we retained a small number of parameters: we observed which parameters were relevant for the classification in the sub-categories (section IV-C2) and we kept only those which were the most correlated in the 4 classifications. They are: *Change Harmony Detection, Attack, Spectrum Entropy, Rolloff, MFCC0, and Irregularity.* We thus obtained 22 correct assignments (33%): the selected parameters were therefore not particularly relevant.

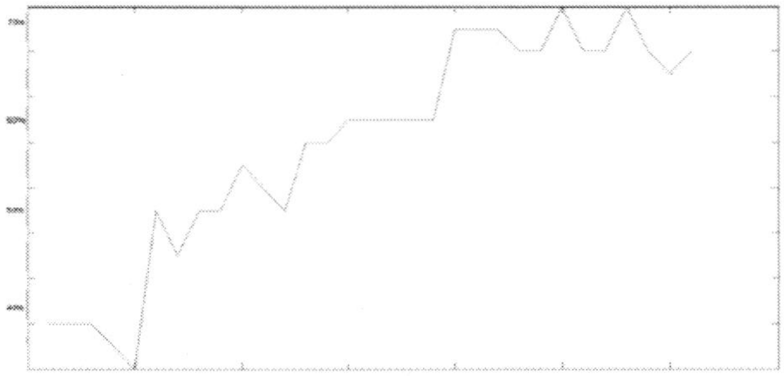

Figure 6. Attribution score based on the number of parameters used. y axis corresponds to the score obtained in function of the number of parameters (x axis).

In the third method, we used the N most correlated parameters in ranking the same way as in the section IV-C1. In Figure 6, we see that the score increases globally with the number of parameters but sometimes decreases when we use a new one. The maximum score (71%) is reached for 25 parameters : all but *3rd, 4th and 6th MFCC, the Spectral Flatness, Inharmonicity and Spectrum Kurtosis*. This method proved to be the best.

V. Conclusion and Prospects

For this experiment, a corpus was built according to a wide range of musicological criteria. Different audio parameters were also computed on the excerpts of the corpus.

Volunteers have performed a free sorting task on this corpus. Analysis of the experimental results let us establish an average human classification of excerpts by volunteers, which has been represented in the form of a dendrogram in which appear four main groups with sub-groups. We noticed that these sub-groups were built according to some of the musicological criteria but also according to 'non expert' criteria such as genres.

In order to automatically reconstruct this human classification, we have established a hierarchy in the parameters relevance depending on their correlation with the volunteers' classification. We saw that this automatic reconstruction is more efficient to distinguish sub-groups within a group instead of groups between them. Finally, the identified parameters can be selected for an application in music recommendation.

References

[1] M. Schedl, E. Gómez, and J. Urbano, "Music information retrieval: Recent developments and applications," Foundations and Trends® in Information Retrieval, vol. 8, no. 2-3, 2014, pp. 127–261.

[2] B. McFee, L. Barrington, and G. Lanckriet, "Learning content similarity for music recommendation," IEEE transactions on audio, speech, and language processing, vol. 20, no. 8, 2012, pp. 2207–2218.

[3] A. Van den Oord, S. Dieleman, and B. Schrauwen, "Deep content-based music recommendation," in Advances in neural information processing systems, 2013, pp. 2643–2651.

[4] E. J. Humphrey, J. P. Bello, and Y. LeCun, "Moving beyond feature design: Deep architectures and automatic feature learning in music informatics." in ISMIR. Citeseer, 2012, pp. 403–408.

[5] M. Schedl and D. Hauger, "Tailoring music recommendations to users by considering diversity, mainstreaminess, and novelty," in Proceedings of the 38th International ACM SIGIR Conference on Research and Development in Information Retrieval. ACM, 2015, pp. 947–950.

[6] Ò. Celma Herrada, "Music recommendation and discovery in the long tail," Ph.D. dissertation, 2009.

[7] M. A. Domingues, F. Gouyon, A. M. Jorge, J. P. Leal, J. Vinagre, L. Lemos, and M. Sordo, "Combining usage and content in an online recommendation system for music in the long tail," International Journal of Multimedia Information Retrieval, vol. 2, no. 1, 2013, pp. 3–13.

[8] R. Bogue, Deleuze's way: Essays in transverse ethics and aesthetics. Routledge, 2016.

[9] G. Deleuze and F. Guattari, A thousand plateaus: Capitalism and schizophrenia. Continuum, 2004.

[10] P. Boulez, Boulez on music today (trans. by Bradshaw, Susan and Rodney Bennett, Richard). London: Faber and Faber, 1971.

[11] P. Gaillard, "Laissez-nous trier ! tcl-labx et les tâches de catégorisation libre de sons." Le sentir et le dire : Concepts et méthodes en psychologie et linguistique cognitive, 2009, pp. 189–210.

[12] http://petra.univ-tlse2.fr/tcl-labx, [Online; accessed 15-January-2019].

[13] J. P. Barthélémy and A. Guénoche, Trees and Proximity Representations. John Wiley and Sons, 1991.

[14] J. H. Ward Jr, "Hierarchical grouping to optimize an objective function," Journal of the American statistical association, vol. 58, no. 301, 1963, pp. 236–244.

[15] G. Saporta, Probabilités, analyse des données et statistique. Editions Technip, 2006.

[16] O. Lartillot, "Mirtoolbox 1.6.1 users manual," 2014.

[17] O. Lartillot, T. Eerola, P. Toiviainen, and J. Fornari, "Multi-feature modeling of pulse clarity: Design, validation and optimization." in ISMIR, 2008, pp. 521–526.

[18] J. M. Grey, An Exploration of Musical Timbre Using Computer-based Techniques. Department of Psychology, Stanford University., 1975.

[19] F. Gouyon, F. Pachet, and O. Delerue, "On the use of zero-crossing rate for an application of classification of percussive sounds," in Proceedings of the COST G-6 conference on Digital Audio Effects (DAFX-00), Verona, Italy, 2000.

[20] P. Laukka, P. Juslin, and R. Bresin, "A dimensional approach to vocal expression of emotion," Cognition & Emotion, vol. 19, no. 5, 2005, pp. 633–653.

[21] B. Logan, "Mel frequency cepstral coefficients for music modeling." in ISMIR, vol. 270, 2000, pp. 1–11.

[22] W. A. Sethares, Tuning, timbre, spectrum, scale. Springer Science & Business Media, 2005.

Images Processing Techniques and Data Analysis Applied to High-Power Laser Systems

Bertrand de Boisdeffre, Mihai Caragea, Ioan Dancus, Daniel Ursescu
ELI-NP project, Laser department
Horia Hulubei National Institute for Physics and Nuclear Engineering
Magurele, Romania
e-mail: bertrand.boisdeffre@eli-np.ro, mihai.caragea@nipne.ro, ioan,dancus@eli-np.ro, daniel.ursescu@eli-np.ro

Abstract — **Extreme-Light Nuclear Physics (ELI-NP) facility in Romania is part of the pan-European distributed facility that addresses laser physics research with emphasis in the field of nuclear physics (in Romania), secondary radiation sources (in the Czech Republic) and attosecond light science (in Hungary). At ELI-NP, experiments will be carried out by using a High-Power Laser System (HPLS) delivered by Thales Company. Within the HPLS, cameras acquire images at different frequencies (from 10 frames per second to 1 frame per minute). They contribute to more than 90% of the data produced each day (around 700 gigabytes). These data are stored in Hierarchical Data Format 5 (HDF5) files on different servers located in the HPLS network. Thus, in this paper, we aim at presenting how digital image processing techniques applied on images can be used to reduce the amount of data that should be stored at the ELI-NP data center. The ensemble of these techniques were grouped and structured in order to form a laser beam detection algorithm. The algorithm was tested on different laser beam intensity profiles (Near-Field and Far-Field). As a conclusion, this paper offers a perspective upon the future development of testing quantitatively the algorithm and improving it.**

Keywords-laser; image processing; HDF5; data analysis.

I. Introduction

Research in the field of laser physics has been growing for the last thirty years especially after the development of the chirped pulse amplification technique [1]. The latter was recognized as one of the most important scientific achievements being awarded the Nobel Prize in Physics in 2018. In 2006, the European Strategy Forum on Research Infrastructures decided to build a pan-European distributed research facility, the Extreme Light Infrastructure (ELI) [2]. The implementation phase is on-going in three countries (the Czech Republic, Hungary and Romania). If the three pillars aim to host different but complementary experiments, all of them are making use of High-Power Laser Systems (HPLS). Such a system is currently being implemented in Romania by Thales.

The HPLS at ELI-NP is partially functional and the data acquired through its complex Distributed Control System (DCS) are already available. The DCS contains more than one hundred laser diagnostics instruments. Complementary metal–oxide–semiconductor (CMOS) cameras are the key instruments when considering the volume of data produced. Some of these cameras are not triggered externally, resulting in the acquisition of images without any laser beams. Our main goal is to eliminate data (images) without valuable information by implementing a laser beam detection algorithm. To our knowledge, this problem was not addressed in other laser facilities. Most of the time, the methods found in the literature aim to perform alignment tasks [3][4] and are based on alignment loop using weighting centroid and pointing algorithms [5]. Specific needs, such as laser beam classifications, led to the development of other techniques based on convolutional neural network, as presented in [6].

Our approach is quite different because we cannot assume that the image contains a beam a priori. Additionally, the dataset we have to process is large and diverse because the images come from different laser subsystems and may capture different profile intensity measurements (e.g., Near-Field and Far-Field). Our algorithm is primarily relying on region-based segmentation [7] and is similar to the autofocus algorithm presented by Gu [8]. If the first part of the two algorithms (filtering and segmentation techniques) is the same, the last part is not. We consider indeed that the laser beam cannot always be modelled as a circle or an ellipse. This assumption was made after we conducted a visual analysis of the laser beam images already available from the HPLS, in particular when looking at Far-Field beam intensity profiles. Instead, we propose to use a convex-hull algorithm [9] that was tested on few images samples.

The structure of the paper is the following: in Section II, we present the structure of the data that had to be processed. Section III describes how a laser beam detection algorithm has been developed by using threshold segmentation techniques combined with non-linear filtering and convex hull algorithm. The paper concludes with the work to be carried out in the future in order to improve the current algorithm.

II. Data structure

The data stored by the HPLS DCS are using a specific Hierarchical Data Format, HDF5 [10]. The HDF5 format is based on an Abstract Data Model relying on three key concepts: File, Group, and Dataset. They are presented in Figure 1.

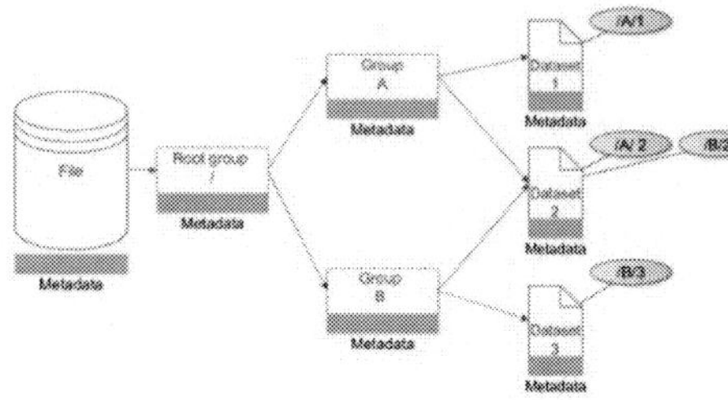

Figure 1. Simplified view of the HDF5 structure

The File is a storage container for organizing objects of mainly two types: Groups and Datasets. A Group is similar to a filesystem directory and contains Groups or Datasets linked together with parent-child relationships. Finally, the dataset is a multidimensional array of data elements. Each dataset relies on diverse properties that characterize it. All the images to be analyzed by the algorithm presented in the next section are stored in such HDF5 files.

III. LASER BEAM DETECTION ALGORITHM

The laser beam detection algorithm is divided into four main steps:

1) Access to input data and creation of python numpy array
2) Segmentation with a threshold algorithm
3) Noise filtering with a median filter
4) Beam detection with the convex hull algorithm

A. Access to input data and creation of numpy array

The access to the data is made by opening the HDF5 file with the use of the h5.py python modules. The matrix of pixels contained in the HDF5 file is stored as a numpy array. This array is used as an input for the algorithm. Numpy array was selected because it uses less memory than classical python lists [11] and a vast number of python packages for image processing were developed around it [12][13].

B. Selection of a threshold algorithm

To isolate a specific object/region in an image, several segmentation techniques exist. In this study, we focused on two threshold techniques: minimum-threshold algorithm and Otsu threshold algorithm [14].

1) Minimum threshold algorithm

The algorithm can be explained by the formula below:

$$g(x,y) = f(x,y), \quad if\ f(x,y) \geq T$$
$$g(x,y) = 0, \quad if\ f(x,y) < T$$

- *f(x,y): value of the pixel located at the (x,y) coordinates in the original image*
- *T: threshold value*
- *g(x,y): value of the pixel located at the (x,y) coordinates after processing*

Usually, the laser beams are modeled with Gaussian, or Super-Gaussian distributions [15]. When considering Gaussian beams, the maximum intensity is located at the center of the beam. The diameter can be measured either at "Full-Width-Half-Maximum" (FWHM), either at "$1/e^2$". In the first measurement, the optical intensity drops to ½ of the maximum intensity value. In the second case, the optical density drops to 13.5% ($1/e^2$) of the maximum intensity. These beam diameters measurements are represented in Figure 2.

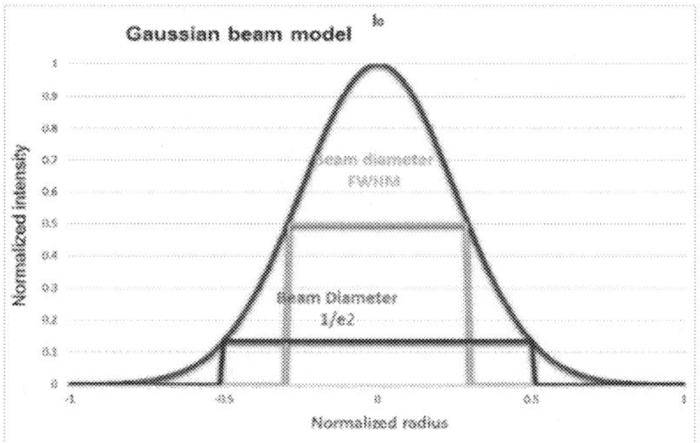

Figure 2. Intensity of a Gaussian beam with the representations of the beam diameters at FWHM and $1/e^2$

Based on these measurements, we defined two threshold values:

- $T_1 = I(FWHM) = I_0/2$
- $T_2 = I(1/e^2) = I_0 * 1/e^2$

I_0: peak intensity of a Gaussian beam

After empiric tests, it appears that the threshold value T_2 is better - the shape of the original beam is preserved - than T_1 (see Figure 3).

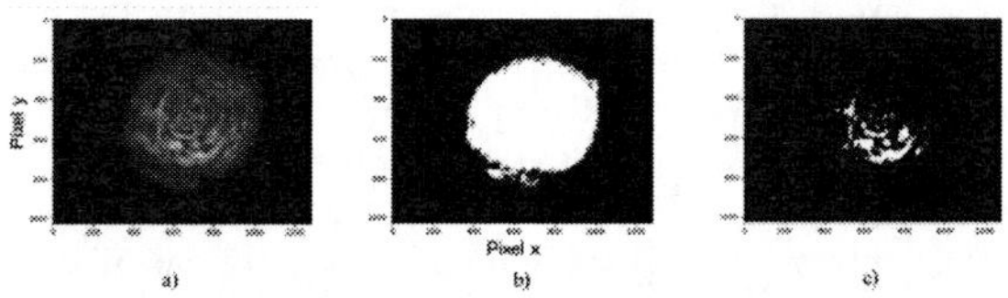

Figure 3. a) Original image; b) image processed with the "$1/e^2$" threshold; c) image processed with "FWHM" threshold

2) Otsu threshold algorithm

This threshold algorithm is named after its inventor (Nobuyuki Otsu). The algorithm is quite complex, but the main idea can be expressed as follows: the algorithm calculates automatically the optimized threshold value to be applied on an image. This calculus is based on the histogram of the image. Nevertheless, the algorithm "assumes" a bimodal distribution of the histogram (the image should be divided between background and foreground pixels).

Additionally, the algorithm needs a sharp valley between the two peaks of the histogram and cannot work if the background and foreground pixels are too different in terms of size (e.g., a small object in comparison with its background). To implement the Otsu algorithm, the scikit-image module was used. "Near-Field" and "Far-Field" beam profile images were processed with this technique (see Figure 4). The threshold values computed for the images are available in the Table 1.

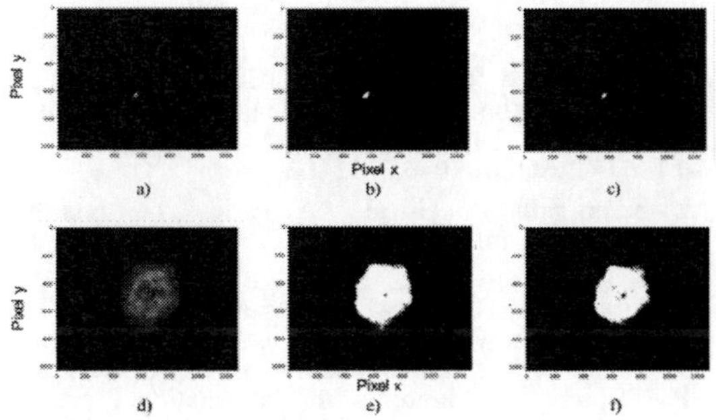

Figure 4. Left column, original images; middle-column, images processed with "$1/e^2$ threshold; right column, images processed with Otsu threshold

TABLE I. EXAMPLE OF THRESHOLD VALUES DEPENDING ON THE THRESHOLD ALGORITHM

Image	Type of image	$1/e^2$ threshold value	Otsu threshold value
a)	Far-Field	470	948
b)	Near-Field	214	296

The Otsu threshold tends to eliminate more information than the minimum threshold "$1/e^2$" (due to a higher threshold value). This is acceptable for "Near-Field" beam profiles but becomes more problematic for the "Far-Field" beam profiles.

As a conclusion, the images are segmented in two regions: beam ("white region") and background ("black region"). To identify the surface of the "white region", the convex hull algorithm is used, however not without a pre-filtering, as we will observe in the next paragraph.

C. Median filtering

The application of threshold methods has a drawback. When a "noise" is present on the original image, both threshold techniques tend to amplify it and produce a "salt" noise (see Figure 5). To eliminate this noise, a median filter [16] is used after the thresholding process. The size of the median filter windows has an influence on the "white segmented region". The median filter tends to smooth the region and the bigger the window is, the smaller the "white region" becomes. Different sizes were tested: from 3 to 15. After the filtering process, the image is segmented in two regions. In an ideal scenario, the white region (laser beam) is either circular, either slightly elliptic and could be easily characterized by its smaller inner/outer circle/ellipse. The reality is quite different because laser beams can have "non-canonic" geometrical forms (see image a) in Figure 4), "critical points" that we define as points located in the white region but having a zero value (see Figure 5).

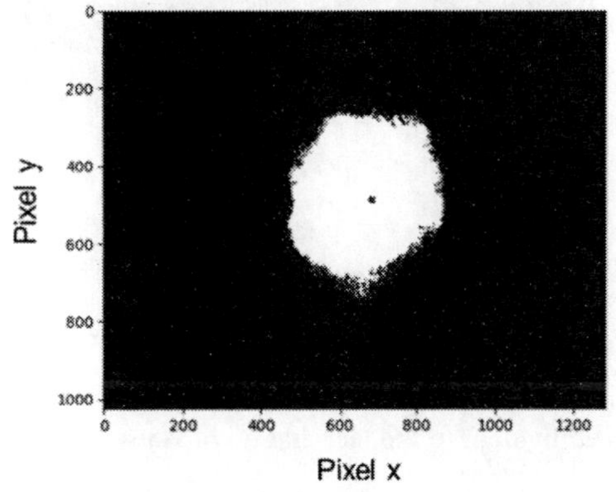

Figure 5. Example of image with a salt noise obtained after threshold algorithm processing

D. Convex hull algorithm and preliminary results

To overcome the issues previously mentioned, we propose to find the smallest convex set that will contain all the points of the "white region". In other words, the set will represent the smallest convex polygon containing all the points of the "white region". The advantage of this technique is that the polygon will be much closer to the form of the laser beam than the classical inner/outer circle/ellipse/rectangle, etc., but only if the image was correctly segmented and filtered before. Figure 6 shows the

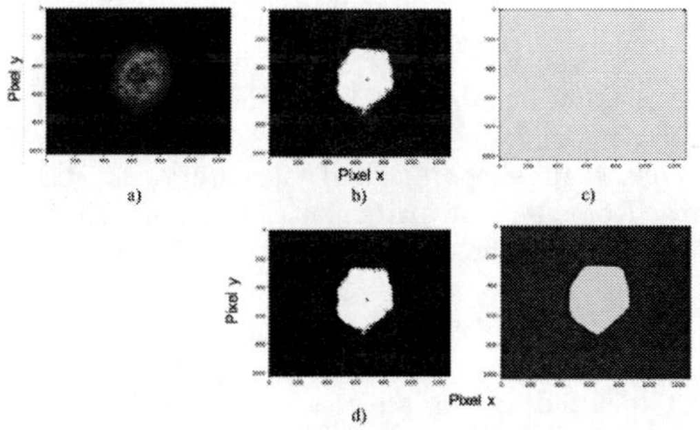

Figure 6. a) Original image; b) & d) segmented image w/out & w/ median filtering; c) & e) results of the convex hull algorithm

problematics encountered when applying this algorithm.

In Figure 6, the polygon containing the white region is filled in yellow. In picture c), the polygon covers almost the entire image due to the noise that was not filtered. In picture e), the polygon shape is close to the original beam shape. Once the polygon is determined, its properties (centroid, perimeter, surface, etc.) can be measured. The resulted properties can be used to characterize the laser beam. Finally, the laser beam detection algorithm was tested on an

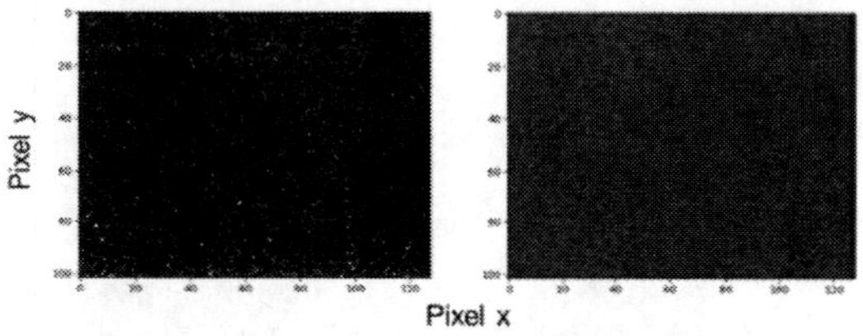

a) b)

Figure 7. a) Original image; b) result of the beam detection algorithm

empty image. The result is presented in Figure 7.

The image b) In Figure 7 does not contain any polygon, which is equivalent to the fact that no beam was detected.

IV. Conclusions

The results obtained with the laser beam detection algorithm are encouraging, but are based on a few image samples. This is the reason why quantitative methods for measuring the information lost during the processing will be tested in the near future. We envisage using the following region-based metrics: Overall Pixel accuracy and Jaccard Index. Additionally, future work will be necessary to implement a real-time algorithm. At this moment, the algorithm is an offline processing made at the ELI-NP data center in order to sort images with beam and images without beam. With a real-time algorithm running directly on the server acquiring images, it would be possible to store only valuable data in the ELI-NP datacenter.

Acknowledgment

This research was supported by the Romanian Ministry of Research and Innovation through the Sovarex project. We would like to thank the director of the project, Mihnea Dulea, for his constant support and Thales Services and Thales Systems Romania, in particular Andrei Gradinariu and Dominique Peter who made the data available to the IFIN-HH team.

References

[1] D. Strickland and G. Mourou, "Compression of amplified chirped optical pulses" Phil. Trans. Optics Communications, Volume 56, number 3, pp. 219-221, December 1985

[2] G. Mourou, G. Korn, W. Sandner and J.L. Collier , "ELI - Extreme Light Infrastructure Science and Technology with Ultra-Intense Lasers Whitebook". [Online] Available from: https://eli-laser.eu/media/1019/eli-whitebook.pdf

[3] R. Ziano, J-B. Accary, B. Ploetzeneder, R. Versaci and B. LeGarrec, "Alignment system for high-power large aperture laser systems", Proc. SPIE High-Power, High-Energy, and High-Intensity Laser Technology II, Volume 9513, id. 95130J, May 2015, doi: 10.1117/12.2178479

[4] K. C. Wilhlelmsen, A. A. S. Awwal, S. W. Ferguson, B. Horowitz, V. J. Miller-Kamm, C. A. Reynolds, "Automati Alignment System for the National Ignition Facility", Proc. ICALEPCS 2007, Oct. 2007, pp. 486-490

[5] A. A. Awwal R. R. Leach, V. J. Miller-Kamm, K. C. Wilhelmsen and R. Lowe-Webb, "Image processing for the Automatic Alignment at the National Ignition Facility", OSA Technical Digest, paper SM2M.3, doi: 10.1364/CLEO_SI.2016.SM2M.3

[6] M. Kaur and P. Goyal, "A review on region based segmentation", Int. J.Sci. Res., vol. 4, pp. 3194 - 3197, April 2015

[7] Z. Alom, A. A. S. Awwal, R. Lowe-Webb and T. M. Taha, "Optical beam classification using deep learning: A comparison with rule- and feature-based classification", Proc. SPIE Optics and Photonics for Information Processing XI, Volume 10395, id 103950J Sep. 2017, doi: 10.1117/12.2282903

[8] C. C. Gu, H. Cheng, K. J. Wu, L. J. Zhang and X. P. Guan, "A High Precision Laser-Based Autofocus Method Using Biased Image Plane for Microscopy", Journal of Sensors, Volume 2018, id 8542680, doi: 10.1155/2018/8542680

[9] D. McCallum and D. Avis, "A linear algorithm for finding the convex hull of a simple polygon", Information Processing Letters, Volume 9, pp. 201-206, December 1979.

[10] The HDF Group. Hierarchical Data Format, version 5, 1997-NNNN http://www.hdfgroup.org/HDF5/, [retrieved: Feb., 2019]

[11] S. Van der Walt, S. C. Colbert and G. Varoquaux, "The Numpy array: a structure for efficient numerical computation", Computing in Science & Engineering, Volume: 13 , Issue: 2 , March-April 2011, pp. 22-30, doi: 10.1109/MCSE.2011.37

[12] K. J. Millman and M. Aivazis, "Python for Scientists and Engineers", Computing in Science & Engineering, Volume 13, Issue 2, March-April 2011, pp. 9-12, doi:10.1109/MCSE.2011.36

[13] F. Pedregosa, "Scikit-learn: Machine Learning in Python", Journal of Machine Learning Research, Oct. 2011, pp. 2825–2830

[14] N. Otsu, "A threshold selection method from gray-level histograms", IEEE Trans. Sys., Man., Cyber, Volume 9, Jan. 1979, pp. 62–66, doi: 10.1109/TSMC.1979.4310076

[15] D. L. Shealy and J. Hoffnagle, "Laser beam shaping profiles and propagation", Applied Optics, Volume 45, Issue 21, Aug. 2006, pp. 5118-5131, doi: 10.1364/AO.45.005118

[16] J. W. Tukey, "Exploratory Data Analysis". Reading, MA. AddisonWesley, 1977.

A Novel Bidirectional Transmission System Based on Passive Optical Network and Wavelength Reuse Technique

Chung-Yi Li
Department of Communication Engineering
National Taipei University
New Taipei City, 23741 Taiwan
e-mail:cyli@gm.ntpu.edu.tw

Wen-Shing Tsai*
Department of Electrical Engineering
Ming Chi University of Technology
New Taipei City 24301, Taiwan
e-mail:wst@mail.mcut.edu.tw

Min-Cian Chen
Department of Electrical Engineering
Ming Chi University of Technology
New Taipei City 24301, Taiwan
e-mail:r943006@gmail.com

***Abstract*—In this paper, a bidirectional transmission system based on Passive Optical Network (PON) and wavelength reuse technology is proposed and demonstrated. A local oscillator, with 16 GHz via first Mach-Zehnder Modulator (MZM) and 1.25-Gb/s data via second MZM, generates the transmitting signal. The signal is separated by Fiber Bragg Grating (FBG) into two optical signals. One is central carrier and the other is subcarrier. The subcarrier signal transports data from Optical Line Terminal (OLT) to Optical Network Unit (ONU) by 25 km Single Mode Fiber (SMF) transmission. The central carrier is reused as upstream light source to achieve bidirectional transmission. The power penalty of the system is < 1.7 dB for downlink with and without enhanced channel, and downlink and uplink transmissions of Bit Error Rate (BER) performances are < 10^{-9}.**

Keywords- Fiber Bragg Grating; Mach-Zehnder Modulator; Passive Optical Network; Radion-on-Fiber; Wavelength Reuse.

I. INTRODUCTION

A Radio-on-Fiber (ROF) system provides broad bandwidth for users to solve transmission congestion. It can be applied to microwave communication systems, such as Wavelength Division Multiplexing (WDM), Optical Add-Drop Multiplexing (OADM) and Orthogonal Frequency Division Multiplexing (OFDM) [1]-[3]. These techniques are often accompanied by high bandwidth and high capacity in order to meet the needs of many users. Hybrid Fiber to The Home (FTTH) systems can achieve this goal [4].Currently, integrated ROF-PON technology [1][2] is the most common application of hybrid FTTH technology. It can transmit microwave signals over a long distance with high fidelity. Such technology can make effective usage of the broad bandwidth and low transmission loss characteristics of the fiber, in order to meet needs for bandwidth and mobility. Optical fiber has lots of advantages in long distance transmission including high bandwidth, low power loss, and immunity to electromagnetic interference. Bidirectional optical fiber transport system has a series of interferences. This is due to the simultaneous uplink data and the downlink data transport, which creates the Rayleigh backscattering (RB) effect [5]. The RB results in power fading, deteriorating system performance and increasing bit error rate because the fiber crystal structure is not uniform in the manufacturing process leading to a shift in the refraction index. To solve the RB of power fading, many schemes and demonstrations have been proposed, such as using different paths or wavelengths between the uplink and the downlink transmissions.

In this paper, we propose a ROF-PON and wavelength reuse system that can increase spectral efficiency. Another advantage is to use only an optical light source that can reduce the RB interference as well as improve the system performance.

II. EXPERIMENT SETUP AND RESULTS

The experimental setup of the bidirectional transmission system based on the passive optical network and wavelength reuse technique is shown in Figure 1. Because the sensitivity of the MZM is affected by polarization, we set a Polarization Controller (PC) before MZM to improve the stability of MZM. The Optical Double Sideband (ODSB) signal is generated by first MZM. After the ODSB signal is separated by FBG, the +1 order sideband signal, the -1 order sideband signal with central carrier are used as downstream signals for different paths transmission. The +1 order sideband signal is reflected by FBG and the -1 order sideband with central carrier signal pass through FBG. The downstream optical signal combines the two ways of optical signals and is amplified by Erbium Doped Fiber Amplifier (EDFA) to avoid transmission power loss for 25 km SMF transport. The downstream signal with 1.25-Gb/s data is generated by the MZM. The combined optical spectrum is shown in Figure 2. Upstream 1.25-Gb/s data is modulated by using another MZM. To compare the downstream and upstream transmissions, the transmission data is in the +1 sideband signal and the -1 sideband with central carrier signal, respectively.

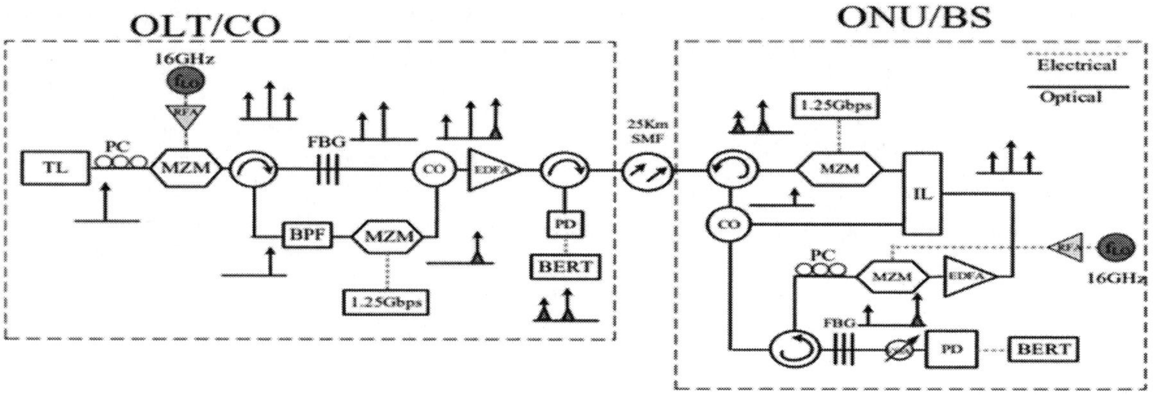

Figure 1. Experimental setup of bidirectional transmission system based on passive optical network and wavelength reuse technique

We reuse part of the downstream optical signal as upstream carrier. The upstream optical signal goes through odd channel then performs Optical / Electrical (O/E) convert by Photodetector (PD) and measures BER performance.

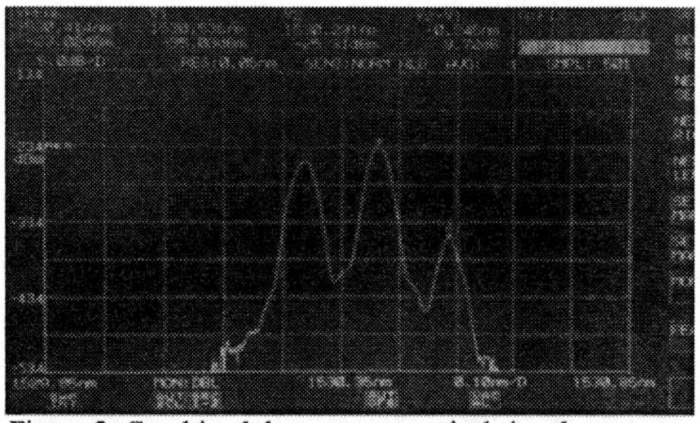

Figure 2. Combined downstream optical signal spectrum.

For the even channel, we let the +1 order sideband signal pass through, even channel enhance the power of the downstream signal to lead the downstream signal with better BER performance. The measured BER curves of the received optical power are presented in Figure 3. The received optical power levels at the BER of 10^{-9} are −23.1 dBm (with even channel enhanced for downlink), −21.4 dBm (without even channel enhanced for downlink), and -20.1 dBm (uplink). A power penalty of approximately <1.7 dB (for downlink) of the fiber link is observed during the BER test for 25 km SMF transmission.

III. CONCLUSION AND FUTURE WORK

We have proposed and demonstrated a bidirectional ROF-PON system. The system has simple and low cost features. Due to the RB effect, using FBG and IL achieve different carrier transmission and enhances the power in even channel. We reuse part of the downstream signal as upstream optical carrier in BS to achieve low cost. As compared with downstream and upstream for transmission, the transmission data is in the +1 sideband single and the -1 sideband with central carrier signal, respectively. The power penalty of the system is < 1.7 dB, downlink and uplink transmission of BER values are < 10^{-9}. The system can be combined with optical network and radio frequency, such as FTTH to implement long-haul transmission.

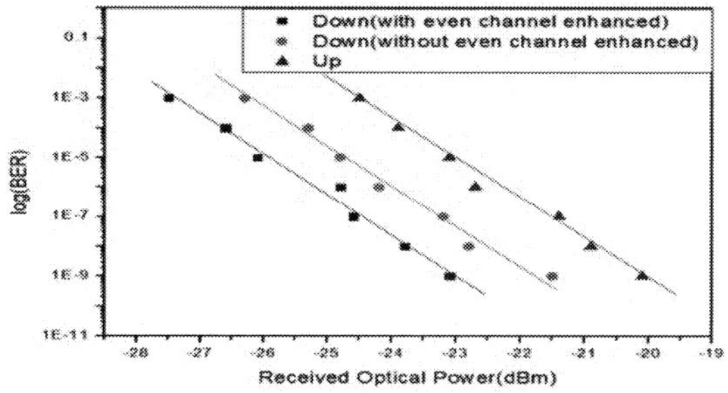

Figure 3. The measure BER curves

REFERENCES

[1] J. Yu, Z. Jia, T. Wang, G. K. Chang, and G. Ellinas "Demonstration of a Novel WDM-PON Access Network Compatible with ROF System to Provide 2.5Gb/s per Channel Symmetric Data Services," 2007 Optical Fiber Communication and National Fiber Optic Engineers Conference (OFC/NFOEC 2007), pp. 1-3, March 25-29, 2007.

[2] J. Prat, J. Lazaro, P. Chanclou and S. Cascelli, "Passive OADM Network Element for Hybrid Ring-Tree WDM/TDM-PON," the 35th European Conference on Optical Communication(ECOC 2009), pp.1-2, Sept. 20-24, 2009, Vienna, Austria.

[3] Y. Liao and W. Pan, "All-optical OFDM Based on Arrayed Grating Waveguides in WDM Systems," International Conference on Electronics, Communications and Control (ICECC), pp.707 – 710, Sept. 9-11, 2011.

[4] R. Llorente, M. Morant, M. Beltran, and E. Pellicer, "Fully Converged Optical, Millimetre-Wave Wireless and Cable Provision in OFDM-PON FTTH Networks," Transparent Optical Networks (ICTON), 2013 15th Int. Conf. on, pp.1-4, Jun. 23-27, 2013

[5] H. H. Lin, C. Y. Lee, S. C. Lin, S. L. Lee and G. Keiser "WDM-PON Systems Using Cross-Remodulation to Double Network Capacity with Reduced Rayleigh Scattering Effects," 2008Optical Fiber communication (OFC) /National Fiber Optic Engineers Conference (NFOEC), pp.1-3, March 24-28, 2008.

Technique for Embedding Information in Objects Produced with 3D Printer Using Near Infrared Fluorescent Dye

*Piyarat Silapasuphakornwong, **Hideyuki Trii, **Kazutake Uehira
Human Media Research Center
Kanagawa Institute of Technology
Atsugi, Japan
E-mail: *silpiyarat@gmail.com, **{torii, uehira}@nw.kanagawa-it.ac.jp

Masahiro Suzuki
Department of Psychology
Tokiwa University
Mito, Japan
E-mail: masuzuki@tokiwa.ac.jp

Abstract—**This paper provides a novel technique to embed information in objects fabricated with a 3D printer using a near infrared fluorescent dye. To embed information inside an object, regions containing a small amount of fluorescent dye are formed inside the object as it is fabricated, and these regions form a pattern that expresses certain information. When this object is irradiated with near-infrared rays, they pass through the resin but are partly absorbed by the fluorescent dyes, and the fluorescent dyes emit near-infrared fluorescence. Therefore, by using a near-infrared camera, the internal pattern can be captured as a high-contrast image and the embedded information can be nondestructively read out. We conducted experiments to confirm the principle of the technique and demonstrate its feasibility. A sample was prepared using a two head fused deposition modeling-type 3D printer. On the basis of the experimental results, it was determined that a bright and high-contrast image could be taken if the pattern was formed at a depth of 1 mm or less from the surface, demonstrating the feasibility of this technique.**

Keywords-3D printer; information hiding; near infrared light; fluorescent dye.

I. Introduction

In recent years, 3D printers have spread rapidly because they have become smaller and cheaper. If consumers have a 3D printer in their own home or office, they can easily obtain a product that they want just by buying the 3D model data through the Internet and print it. Therefore, it is expected that 3D printers may bring a revolution in the manufacturing industry and logistics [1]-[3].

Moreover, 3D printers use a process called additive manufacturing in which thin layers are formed one by one to form an object. This makes it possible to form a fine structure inside the object. Using this process, we have been studying techniques that can embed information inside an object by forming fine patterns that express information in the object while it is fabricated. We have also been studying techniques that can read out such information nondestructively from the outside.

The embedding of information inside 3D printed objects will enable extra value to be added to 3D printed objects, expanding their applications. For example, we can embed information that usually comes with newly purchased products (e.g., user manuals) into the objects. We can also embed watermarks to protect the copyright of the original 3D model data. Although this is similar to conventional watermarking for digital content [4], the final product is not digital data but a real physical object. Therefore, a watermark needs to be embedded into it. Moreover, it will be also possible to use the object as a "thing" of Internet of Things (IoT) connecting the Internet.

To develop a nondestructive information readout technology, we examined a method using thermography [5] [6] and a near infrared camera [7] [8]. We formed small cavities inside an object as fine patterns at shallow depths from the surface using thermography. Since a cavity has a very low thermal conductivity, the temperature of the surface above them becomes higher than other areas when the surface is heated, therefore, we can know where cavities are in the object and read out the information.

We formed the fine patterns using a resin that has a high reflectivity or high absorption rate for infrared light when using an infrared camera. We can obtain the pattern in this case too because most resin materials transmit infrared rays.

As related work, the technique of embedding information inside 3D printed objects using a thin plate with a cutout pattern has been studied in recent years. Willis and Wilson [9] first created some product parts, one of which had a visible pattern, and then assembled these parts into one product so that the patterned part was inside it. They read out the patterned information inside by using terahertz wavelength light. However, in practical terms, it was too complicated to apply it to common 3D printing. In contrast, the fine patterns in our technique are integrally formed using the body-utilizing additive manufacturing process of 3D printers, which eliminates any additional processes.

In this paper, we propose a new technique for forming an inside pattern containing a small amount of fluorescent dye. In Section 2, we describe the principle of the proposed technique. Since the dye emits fluorescence, it is expected that high-luminance, high-contrast pattern image can be captured. This paper also describes the experiment we conducted to confirm the feasibility of this technique in Sections 3 and 4. We conclude this paper in Section 5.

II. INFORMATION EMBEDDING USING FLUORESCENT DYE

Figure 1 shows the basic principle of the proposed technique. This technique assumes that the resin is used as an object material. Pattern regions inside the object are formed using the same resin as that of the other regions, but they contain a small amount fluorescent dye. Since resin has high transmittance for near infrared, when the object is irradiated with near-infrared rays from the outside, the rays reach the internal fluorescent dyes. The light source irradiates light with wavelength λ_E, which excites the fluorescent dye. The fluorescent dye is excited and emits fluorescence. Therefore, a bright image of the patterns inside the resin object can be captured.

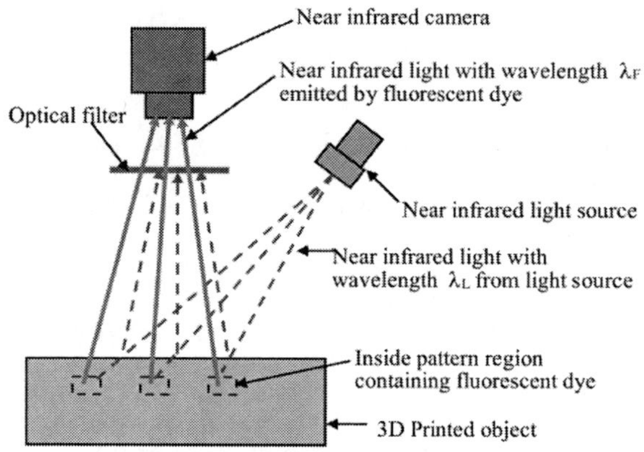

Figure 1. Basic concept of proposed technique

Since wavelength λ_F of the dye's fluorescence differs from wavelength λ_E of the irradiated light, only light the fluorescent dye emits enters the camera, using an optical filter that blocks the light from the light source. In our previous studies where near infrared rays were used, reflective light from the object surface also entered the camera as noise. This decreased readability of the embedded information. In contrast, since the technique in this study can block such reflective light from the surface, it is expected that a low noise image of the pattern can be obtained, enhancing the readability.

Using the same color of resins for the body and internal patterns, the patterns cannot be seen from the outside even if they are formed in a very shallow position from the surface. This is because the amount of the fluorescent dye contained in the resin is very small, and this hardly changes the color of the resin. This is important for applications requiring embedded information to remain hidden.

III. EXPERIMENTS

A. *Sample preparation*

Figure 2 shows the designed layout of the sample. In many practical cases of fabricating an object with a resin material, its inside is hollow as shown Figure 2, requiring only thin walls to maintain the strength of its body (the

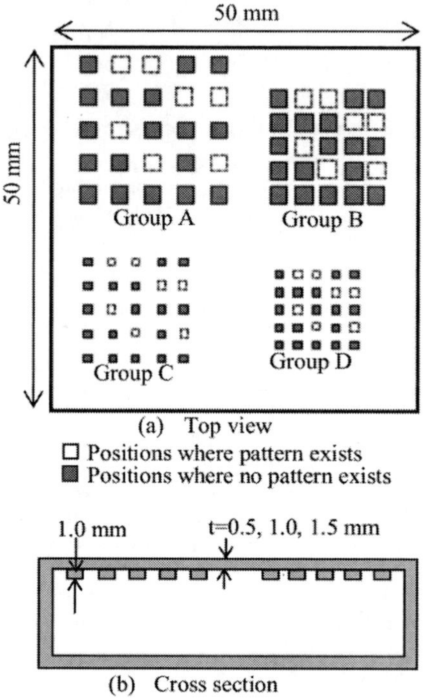

Figure 2. Layout of sample

TABLE 1 LAYOUT PARAMETERS OF PATTERNS IN SAMPLE

	Size	Space
Group A	2	2
Group B	2	1
Group C	1	2
Group D	1	1

(mm)

walls are omitted in this figure). Therefore, even in this study, samples whose insides are hollow were prepared. As shown in the figure, the internal patterns contact the inner wall of the outer shell. The sizes of the internal pattern and spaces between them were changed as experimental parameters as listed in Table 1. The thickness of the outer shell of the main body was also changed from 0.5 to 2 mm as an experimental parameter.

Figure 3 shows a photo of the 3D printer used to fabricate the samples. We used a fused deposition modeling (FDM)-type dual-nozzle 3D printer, Mutoh Value3D MagiX 2200D, to use two materials for one single object.

The body structure was fabricated using pure Acrylonitrile Butadiene Styrene (ABS) resin, and the inside patterns were formed using the same color of ABS resin as that for body, however, it contained a small amount of florescent dye (less than 1%). Figure 4 shows an example of the samples whose outer shell thickness t is 0.5 mm, in which the internal patterns cannot seen from the outside at all.

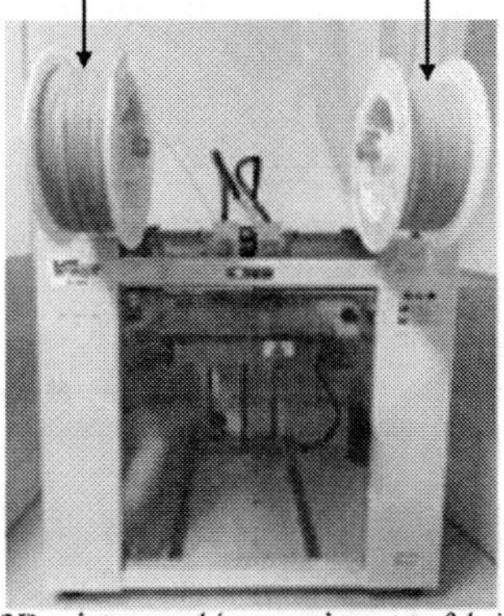

Figure 3. 3D printer used in experiment to fabricate samples

Figure 4. Example of samples.

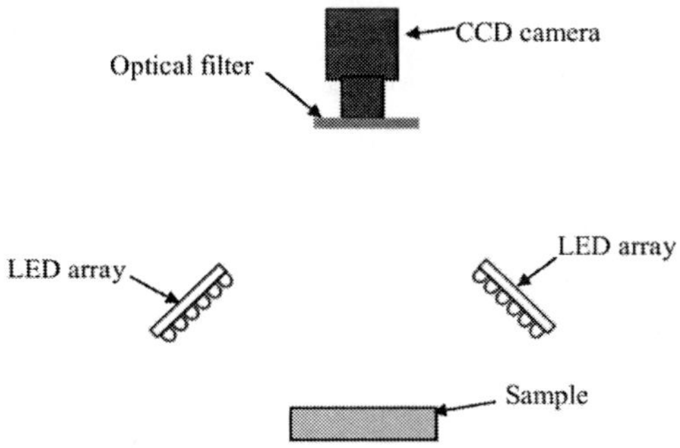

Figure 5. Layout of equipment to capture near infrared images

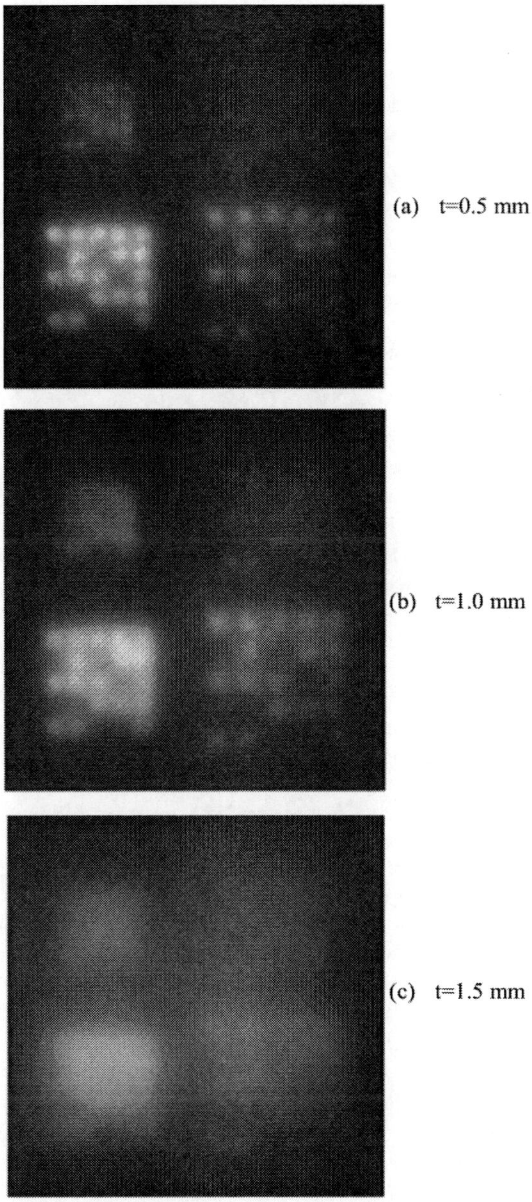

Figure 6. Captured images with CCD camera

B. *Capture of near infrared image*

Figure 5 illustrates the layout of the equipment used to capture a near infrared image. We used two sets of LED arrays as near infrared light sources. A CCD camera with 2048 x 1088 pixels, which was sensitive to light with wavelengths up to 1100 nm, was set at the same side as above the sample, between the LED arrays. An optical filter was placed in front of the camera.

IV. RESULTS AND DISCUSSION

Figure 6 shows the images captured with CCD camera. For all groups in the sample with t=0.5 mm, we can clearly determine the presence or absence of internal patterns at predetermined positions. For the sample with t=1.0 mm, although the image is blurred, it can barely be determined whether there is a pattern at a predetermined position. However, we cannot determine the presence or absence of any patterns in any group of the sample with t=1.5 mm due to the large degree of blur in the image. From this result, it can be seen that binary information can be read out if the distance from the object surface to the pattern is within 1 mm and the pattern size and the interval are 1 mm or more.

The captured images shown in Figure 6 have low noise and high contrast. These make it easy to distinguish whether or not a pattern exists. This demonstrates that the proposed technique using a fluorescent dye has the effect we expected.

The blur in the image occurs because the near infrared rays are scattered as it passes through the ABS resin. Therefore, as the path becomes shorter, the blurring becomes less, that is, in order to reduce blurring, it is necessary to shorten the distance from the surface of the object to the region containing the fluorescent dye. Since thinning the outer shell decreases the strength of the object's body, a method of forming a region containing a fluorescent dye in a part of the outer shell without reducing the thickness of the outer shell can be a candidate countermeasure. Verification of the effectiveness of this idea is a future task.

V. Conclusion

We have studied a technique of forming an internal pattern region in a 3D printed object with ABS resin containing a very small account of fluorescent dye to enhance contrast and decrease noise in images of the patterns and to enhance readability of the embedded information the patterns express.

From the experiments we conducted, we clarified that bright and low-noise images of the internal pattern could be captured as expected and it enhanced readability for embedded binary information.

In future work, we will decrease image blur of internal patterns by shorten the distance from the object surface to the internal pattern to enable higher density information embedding.

Acknowledgment

This research was supported by Japan Society for the Promotion of Science Grant-in-Aid for Scientific Research 15H02707. Moreover, we would like to thank DIC Corporation for providing the fluorescent dye contained in the ABS resin in this research.

References

[1] B. Berman, "3-D printing: The new industrial revolution," Business horizons, vol. 55, no. 2, pp. 155–162, March–April 2012.

[2] B. Garrett, "3D printing: New economic paradigms and strategic shifts," Global Policy, vol. 5, no. 1, pp. 70–75, February 2014.

[3] C. Weller, R. Kleer, and F. T. Piller, "Economic implications of 3D printing: Market structure models in light of additive manufacturing revisited," International Journal of Production Economics, vol. 164, pp. 43–56, June 2015.

[4] F. Hartung and M. Kutter, "Multimedia watermarking techniques" Proc IEEE, Vol. 87, No. 7, pp. 1079-1107, 1999.

[5] M. Suzuki, P. Silapasuphakornwong, K. Uehira, H. Unno, and Y. Takashima, "Copyright protection for 3D printing by embedding information inside real fabricated objects," International Conference on Computer Vision Theory and Applications, pp. 180–185, March 2015.

[6] M. Suzuki, et al., "Embedding Information into Objects Fabricated With 3-D Printers by Forming Fine Cavities inside Them", Proceedings of IS&T International symposium on Electronic Imaging, Vol. 2017, No. 41, pp. 6-9, 2017 .

[7] P. Silapasuphakornwong, et al., "Nondestructive readout of copyright information embedded in objects fabricated with 3-D printers", The 14th International Workshop on Digital-forensics and Watermarking, Revised Selected Papers, pp.232-238, 2016.

[8] K. Uehira, et al., "Copyright Protection for 3D Printing by Embedding Information Inside 3D-Printed Object", The 15th International Workshop on Digital-forensics and Watermarking Revised Selected Papers, pp.370-378, 2017.

[9] K. D. D. Willis and A. D. Wilson, "Infrastructs: Fabricating Information Inside Physical Objects for Imaging in the Terahertz Region", ACM Transactions on Graphics, Vol. 32, No. 4, pp. 138-1–138-10 July 2013.

Deep Reinforcement Learning in VizDoom First-Person Shooter for Health Gathering Scenario

Dmitry Akimov and Ilya Makarov
National Research University Higher School of Economics
Moscow, Russia
deakimov@edu.hse.ru, iamakarov@hse.ru

Abstract—**In this work, we study the effect of combining existent improvements for Deep Q-Networks (DQN) in Markov Decision Processes (MDP) and Partially Observable MDP (POMDP) settings. Combinations of several heuristics, such as Distributional Learning and Dueling architectures improvements, for MDP are well-studied. We propose a new combination method of simple DQN extensions and develop a new model-free reinforcement learning agent, which works with POMDP and uses well-studied improvements from fully observable MDP. To test our agent we choose the VizDoom environment, which is old first person shooter, and the Health Gathering scenario. We prove that improvements used in MDP setting may be used in POMDP setting as well and our combined agents can converge to better policies. We develop an agent with combination of several improvements showing superior game performance in practice. We compare our agent with Recurrent DQN using Prioritized Experience Replay and Snaphot Ensembling agent and get approximately triple increase in per episode reward.**

Keywords–Deep Reinforcement Learning; VizDoom; POMDP; First-Person Shooter.

I. INTRODUCTION

The 3D shooter is a video game genre where a player controls the virtual combatant and tries to achieve some predefined goal, such as make their way trough the maze or capture the flag or fight other players with a ranged weapon. There are several game modes in which players can compete or cooperate with each other. Usually, such games are very demanding on player skill, reaction and cleverness.

3D shooters are challenging task for Reinforcement Learning (RL) algorithms. In terms of reinforcement learning concept, we can describe a 3D shooter as sophisticated environment with one general goal, for example, to maximize kill-death ratio during one game session or episode, and with many simpler tasks, such as map navigation or enemy detection. Learning behaviour policy in 3D shooters is difficult: rewards are extremely sparse and usually highly delayed. It means that an agent may receive reward signal for action it performed hundreds frames ago. Also, information received by the agent from the environment is incomplete: enemies positions are unknown and angle of view is limited by 90-110 degrees. Maps can be complex mazes, and the navigation inside is challenging for the agent as well. The only information that Deep RL agent can use for action choice is a game screenshot (image captured from rendered scene).

We decided to focus on First-Person Shooter (FPS) videogame, which we have previously simulated and studied related to intelligent path planning [1] [2] and building RL agent for weapon choice [3].

In this work, we choose VizDoom [4] as simulation environment. There are many maps (scenarios) in VizDoom, each with different goals and gameplay features. We choose the Health Gathering scenario to teach an agent to detect health packs and navigate inside a room with acid on the floor.

We combine several existing improvements for RL agents to propose a new model-free approach for general RL problems. We conduct experiments proving effectiveness of the proposed agent. We show that our agent outperforms well studied baseline methods, as well as their modifications.

The paper is organized as follows. Related work for deep reinforcement learning is overviewed in Section 2. We introduce basic concepts in Section 3 and describe chosen scenario for VizDoom in Section 4. Then, in Section 5–7, we describe proposed approach, experiments and analyze obtained results. Finally, in Section 8, we make a conclusion and describe future work.

II. RELATED WORK

A. Rainbow

In the Rainbow paper [5] authors combined several of the DQN extensions. Particularly, authors propose to use Double Learning, Dueling Architecture, Multi-step learning, Prioritized Replay, C51 and Noisy Networks for exploration all together. Their combined agent learn up to 8 times faster than simple DQN. Also authors investigate effects of combining all the five out of these methods.

However, they tested combined agent on the Atari games, which were implemented in The Arcade Learning Environment [6], in MDP manner, and, thus, effects of this combination in environments with incomplete information is unknown.

B. Arnold paper

In ‘Arnold’ paper [7], authors develop an agent to play a deathmatch scenario in VizDoom environment. Authors used several useful learning tricks. They implemented augmentation of the agent with in-game features, which are accessible during training, and enemy-detection layer, which greatly speeds up training and helps agent to converge to a good policy. Also, authors did reward shaping presented as small reward signals for good actions, which do not directly correspond to the main objective, separate networks for action and navigation for faster leanring, and added dropout layer after convolutions, preventing neural network from overfitting and making agent’s policy more robust to previously unseen in-game situations. Their final agent substantially outperforms build-in AI agent of the game and, surprisingly, humans. However, the ‘Arnold’ agent is relatively simple: authors did not exploit Q-learning extensions that could significantly improve agent's performance.

C. DRQN with Prioritized Experience Replay, Double Q-learning and Snapshot Ensembling

Prioritized Experience Replay (PER) [8] is a smart way to speed-up training. In this method, the examples for Experience Replay are sampled with non-uniform probabilities, assigned to each tuple $\langle s, a, r, s' \rangle$ or $\langle o, a, r, o' \rangle$ in case of POMDP setting, according to loss value on this example. Examples with higher error values carry more information than ones with low error value, so we prefer to sample them more often. This approach has shown its potential and superior performance compared to DQN in Atari games. Authors of [9] combined PER with Double Q-learning and Snapshot Ensembling and tested their agent in VizDoom Defend The Center scenario, in which the agent stand at certain point and rotate in order to shoot the enemies closing to the agent. Also, authors integrated an enemy detector and trained it jointly with Q-function. We compare our results with [9] below.

Deep Reinforcement Learning improvements for MDP achieved super-human performance in many games. However, this improvements had not been considered in POMDP setting before. We think that it is essential to combine such simple heuristics from MDP with POMDP to push up state-of-the art methods considering several scenarios for first-person shooter (FPS) according to VisDoom Deep RL competition.

III. Deep Reinforcement Learning Overview

General reinforcement learning goal is to learn optimal policy for an agent, which maximizes scalar reward by interacting with the environment.

At each time step t an agent observes the state s_t of the environment, makes a decision about the best action a_t according to its policy π and gets the reward r_t. This process well known as *Markov Decision Process* (MDP) denoted as a tuple (S, A, R, T), where S indicates a finite state space, A indicates a finite action space, R is a reward function, which maps pair $(s, a) \in (S, A)$ into stochastic reward r, and last but not least T is a transition kernel: $T(s, a, s') = P(S_{t+1} = s' | S_t = s, A_t = a)$.

Discounted return from state s_t is expressed by the following formula:

$$G_t = \sum_{i=0}^{\infty} \gamma^i r_{t+i},$$

where $\gamma \in (0, 1)$ is a discount factor reducing the impact of reward on previous steps. Typically, the choice of γ depends on the length of the game. An agent with the greater values of gamma concentrates on dilated rewards, which is important in the long game sessions, and an agent with small gamma concentrates on short-term rewards.

In order to choose the actions, an agent uses a policy $\pi = P(a|s)$. We will call a policy π *optimal* if it maximizes expected discounted reward and mark it with a star:

$$\pi^* = \operatorname*{argmin}_{\pi} \mathbb{E}_\pi (G_t)$$

There may be several optimal policies as well.

In this work, we consider *Q-learning*, a *value-based* method, because of its popularity and effectiveness. All required information about the methods is presented below.

A. Q-learning

To measure the quality of a given policy π one can use action-value function Q^π defined as:

$$Q^\pi(s, a) = \mathbb{E}_\pi \left[G | s_0 = s, a_0 = a \right] \tag{1}$$

Q is expected over all possible action and states reward that can be obtained by the agent with the policy π started from state **s** and performed action **a** and then following its policy. If the true Q-function (Q^*) is given for us, we can derive optimal policy by taking action a that maximizes Q for each state s: $a = \operatorname{argmax}'_a Q(s, a')$

To learn Q for the optimal policy we use *Bellman equation* (1):

$$Q^\pi(s, a) = r(s, a) + \gamma \max_{a'} Q^\pi(s', a') \tag{2}$$

It is proven in [10] that this sequential assignment will converge from any given Q to desired Q^* eventually if action and state spaces are finite and each pair of state and action are presented repeatedly. If we start learning procedure from some Q-function approximation we will learn nothing because of the max operator: agent has no will to explore environment, it will simply perform 'best' action according to its policy. So we must add *exploration* to the agent: we may sample actions with probabilities $p(a_i) = \frac{\exp Q(s, a_i)}{\sum_j \exp Q(s, a_j)} = softmax(a_i)$ (Boltzmann approach) or we can apply *epsilon-greedy* sampling: take random action with probability ϵ and take the best action with probability $1 - \epsilon$. It is recommended to start with epsilon close to 1 and gradually reduce it during training.

To tackle with infinite state spaces we can approximate Q-function with deep neural networks.

1) Deep Q-Network (DQN): The first attempt to use Deep Neural Networks to our knowledge was made in [11]. The authors presented an agent achieving super-human performance in several games. This work marks a milestone in deep reinforcement learning. To make it works, the authors propose to use 2-layer convolutional neural network (CNN) as feature extractor and stack two more fully-connected layers on top to approximate Q-values. This network takes a raw image as input of state and produces Q-values, one output per action.

Because of using a neural network as Q-function estimator, the authors of [11] can not directly apply the rule (2) and instead compute *Temporal Difference* error (TD):

$$TD = Q(s_i, a_i) - (r_i + \gamma \max_{a'} Q(s'_i, a')) \tag{3}$$

and then minimize square of it. Authors used an *online network* to estimate $Q(s_i, a_i)$ term and a *target network* to estimate $\max_{a'} Q(s'_i, a')$ term. The online network was trained via backpropagation, while a value produced by the target network is considered as a constant. The target network's weights were fixed during the online network training and were periodically updated to trained online network.

If we denote parameters of the online network as θ and parameters of the target network as $\tilde{\theta}$, then loss can be expressed as:

$$L = \sum_i \left(Q(s_i, a_i; \theta) - (r_i + \gamma \max_{a'} Q(s'_i, a'; \tilde{\theta}) \right)^2, \quad (4)$$

where summation taken over a batch (defining the number of samples that will be propagated through the network).

To form a batch authors in [11] propose to use *experience replay*, which contains tuples $\langle s, a, r, s' \rangle$ of state, performed action, reward and next state. During training, authors uses estimation of $Q(s, a)$ not for all actions, but only for the performed ones, and, thus, backpropagate the error through neurons corresponding only to these actions.

Although DQN have shown good results in playing Atari video games, it has several problems, such as slow and unstable training [12], and overestimating of expected reward [13], from which we want to get rid off. There are several extensions to DQN, which can fix these drawbacks or boost up resulting performance.

2) Double Q-learning: Conventional Q-learning suffers from max operator in (2) and agent always overestimates obtained reward. There is simple solution called *Double Q-learning* [13] that is to replace $max_{a'} Q(s, a)$ with

$$Q(s', \operatorname*{argmax}_{a'} Q(s'a); \theta) \quad (5)$$

leading to faster and more stable training process.

3) Dueling Networks: The *Dueling network* [12] is a specific architecture, which explicitly uses the Q-function decomposition: $Q(s, a) = V(s) + A(s, a)$, where $V(s)$ is *value* and $A(s, a)$ is advantage. In order to solve the problem of unidentifiability in the sense that given Q we cannot recover V and A uniquely, we present Q-function estimator now has two streams: one for $V(s)$ and one for $A(s, a)$ approximations, and Q-function is computed as following:

$$Q(s, a) = V(s) + A(s, a) - \frac{1}{N_a} \sum_j^{N_a} A(s, a_j) \quad (6)$$

Dueling network may result in a huge performance boost.

B. Recurrent Q-learning

Simple Q-learning and extension works under assumption that we have full access to the environment state at any time. However, in practice we do not. In many cases, we can only *observe* part of the environment state, and observation may be incomplete or noisy. In such a case, it is better to use *Partially Observable Markov Decision Process* (POMDP) formalism. POMDP is a tuple (S, A, R, T, Ω, O), where first four items come from MDP, Ω indicates *observation* set and O indicates *observation function*: $O(s_{t+1}, a_t) = p(o_{t+1} | s_{t+1}, a_t), \forall o \in \Omega$. Due to no available knowledge of environment's state, the agent makes a decision by interacting with the environment and receiving new observations. The agent updates its distribution of belief in true state based on distribution of the current state.

1) Deep Recurrent Q-Network (DRQN): Since we do not have state s_t in POMDP, we could not estimate $Q(s_t, a_t)$ like in DQN. However, there is a simple solution to it. One needs to equip an agent with memory h_t and approximate $Q(s_t, a_t)$ by $Q(o_t, h_{t-1}, a_t)$. One of the most popular approaches is to use recurrent neural networks to solve the problem. Dependence on o_t can be eliminated by modelling $h_t = LSTM(o_t, h_{t-1})$ called long-short term memory block [14]. Such networks are called Deep Recurrent Q-Network (DRQN) [15].

Experience replay now contains tuples $\langle o, a, r, o' \rangle$ denoting observation, performed action, reward and next observation. It is essential to sample sequences of consecutive observations from experience replay to make use of agent memory: without such sampling it can not learn sequences. It is natural to learn only from several last observations, because agent has to form its memory from a few observations. All previously mentioned extensions of DQN can be integrated into DRQN model.

2) Multi-step learning: DQN is trained on a single time step, although DRQN trained on a sequence. One may use this in the loss construction as follows: to replace single-step temporal difference (3) by n-step temporal difference [16]:

$$TD(n) = Q(s_i, a_i) - \\ - (r_i + \gamma r_{i+1} + \ldots + \gamma^{n-1} r_{i+n-1} + \gamma^n \max_a Q(s_{i+n}, a')) \quad (7)$$

This also provides faster and more stable training, especially with delayed rewards, but n has to be properly tuned [17].

3) Distributional RL: Instead of learning Q-function, which is an expectation of discounted reward, it is possible to learn distribution of discounted reward [18] [19]. These distributions can be presented by probability masses, placed on a discrete support z with N atoms, $z_i = V_{min} + i * \Delta z, i = 0, \ldots, N$, where $\Delta z = (V_{max} - V_{min})/(N - 1)$ and (V_{min}, V_{max}) represent admissible value interval. Authors denote the value distribution as Z, then distributional version of (2) holds: $Z(x, a) \overset{D}{=} R(x, a) + \gamma * Z(X', A')$, which may be used for training. They proposed loss function and exact algorithm to learn such discounted reward distribution and name it Categorical 51 (C51), where 51 is the number of atoms z_i. It has been shown that an agent trained in distributional manner has richer expressiveness and usually converges to a better policy.

IV. Health Gathering Scenario

In "Health gathering" scenario, the agent spawns in square room with lava on the floor. The agent has no access to its health and can only turn left, right and move forward (see screenshot of agent view at Fig. 1). There is a bunch of health kits, which increase agent's health and make it survive longer. We used the following reward shaping: agent receives +1 for every step, -100 if it dies, and + *amount of healing*, which is equal to $health(o_t) - health(o_{t-1})$ if this value is bigger than zero, where $health(o)$ represents the agent health in the game.

Figure 1. A Screenshot of Health Gathering Scenario

An episode ends if the agent dies or if 2100 tics done. We assume that such shaping will force agent to pick up health kits with some latency and do it only if it has been badly wounded. Agent trained with frameskip 4 and screen resolution of 108×60.

V. Proposed Approach

In this section we describe our baseline models, as well as combined agent architectures. We use two agents as a baseline to compare with: simple DQN and DRQN with LSTM. Also we use two modified versions: first is DRQN with Dueling architecture and Double Q-Learning and dropout with keeprate=0.5 (D4RQN), and second in addition with C51 and Multi-step (C51M).

We decide to use simplified neural network architecture for all agents in this scenario. Also, all the agents preprocess game screenshot by convolutional feature extractor with the same architecture, presented in Table I. CR denotes Convolution + Relu, n denotes number of convolution filters, k denotes kernel size, s denotes stride.

TABLE I. CONVOLUTIONAL FEATURE EXTRACTOR

Input size	Basic	Input size	Other
$30 \times 45 \times 1$	CR, n=8, k=6, s=3	$60 \times 108 \times 3$	CR, n=32, k=8, s=4
$9 \times 14 \times 8$	CR, n=8, k=3, s=2	$14 \times 26 \times 32$	CR, n=64, k=4, s=2
$4 \times 6 \times 8$		$6 \times 12 \times 64$	CR, n=64, k=3, s=1
		$4 \times 10 \times 64$	

After convolutions, the feature map is reshaped to vector form and is feeded into next layers. DQN network has dense layer with 512 units , with Relu activation in both cases. DRQN has LSTM cell with 128 and 512 units respectively. Both DQN and DRQN has one more dense layer at the end with *number of actions* units and linear activation.

D4RQN and C51M has dropout layer after convolutions with keep rate = 0.5. After this they both have LSTM layer with 512 units. D4RQN splits computation into two streams: *value* stream and *advantage* stream by dense layers with 1 and *number of actions* units with linear activation. Outputs from streams are combined by formula (6) and targets during optimization are picked according to (5) thus combining Double Q-learning and Dueling Networks.

There are atoms in C51M algorithm supporting discounted reward distribution. Each atom has the probability, calculated as softmax over atoms. We split LSTM output into two streams: *value* stream with *number of atoms* units and *value* stream with *number of actions* linear layers, each with *number of atoms* units. For each atom these streams combined by formula (6) and then softmax function applied. To compute Q-value from this distribution we use formula: $Q(s,a) = \sum_i^{n\_atoms} z_i p_i(s,a;\theta)$, where z_i and p_i is the i-th atom support and probability and θ represents network parameters. An illustration of the network architecture for C51M algorithm is presented in Fig. 2.

We choose 51 atoms as in the original algorithm for our scenario. It is crucial to pick right values for V_{min} and V_{max} in atom support. These values must represent lowest and highest possible discounted reward. Indeed, if we choose V_{min} and V_{max} too close to each other, agent will not have rich enough expressiveness, but if we choose the gape too much then only few atoms will be used during training and agent degrades down to DQN.

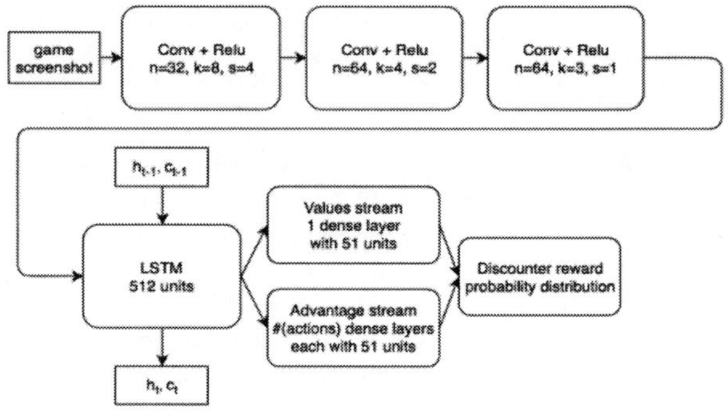

Figure 2. Neural Network for C51M Architecture

In Health Gathering scenario we set these values to -5 and 195. The maximum possible reward equals to maximum episode length which is 2100, and can not be precisely precomputed for shaped reward because of environment randomness. We also decide to focus on small rewards for the agent and significantly reduced range of rewards.

VI. Experiment Design

In this section we provide training procedure details. We set experience replay size to 10^5 . It is important to sample sequences of consecutive observations from experience replay, such that only the last observation may be terminating. We decide to do it by simply checking if any of observations in a sequence is terminal, except the last one, and if there is one, we resample until there are no such cases. By doing so, we greatly reduce total amount of terminate observations to train on. It is important in Health Gathering scenario, because agent receives huge penalty at the last observation if it dies. We set batch size and sequence length to 128 and 10, respectively. We use first four observations to update agent's memory and last six to train on. We set number of steps for gradient descent per epoch to 8000 and number of steps before sampling from experience replay to 15. We also reduce learning rate to 0.0002.

VII. Results

In this section we describe our experimental results and compare performance of all the described agents. For each scenario, we compare learning stability by measuring TD loss at each gradient descent step, learning speed by measuring per-episode reward changes during training and performance of agents after each training epoch. For Fig. 3 the visualization is the following: C51M (dark-blue), DQN (red), DRQN (light-blue) and D4RQN (orange). For TD loss plots we visualize C51M separately, so that we could see the difference between this model and other agent architectures.

A. Health Gathering

TD loss for all the agents can be seen at Fig. 3(a) and 3(b). Again, all agents, except DQN, show stable learning process. Rewards obtained during training can be observed at Fig. 3(c) (plot is constructed in relative time-scale). D4RQN obtains max score more than in half of training episodes, but other agents do not show stable performance. Test rewards presented at Fig. 3(d). C51M has lower performance while D4RQN unexpectedly has highest reward while training than while testing with turned off dropout. We further study agents' performance with and without dropout at testing time.

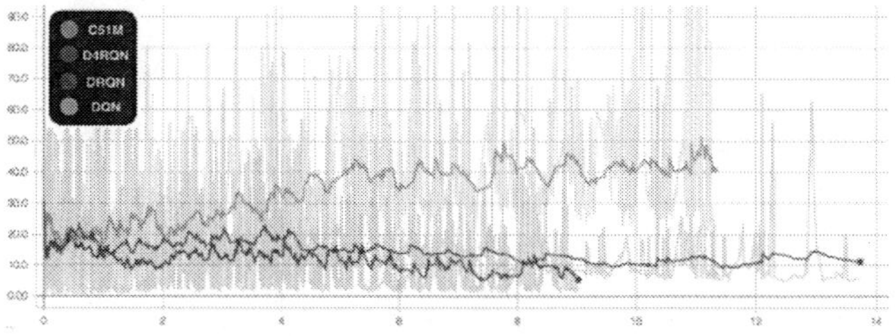

(a) TD Loss for All Agents except C51M

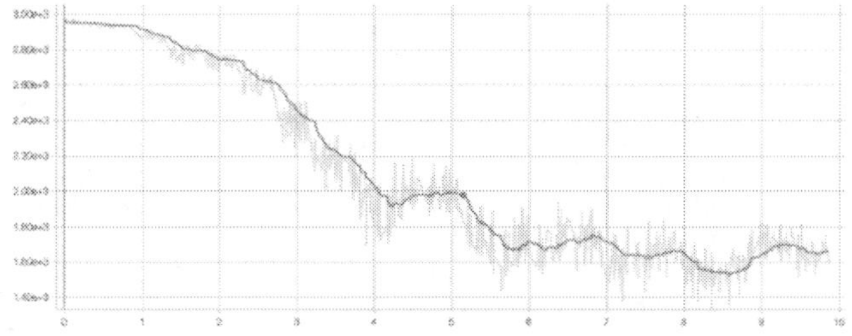

(b) TD Loss for C51M Agent

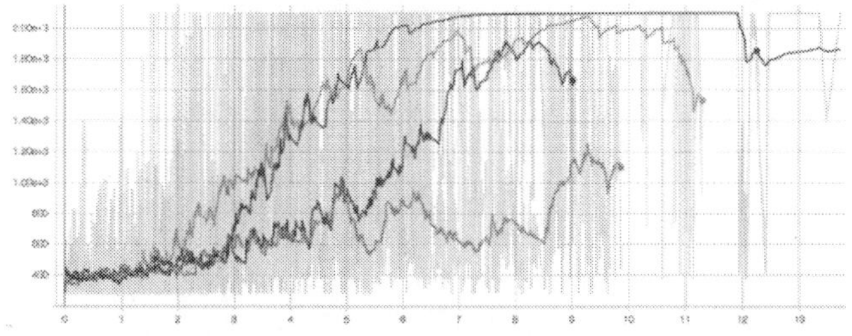

(c) Rewards per Training Episodes

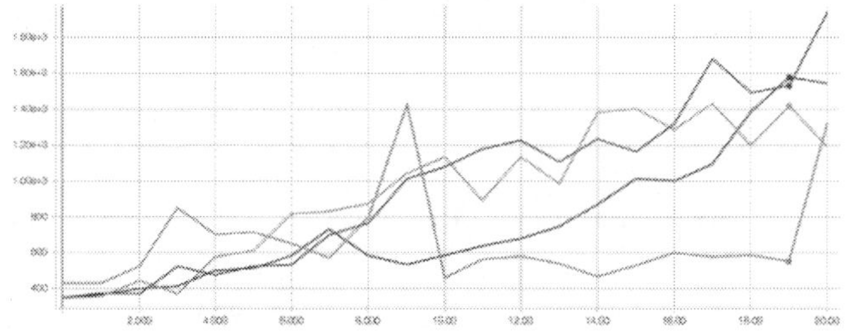

(d) Rewards per Testing Episodes

Figure 3. Health Gathering Scenario Comparison

We noticed that D4RQN detects health packs very well and goes directly to them. With this strategy agent is able to survive all 2100 frames, which is length of the episode, and dies rarely. However, if there are multiple health packs in different sides and approximately on the same distance, agent can not decide where to go and jiggles screen some time in attempt to go both directions at once before deciding which direction it wants to go. DQN does not detect health pack as well as D4RQN and may just move into a wall and die. DRQN plays pretty well, but agent's behaviour was not interpretable in terms of similarity to any reasonable humans' behaviour.

C51M is good at detecting health packs, too. But it scores lower than D4RQN and DRQN have, because it tries to wait several frames before pick up a health pack. We believe that such behaviour occurs, because of our reward shaping and experience replay design. If agent has low health it will obtain bigger reward than if it will pick up health pack will full health. Agent trains on terminal observations rarely due to our sampling method. Also, we believe that human players tend to do the same: it is optimal to pick up health pack when you have only, for example, 50 health points, instead of 90 or more. In situations where health is not observable, skilled players will wait optimal time, learned after several deaths. Alas, C51M did not learn it in our experiment and usually waited too long.

B. Summary results

Since Health Gathering scenario forced to end after 2100 steps during training, it is interesting to test agents without this forced ending. So, we modified config file and set episode length to 10000 and call it Health Gathering Expanded. We add this version of scenario in Table II that contains final performance of all trained agents in order: DQN, DRQN, D4RQN dropout off, D4RQN dropout on, C51M dropout off, C51M dropout on. Values in Table II equal to $mean(R) \pm std(R)$, where R is non-shaped rewards over 100 episodes.

From Table II we can observe that dropout at *testing time* may increase agent's performance: Health Gathering scenario

TABLE II. RESULTS COMPARISON

Model	HG	HG Expanded
DQN	1262.0 ± 631.0	1469.6 ± 1257.0
DRQN	1578.1 ± 665.9	3173.5 ± 2842.3
D4RQN	1890.0 ± 434.3	4781.7 ± 2938.8
D4RQNd	2078.8 ± 144.5	9291.4 ± 2231.2
C51M	1451.7 ± 708.9	2466.4 ± 1766.5
C51Md	1593.7 ± 702.3	4138.4 ± 3634.6

for both D4RQN and C51M. Our results are available via link https://github.com/DEAkimov/vizDoom

VIII. CONCLUSION

In this work, we were the first to present a new model-free deep reinforcement learning agents in POMDP settings for 3D first-person shooter. The presented agents drastically outperformed baseline methods, such as DQN and DRQN. Our agent successfully learned how to play several scenario in VizDoom environment and show human-like behaviour. We aim to further compare such an agent with our other deterministic intelligent agents developed for imitating human behavior [20] [21].

We aim to present our other experiments on Basic and Defend the Tower scenarios in Vizdoom, as well as use our agent as backbone architecture for more challenging task, like Deathmatch scenario, which is exactly our plan for future work. Moreover, our agent could be easily combined with Action-specific DRQN [22], Boltzmann exploration [16], Prioritized Experience Replay [8], and can be modified to use in-game features as well as separate networks for action and navigation to improve further.

ACKNOWLEDGEMENTS

The work was supported by the Russian Science Foundation under grant 17-11-01294 and performed at National Research University Higher School of Economics, Russia.

REFERENCES

[1] I. Makarov and P. Polyakov, "Smoothing voronoi-based path with minimized length and visibility using composite bezier curves." in AIST (Supplement), vol. 191. Ceur WP, 2016, pp. 191–202.

[2] I. Makarov, P. Polyakov, and R. Karpichev, "Voronoi-based path planning based on visibility and kill/death ratio tactical component," in AIST (Suppl). Ceur WP, 2018, pp. 129–140.

[3] I. Makarov and et al., "Modelling human-like behavior through reward-based approach in a first-person shooter game," in EEML, vol. 1627. Ceur WP, 2016, pp. 24–33.

[4] M. Kempka, M. Wydmuch, G. Runc, J. Toczek, and W. Jaśkowski, "Vizdoom: A doom-based ai research platform for visual reinforcement learning," in Computational Intelligence and Games (CIG), 2016 IEEE Conference on. IEEE, 2016, pp. 1–8.

[5] M. Hessel and et al., "Rainbow: Combining improvements in deep reinforcement learning," arXiv preprint arXiv:1710.02298, 2017, pp. 1–14.

[6] M. G. Bellemare, Y. Naddaf, J. Veness, and M. Bowling, "The arcade learning environment: An evaluation platform for general agents," in Proceedings of the 24th International Conference on Artificial Intelligence, ser. IJCAI'15. AAAI Press, 2015, pp. 4148–4152. [Online]. Available: http://dl.acm.org/citation.cfm?id=2832747.2832830

[7] G. Lample and D. S. Chaplot, "Playing fps games with deep reinforcement learning." in AAAI, 2017, pp. 2140–2146.

[8] T. Schaul, J. Quan, I. Antonoglou, and D. Silver, "Prioritized experience replay," arXiv preprint arXiv:1511.05952, 2015, pp. 1–21.

[9] C. Schulze and M. Schulze, "Vizdoom: Drqn with prioritized experience replay, double-q learning, & snapshot ensembling," arXiv preprint arXiv:1801.01000, 2018, pp. 1–9.

[10] C. J. C. H. Watkins and P. Dayan, "Q-learning," Machine Learning, vol. 8, no. 3, May 1992, pp. 279–292. [Online]. Available: https://doi.org/10.1007/BF00992698

[11] V. Mnih and et al., "Human-level control through deep reinforcement learning," Nature, vol. 518, no. 7540, 2015, pp. 529–533.

[12] Z. Wang, T. Schaul, M. Hessel, H. Van Hasselt, M. Lanctot, and N. De Freitas, "Dueling network architectures for deep reinforcement learning," arXiv preprint arXiv:1511.06581, 2015, pp. 1–15.

[13] H. Van Hasselt, A. Guez, and D. Silver, "Deep reinforcement learning with double q-learning." in AAAI, vol. 16, 2016, pp. 2094–2100.

[14] S. Hochreiter and J. Schmidhuber, "Long short-term memory," Neural Computation, vol. 9, no. 8, 1997, pp. 1735–1780. [Online]. Available: https://doi.org/10.1162/neco.1997.9.8.1735

[15] M. Hausknecht and P. Stone, "Deep recurrent q-learning for partially observable mdps," CoRR, abs/1507.06527, 2015, pp. 1–9.

[16] R. S. Sutton, "Learning to predict by the methods of temporal differences," Machine learning, vol. 3, no. 1, 1988, pp. 9–44.

[17] R. S. Sutton and A. G. Barto, Reinforcement learning: An introduction. MIT press Cambridge, 1998, vol. 1.

[18] M. G. Bellemare, W. Dabney, and R. Munos, "A distributional perspective on reinforcement learning," arXiv preprint arXiv:1707.06887, 2017, pp. 1–19.

[19] I. Makarov, A. Kashin, and A. Korinevskaya, "Learning to play pong video game via deep reinforcement learning," in Proceedings of AIST'17. Ceur WP, 2017, pp. 236–241.

[20] I. Makarov, M. Tokmakov, and L. Tokmakova, "Imitation of human behavior in 3d-shooter game," in AIST2015 Analysis of Images, Social Networks and Texts. Ceur WP, 2015, pp. 64–77.

[21] I. Makarov and et al., "First-person shooter game for virtual reality headset with advanced multi-agent intelligent system," in Proceedings of the 24th ACM International Conference on Multimedia, ser. MM '16. New York, NY, USA: ACM, 2016, pp. 735–736.

[22] P. Zhu, X. Li, P. Poupart, and G. Miao, "On improving deep reinforcement learning for pomdps," arXiv preprint arXiv:1804.06309, 2018, pp. 1–7.

Using HTML5 for M-Learning Environments

Sandra Sendra[1,2], Jaime Lloret[2], Ana Isabel Túnez-Murcia[1], Laura Garcia[2,3]
[1]Departamento de Teoría de la Señal, Telemática y Comunicaciones (TSTC), Universidad de Granada. Granada, Spain
[2]Instituto de Investigación para la Gestión Integrada de zonas Costeras, Universitat Politècnica de València, Valencia, Spain
[3]University of Haute Alsace, Mulhouse-Cedex, France

e-mail: ssendra@ugr.es, jlloret@dcom.upv.es, anatunez@correo.ugr.es, laugarg2@teleco.upv.es

Abstract—**Currently, there are several remote learning platforms based on video streaming. In most situations, these multimedia resources are displayed using smartphones that can be wirelessly connected to networks with deficient capabilities. In this scenario, the levels of Quality of Service (QoS) and Quality of Experience (QoE) perceived by users can be very low. Therefore, with the aim of finding the most efficient combination of Web browsers, codecs and containers, this paper presents a study to analyze how the encoding used in videos can affect the network performance in terms of data transfer rate, transmission delays, transmission errors and throughput. The tests are performed using mobile devices with Android as the operating system. Different Web browsers, containers and codecs supported by HyperText Markup Language V.5 (HTML5) are also included in this study. The browsers used in this study are Google Chrome, Firefox and Opera while the containers considered to carry out our tests are MP4 and WebM. Results show that MP4 could be a good option to transmit high resolution videos while WebM would be the best option for low quality videos.**

***Keywords-** HyperText Markup Language (HTML5); multimedia; m-learning; audio; video; live streaming; codecs.*

I. INTRODUCTION

The constant evolution of the industry sector and the Information and Telecommunications Technology (ICT) has led society to require better skilled graduates [1]. This fact is changing the way of teaching. It is changing from traditional methods, based on magisterial classes, to a new way of teaching based on new technologies. Today, electronic devices are an essential part our daily life and they are present in our day-to-day tasks in home environments, the workplace or in the academic field [2].

Blended and remote learning [3] is a new way of understanding teaching. It is characterized by accessing teaching resources from the Internet and personalizing the learning systems, which are designed for either personal computers (e-learning) or mobile devices (m-learning) [4]. Furthermore, e-learning and m-learning are characterized by:

- Their simplicity of use.
- There is no distance between professors and students.
- Their price is affordable for the students.
- They permit the interactivity between professors and students.
- They allow the ubiquity and the access to courses anywhere.

Among digital resources, m-learning, the use of video tutorials and live streaming videos with teaching purposes [5] [6] could be the ones that require knowledge of the network architecture and the features of end devices.

Historically, these platforms have been designed using Adobe Flash to allow the compatibility of this type of content on a greater number of devices. However, many mobile devices are not capable of supporting this technology. HyperText Markup Language V.5 [7] is the fifth major revision of the basic language of the World Wide Web. It is supported on a wide range of platforms and browsers which allows a greater number of devices to be able to access the contents of these learning platforms. The use of this kind of resources implies focusing part of the effort in guarantying the correct reception of content, i.e., reaching good levels of quality of service and quality of experience [8]. Issues in network capacity limit the volume of data the users can receive and thus the quality of video [9]. So, it is important to know the most adequate way of encoding the video to be transmitted.

So, considering the aforementioned arguments, this paper presents a practical study on how the encoding used in videos can affect network parameters such as data transfer rate, transmission delays, transmission errors and throughput when distributing and playing multimedia content in mobile devices, using Android as the operating system. Different Web browsers, containers and codecs supported by HTML5 are also included in this study. The browsers used in this study are Google Chrome, Firefox and Opera while the used containers are MP4 and WebM.

The rest of this paper is structured as follows. Section 2 presents some interesting previous works related to proposals of m-learning tools based on new technologies and practical tests to improve the efficiency in video transmission. The scenario, tools and the videos used to carry out or test bench are presented in Section 3. Section 4 presents the obtained results and a discussion regarding to the results. Finally, Section 5 shows the conclusion and future work.

II. RELATED WORK

This section presents some interesting works related to the use of HTML5 for teaching purposes and different practical experiments where the use of containers and codecs is analyzed for achieving the best QoS and QoE.

The current trend in academic and professional training is the implementation of distance and blended courses [3]. Many of these courses are based on the use of remote labs, video-tutorials [10] and live streaming of videos [11] that students can play on any type of device, i.e., laptops, tables, personal computers and even smartphones. Between all these devices, the one that can present the greatest limitations are smartphones because the connection to access to these teaching resources may be deficient.

Considering these issues, there are several studies related to the optimization of video transmission. One of the most important aspects, regarding these optimization tasks, is the enhancement of QoS and QoE with the use of the most suitable codecs and containers for the type of device and, even the restrictions of the networks. In this sense, I. Mateos-Cañas et al. [12] presented the design and test of an autonomous decision algorithm that was able to analyze video content and network constraints. According to the measurements results, the system extracted the predominant color of the requested video and determined the most optimal compression codec for transmitting the video through that network. The proposal was tested with videos of different resolutions and predominant colors to measure the levels of QoS and QoE. The results showed that codecs, such as H264 (MPEG-4) would be a good option when the predominant color of videos were black or white while XVID [13] would be the best codecs to transmit videos with red, green or blue as predominant colors.

A. López-Herreros et al. [14] presented an analysis about the characteristics of some video compression codecs included in HTML5. The authors analyzed several parameters such as the type of browser, frame rate, bitrate, encoding time and final quality of the video. The results showed that values registered for PAL (Phase Alternating Line) [15] are better than the ones obtained in NTSC (National Television System Committee) [16] system in terms of compressed file size, being very similar in both MP4 (H.264) and Ogg (Theora) for PAL systems while WebM (VP8) results are identical in PAL and NTSC.

Another important front in the field of m-learning is the development of platforms that make easy the access to teaching resources or remote laboratories. N. Wang et al. [17] presented a mobile-optimized application architecture for incorporating remote laboratory practices in M-Learning environments. Through the developed platform, students can perform different experiments in a similar way as they would physically in a laboratory. The system has been developed for different mobile platforms, such as iOS, Android, Windows Mobile and Blackberry. To test the system, authors proposed the realization of practices of proportional–integral–derivative controls. The system was tested using the Baidu mobile cloud testing bed with interesting and successful results.

Finally, M. Truebano and C. Munn [10] evaluated the use of a video tutorial during active learning laboratory-based sessions. The performed study comprised undergraduate students divided into three groups, one that received face-to-face training, one that received training only through the videos and one that received a mix of both methodologies. The tests were performed in terms of behavior, the end result of the procedure and the answers to a questionnaire. Results showed that a blended approach yielded the greatest success when performing the procedure alone. So, video tutorials can be considered as a good tool to complement a blended learning to teach practical skills.

As we have seen through these works, there is a great interest in the development of systems to facilitate the implementation of remote and blended learning. However, none of the proposals and others we have read, present real experiments on video streaming on mobile devices. Therefore, this article tries to collect these values. We think this study can serve as a reference for the development of future remote learning platforms.

III. TOOLS AND EQUIPMENT USED IN TEST BENCH.

This section presents the different pieces equipment as well as the tools used to carry out our test benches.

A. Scenario

In order to perform our experiments and test bench, we have implemented the network shown in Figure 1. It is composed by 2 different mobile Android devices with very similar characteristics but different operating systems. Videos were stored in the server and were transmitted wirelessly to the smartphones. Both devices are connected to a router (192.168.0.1/24), which establishes the link between the end devices and the video server (192.168.0.10/24). Wireless devices are connected using the IEEE 802.11n standard and the connection between the router and server is a Cat5e link.

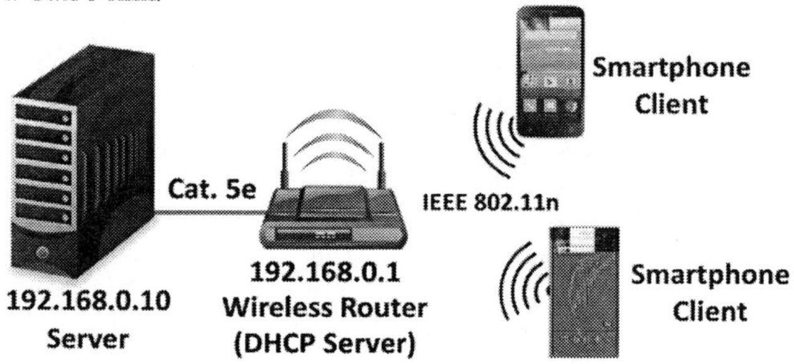

Figure 1. Scenario used during the test bench.

The hardware features of these devices are shown in Table 1.

B. Videos used to perform to tests

In order to carry out our test benches, we have selected a free distribution video developed by the Blender Institute called Big Buck Bunny [18]. The original features of this video are shown in Table 2.

When transmitting videos through Web pages, they are usually adapted to the different devices that requested them. This fact gives us videos with different resolutions. In mobile devices, the kind of networks that give them Internet access should also be considered when video is streamed. Therefore, in order to consider the final quality of the displayed videos, we have encoded the video with different codecs. In this case, H.264 [19] and WEBM [20] has been considered in this paper. Regarding to the video resolutions, we have used video resolutions of 360p, 480p, 720p and 1080p. Table 3 shows the characteristics of the encoded videos.

C. *Web browsers and mobile operating systems*

In order to decide which operating systems and browsers we want to include in our study, it is interesting to firstly analyze their uses. As Figure 2 shows, the number of users of mobile devices (44.2%) is almost the same of Desktop users (52%) in contrast to the number of users of tables which is very low (< 4%) [21]. Regarding the most used operating system (see Figure 3) [22], it is easy to see the predominant domain of Android as a mobile operating system with a percentage of users of 72.23% followed by iOS with a percentage of users near to 24%. Finally, regarding the use of Web browsers [23], Figure 4 shows that Chrome is the Web browser that presents the biggest percentage (47.20%). So, it will be included in our experiments. Firefox and Opera which are also included in our tests present a percentage of 3.35% and 5.01%, respectively.

TABLE I. FEATURES OF SMARTPHONES USED DURING THE TESTS

Device	Smartphone features				
	Model	*Processor*	*Graphic Card*	*O. S.*	*Max. Resolution*
Xiaomi Mi A1	Snapdragon 625 octa-core 2.2GHz	Android 8 One	Android 8 One	5.5"	1920 x 1080
Samsung Galaxy S4	Snapdragon 400 dual-core 1.7 GHz	Android 4.2.2 Jelly bean	Android 4.2.2 Jelly bean	4.3"	540 x 960

TABLE II. FEATURES OF THE ORIGINAL VIDEO USED IN OUR TESTS

Video	Original video features						
	Size	*Original Container*	*Video format*	*Audio format*	*Duration*	*Overall bit rate*	*Width x Height (pixels)*
Original	85.5 MiB	MPEG-TS	AVC	MPEG Audio	56" 382ms	12.7 Mbps	4000x2250

TABLE III. FORMATS, RESOLUTION, FRAME RATE, BITRATE AND SIZE OF THE DIFFERENT VIDEOS USED IN OUR TESTS

Codec	Features						
	Video	*Resolution*	*FPS*	*Bitrate (KBPS)*	*Size (MIB)*	*Video Format*	*Audio Format*
None	Original	2250	60	127000	85.5	AVC	MPEG Audio
		2160	30	3950	77.4	AVC/AAC	MPEG Audio / AC-3
MP4		720	30	1992	13.4	AVC/AAC	MPEG Audio / AC-3
MP4		480	30	965	6.41	AVC/AAC	MPEG Audio / AC-3
MP4		360	30	774	5.16	AVC/AAC	MPEG Audio / AC-3
WebM		1080	30	0.167	12	VP8	Vorbis
WebM		720	30	0.055	5.69	VP8	Vorbis
WebM		480	30	0.021	2.21	VP8	Vorbis
WebM		360	30	0.036	2.61	VP8	Vorbis

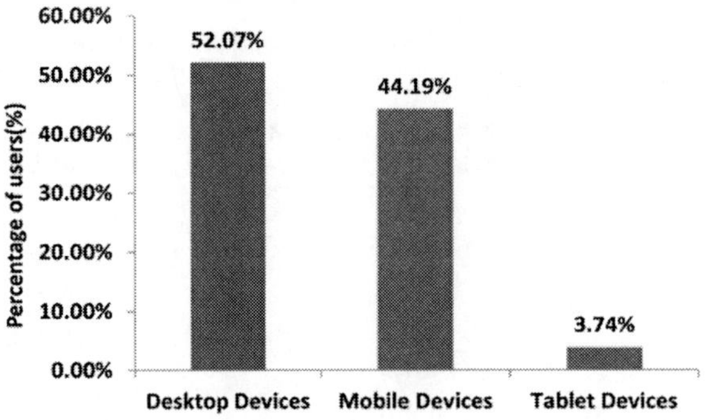

Figure 2. Desktop vs Mobile vs Tablet Market Share Worldwide

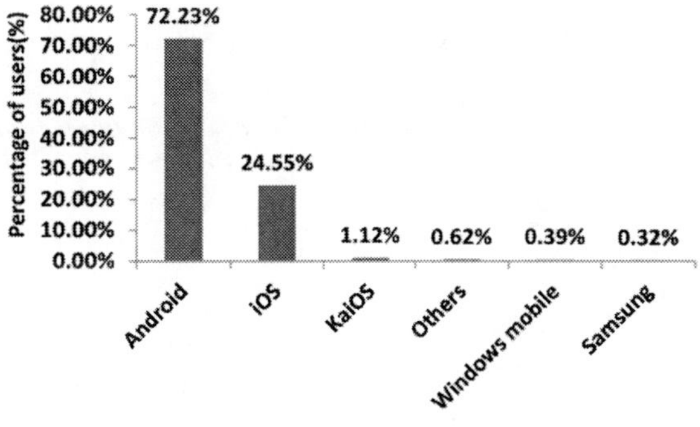

Figure 3. Mobile Operating System Market Share Worldwide

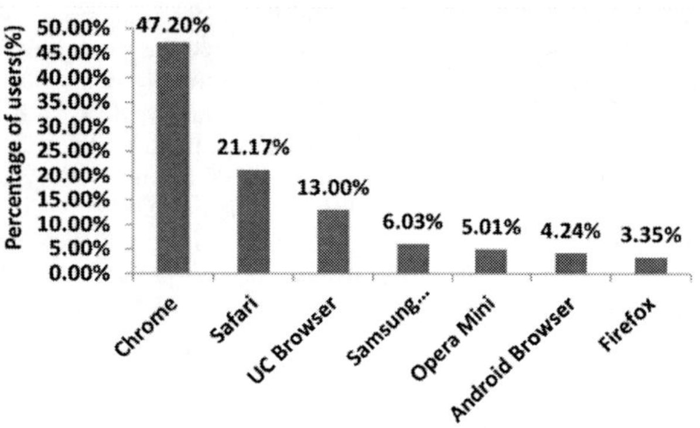

Figure 4. Browser Version Market Share Worldwide

After considering the statistics shown in this section, we decided to use Android as the mobile operating system and Chrome, Opera and Firefox as Web browsers because all of them are capable of supporting the requirements of HTML5 videos.

IV. RESULTS

This section presents the results obtained after performing our tests for both devices using different Web browsers and containers. Results have been divided by operating system, showing the average value of the studied parameter.

A. *Results for Android One*

Figure 5 shows the values of data transfer rate as a function of the video resolution on Android One devices wirelessly connected to an IEEE 802.11n network. As we can see, the browser that, in general, registers a higher data transfer rate is Firefox when using MP4 container, reaching values of 3 Mbps in 720px video resolution. Opera browser in combination to MP4 registers the biggest value of data transfer rate for 720px videos. Comparing the behavior of the three browsers, the one that presents the best values is Chrome with values around 1Mbps for the videos with the highest resolution.

Figure 6 shows the delay (in ms.) as a function of the video resolution for Android One devices. In this case, the browser that presents the worst results is Chrome when videos are encoded using WebM. The combinations that show the best results are the use of Firefox and Opera, using a MP4 container.

Regarding the error rate (see Figure 7), the behavior of all Web browsers and containers present values of error rate lower than 2% being the Chrome-WebM combination the one that presents the worst results with a percentage error of 1.58%.

Finally, Figure 8 shows the throughput registered for Android One devices as a function of the selected browsers and containers. As we can see, the general trend is that the average throughput is between 0.5 and 1.3 Mbps, highlighting the case of Opera- MP4 for 720px videos which presents a value of 5 Mbps.

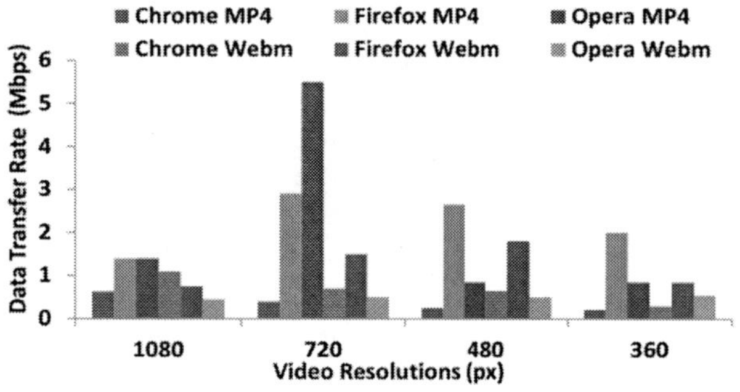

Figure 5. Data transfer rate as a function of the video resolution on Android One

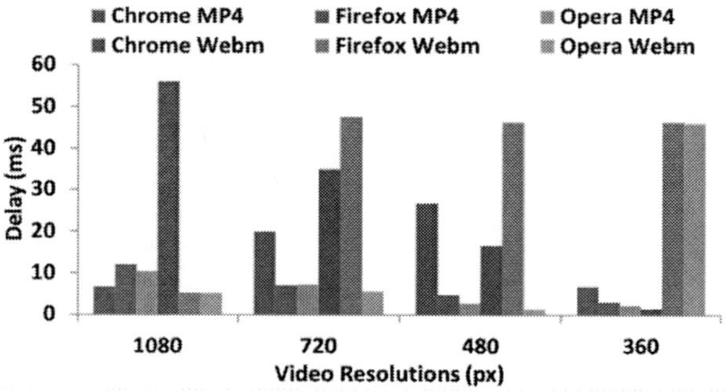

Figure 6. Delay as a function of the video resolution on Android One

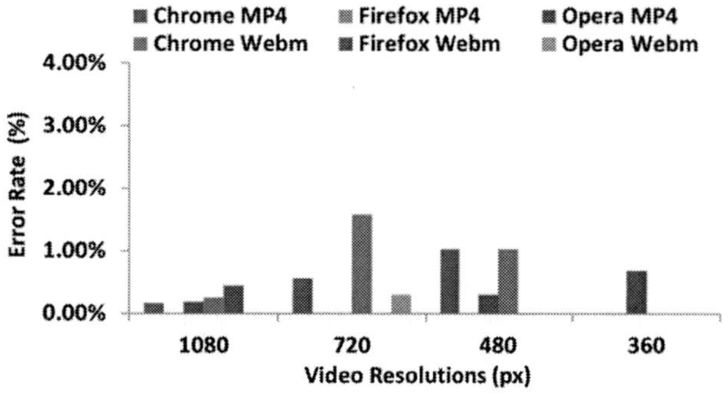

Figure 7. Error rate as a function of the video resolution on Android One

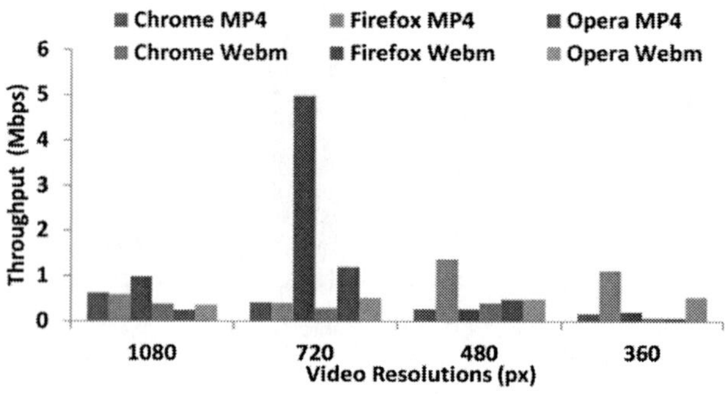

Figure 8. Throughput as a function of the video resolution on Android

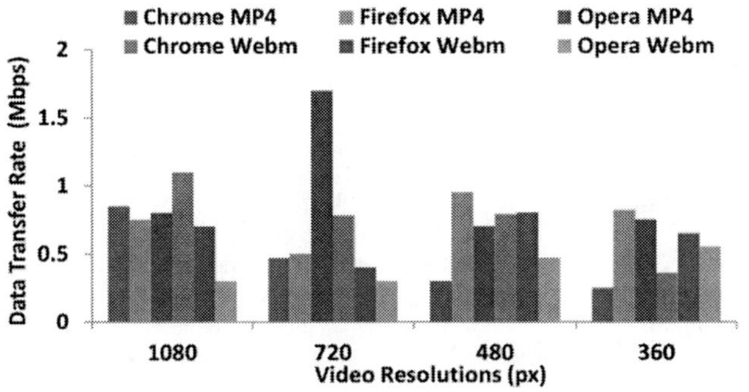

Figure 9. Data transfer rate as a function of the video resolution on Android Kit Kat

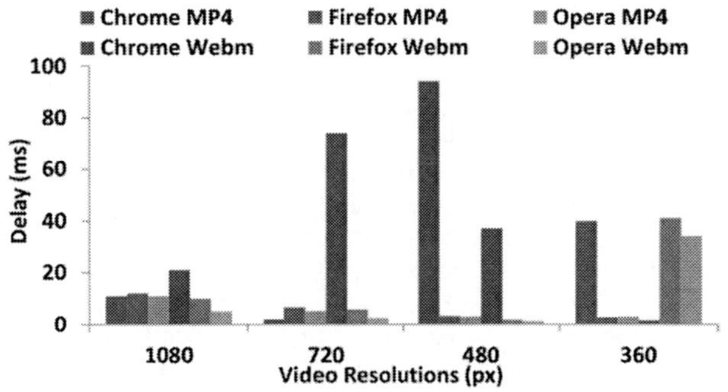

Figure 10. Delay as a function of the video resolution on Android Kit Kat.

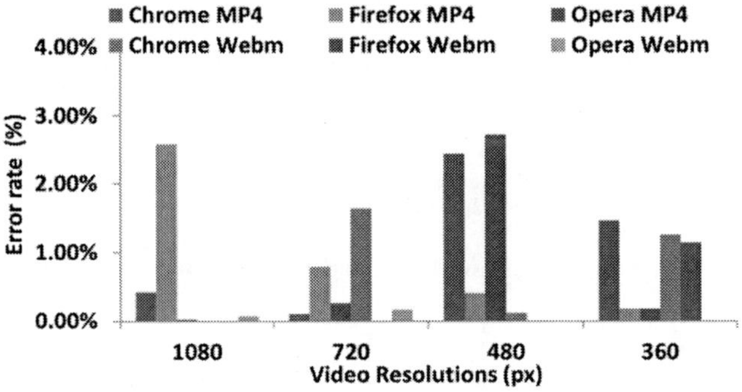

Figure 11. Error rate as a function of the video resolution on Android Kit Kat.

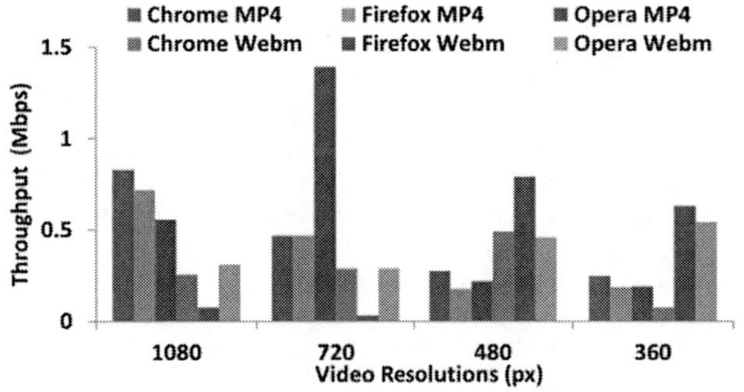

Figure 12. Throughput as a function of the video resolution on Android Kit Kat

B. *Results for Android Kit Kat*

Figure 9 shows the values of data transfer rate in Mbps for different video resolution and Web browsers for Android Kit Kat devices wirelessly connected to an IEEE 802.11n network. As Figure 9 shows, the browser that registers the highest data transfer rate for high resolution videos is Chrome, reaching values of 1.1 Mbps when a WebM container is used. Firefox registers the biggest value of data transfer rate when 480px videos are transmitted using MP4 containers. Finally, Opera browser in combination to MP4 registers the biggest value of data transfer rate for 720px videos. Comparing the behavior of the three browsers, the one that presents the best values is Opera with values around 0.33 Mbps for the videos with the highest resolution.

Figure 10 shows the delay (in ms.) as a function of the video resolution for devices running Android Kit Kat. In this case, the browser that presents the worst results is Chrome when videos are encoded in any of the containers under study, with values higher than 80 ms. For transmitting videos with the highest resolution, the best option is to use Opera in combination to WebM containers, with average values of delay lower than 5ms.

Regarding the error rate (see Figure 11), we can see that the worst cases present values of error rate lower than 3%. Opera in combination with WebM is the combination that presents the best results, reaching values lower than 0.2% in the worst case (values for videos of 720px).

Finally, Figure 12 shows the throughput registered for devices running Android Kit Kat as a function of the selected browsers and containers. As we can see, MP4 is the container that presents the best results for high resolution videos although it is the worst option for transmitting low resolution videos. In contrast to this fact, WebM presents the best results for low resolution videos. Finally, Opera in combination with WebM is the combination that presents the best results for 720px videos, reaching values higher than 1.35 Mbps.

V. CONCLUSION AND FUTURE WORK

The growing interest in the development of remote learning platforms has led to the need of improving the capabilities of networks to facilitate the access of users to multimedia resources and to improve their QoE. To this end, one of the strategies is the choice of the most appropriate codec and container for transmitting multimedia files such as video. Therefore, this paper has presented a practical test bench to analyze the network parameters when videos are processed with different containers for finally reproducing them in different Web browsers based on HTML5. The videos have been reproduced using smartphones running Android One and Android Kit Kat operating systems. After carrying out our tests, we extract the following conclusions:

For the Chrome browser, MP4 is presented as the best container in terms of lower data transfer rate. In terms of delay and error rate, MP4 presents better statistics in high resolution videos while WEBM is the best option for low quality videos. In the case of Firefox, MP4 appears as the container with the highest data transfer rate and throughput. However, it has a greater delay and error rate. WEBM is the container that presents the better delay, although the values of throughput and error rate are high. Finally, the use of Opera in combination with the WEBM container presents the best results in terms of delay and throughput while MP4 has better behavior in terms of error rate and data transfer rate for high resolution videos.

As future work, we want to perform similar tests to other kind of devices and operating systems and finally, we think it could be interesting to consider the design of an intelligent algorithm for real-time transcoding [24] to transmit video in different media and platforms based on HTML5 through the new generation of networks (5G) [25].

ACKNOWLEDGMENT

This work has been partially supported by the European Union through the ERANETMED (Euromediterranean Cooperation through ERANET joint activities and beyond) project ERANETMED3-227 SMARTWATIR, by the "Ministerio de Economia, Industria y Competitividad", through the "Convocatoria 2016 - Proyectos I+D+I - Programa Estatal De Investigación, Desarrollo e Innovación Orientada a los retos de la sociedad" (Project TEC2016-76795-C6-4-R), through the "Convocatoria 2017 - Proyectos I+D+I - Programa Estatal de Investigación, Desarrollo e Innovación, convocatoria excelencia" (Project TIN2017-84802-C2-1-P) and by the "Ministerio de Ciencia, Innovación y Universidades" through the "Ayudas para la adquisición de equipamiento científico-técnico, Subprograma estatal de infraestructuras de investigación y equipamiento científico-técnico (plan Estatal I+D+i 2017-2020)" (project EQC2018-004988-P).

REFERENCES

[1] S. Aronowitz, Technoscience and cyberculture. Francis and Taylor Group, 1st Edition, 2014.

[2] K. Oshima and Y. Muramatsu, "Current situation and issues related to ICT utilization in primary and secondary education," Fujitsu Scientific & Technical Journal, vol. 51, no. 1, pp.3-8, 2015.

[3] S. Sendra, J. M. Jimenez, L. Parra Boronat, and J. Lloret, "Blended Learning in a Postgraduate ICT course,". Proc. 1st International Conference on Higher Education Advances (HEAD' 15). June 24-26, 2015. Valencia, Spain. pp. 516-525.

[4] P. Nedungadi and R. Raman, "A new approach to personalization: integrating e-learning and m-learning,", Education Tech Research Dev, vol. 60, no. 4 ,pp. 659–678, 2012.

[5] A-R. Bartolomé-Pina and K. Steffens, "Are MOOCs Promising Learning Environments?", Comunicar, vol. 22, no. 44, pp. 91-99, 2015.

[6] A. J. Estepa, R. Estepa, J. Vozmediano, and P. Carrillo, "Dynamic VoIP codec selection on smartphones", Network Protocols and Algorithms, vol. 6, no. 2, pp. 22-37, 2014.

[7] G. Anthes, "HTML5 leads a web revolution". Communications of the ACM, vol. 55, no. 7, pp. 16-17, 2012.

[8] J. Lloret, M. García, and F. Boronat, "IPTV: the television on the Internet", Editorial Vértice, Málaga (Spain), 1st Edition, 2008.

[9] L. Fabrega and T. Jove, "A review of the architecture of admission control schemes in the Internet", Network Protocols and Algorithms, vol. 5, no. 3, pp.1-32, 2013.

[10] M. Truebano and C. Munn, "An evaluation of the use of video tutorials as supporting tools for teaching laboratory skills in biology". Practice and Evidence of the Scholarship of Teaching and Learning in Higher Education, vol. 10, no. 2, pp. 121-135, 2015.

[11] T. C. Thang, H. T. Le, A. T. Pham, and Y. M. Ro, "An Evaluation of Bitrate Adaptation Methods for HTTP Live Streaming," in IEEE Journal on Selected Areas in Communications, vol. 32, no. 4, pp. 693-705, 2014.

[12] I Mateos-Cañas, S Sendra, J. Lloret, and JM Jimenez, "Autonomous video compression system for environmental monitoring", Network Protocols and Algorithms, vol. 9, no. 1&2, pp. 48-70, 2017.

[13] Xvid Web site. Available at: https://www.xvid.com/ [Last access: March 13, 2019]

[14] A. López-Herreros, A. Canovas, J. M. Jiménez, and J. Lloret, "A new IP video delivery system for heterogeneous networks using HTML5," Proc.2015 IEEE International Conference on Communications (ICC), London, UK, June 8-12, 2015, pp. 7053-7058.

[15] PAL ITU-R recommendation web site. Available at: https://www.itu.int/rec/R-REC-BT.1197/en [Last acess: March 13, 2019]

[16] NTSC ITU-R recommendation web site. Available at : https://www.itu.int/rec/R-REC-BT.1298/en [Last access: March 13, 2019]

[17] N. Wang, X. Chen, G. Song, Q. Lan, and H. R. Parsaei, "Design of a New Mobile-Optimized Remote Laboratory Application Architecture for M-Learning", IEEE Transactions On Industrial Electronics, vol. 64, no. 3, pp. 2382-2391, 2017.

[18] Big Buck Bunny video. In Blender Foundation Web site. Available at: https://peach.blender.org/download/ [Last access: Dec. 5, 2018]

[19] Y.-K. Wang, R. Even, T. Kristensen, and R. Jesup, "RTP Payload Format for H.264 Video (RFC 6184)". In Internet Engineering Task Force (IETF) Web site. Available at: https://tools.ietf.org/html/rfc6184 [Last access: Dec. 5, 2018]

[20] WebM codec features Project. In WebMproject Web site. Available at: https://www.webmproject.org/docs/container/[Last access: Dec. 5, 2018]

[21] Statistics of worldwide use of electronic devices. In Statcounter Web site. Available at: http://gs.statcounter.com/platform-market-share/desktop-mobile-tablet#monthly-201707-201707-map [Last access: Dec. 5, 2018]

[22] Statistics of worldwide mobile operating systems users. In Statcounter Web site. Available at: http://gs.statcounter.com/os-market-share/mobile/worldwide#monthly-201707-201707-map [Last access: Dec. 5, 2018]

[23] Statistics of worldwide mobile web browser users. In Statcounter Web site. Available at: http://gs.statcounter.com/browser-version-market-share [Last access: Dec. 5, 2018]

[24] H. Wu and H. Ma, "An Optimal Buffer Management Strategy for Video Transmission in Mobile Opportunistic Networks", AHSWN Volume 34, Number 1-4 (2016). p. 129-146.

[25] C. Lai, R. Hwang, H. Chao, M. M. Hassan, and A. Alamri, "A buffer-aware HTTP live streaming approach for SDN-enabled 5G wireless networks," in IEEE Network, vol. 29, no. 1, pp. 49-55, 2015.

Recognition of Human Actions Through Deep Neural Networks for Multimedia Systems Interaction

Marco La Cascia
Dipartimento di Ingegneria
University of Palermo
Palermo, Italy
Email: marco.lacascia@unipa.it

Ignazio Infantino, Filippo Vella
Istituto di calcolo e reti ad alte prestazioni
CNR - National Research Council of Italy
Palermo, Italy
Email: name.surname@icar.cnr.it

***Abstract*—Nowadays, interactive multimedia systems are part of everyday life. The most common way to interact and control these devices is through remote controls or some sort of touch panel. In recent years, due to the introduction of reliable low-cost Kinect-like sensing technology, more and more attention has been dedicated to touchless interfaces. A Kinect-like devices can be positioned on top of a multimedia system, detect a person in front of the system and process skeletal data, optionally with RGBd data, to determine user gestures. The gestures of the person can then be used to control, for example, a media device. Even though there is a lot of interest in this area, currently, no consumer system is using this type of interaction probably due to the inherent difficulties in processing raw data coming from Kinect cameras to detect the user intentions. In this work, we considered the use of neural networks using as input only the Kinect skeletal data for the task of user intention classification. We compared different deep networks and analyzed their outputs.**

Keywords–Multimedia system interaction; gesture recognition; neural networks.

I. INTRODUCTION

In 2010, when Microsoft introduced Kinect, this new device was intended to change the way people play games and how they experience entertainment. However, the potential of the device was immediately clear and applications in different fields leveraging the sensing technology of Kinect have been explored. This is what Microsoft called the "Kinect Effect" [1]. From the early days of introduction to current days several scientific papers reported possible applications in disparate fields. For example in 2011, in [2], a study on the potential of Kinect in education was published. The author states that the use of Kinect can create unprecedented opportunity to enhance classroom interaction, to improve teachers ability to present and manipulate multimedia and multimodal materials and much more.

Interactive media control using gesture was also immediately perceived as a viable application. In [3], the authors propose probably the first system using a Kinect to interact with multimedia content. They defined gestures to activate controls on a media device and used the depth image to detect and track the hand and gestures. Gestures were defined in terms of distance variances along the 3D axes.

Multimedia presentation systems using a gesture based interface could also be used as information provision systems. In [4], the authors developed a platform to develop interactive systems based on depth image streams and demonstrated its potential in a museum application. The importance of touchless gestural systems has been deeply stressed also in [5] where the authors report a case study on an information provision system in a University campus using Kinect-like devices.

In addition to media and entertainment, these sensors can also be used in very specific professional fields. For example, another interesting use of gestural interaction has been recently introduced in [6] where the authors reported the use of Kinect and gesture recognition to give interactive presentations in a more effective manner compared to a traditional pointer, mouse or keyboard. In other cases, touchless interaction is mandatory as the user cannot touch any device for different reasons. For example in [7], gesture recognition and Kinect have been used for touchless visualization of hepatic anatomical models in surgery.

However, while it is rather easy to collect a significant amount of sensors observations, the great challenge is to properly recognize meaningful patterns in the raw data that can be ascribed to user actions and intentions [8] [9]. Only in simple cases skeletal data or RGBd is sufficient to detect actions with little processing. In many cases quite complex processing is needed to detect user intentions. Machine learning approaches are then exploited to process gestural data. These approaches rely on definition, extraction and analysis of the features most useful to detect the human intention. For example in [10], a simple gesture recognition system based on Kinect skeletal data is proposed. Based on joints information a low-dimensional feature is defined and used for action classification with a support vector machine. The authors claim they can discriminate between 10 different basic actions using 3 seconds sequences at 30fps.

The variable time duration of a gesture performed by different users can also pose significant difficulties. In [11] to cope with different duration of the actions without explicitly use dynamic time warping techniques the authors proposed to model action as the output of a sequence of atomic Linear Time-Invariant (LTI) systems. The sequence of LTI systems generating the action is modeled as a Markov chain, where a Hidden Markov Model (HMM) is used to model the transition from one atomic LTI system to another. LTI systems are modeled in terms of Hankel matrices.

To cope with this increasing complexity and to discriminate between several actions across different users The use of neural networks has recently been explored. For example in [7] the authors use a deep convolutional neural network to recognize various hand gesture. In particular they used a deep network architecture consisting of two convolutional layer, each followed by pooling, and three fully connected layers. The input of the network is a 32x32 segmented and filtered depth image coming from Kinect. The final output is the gesture detected.

Among the existing gestures recognition modules it is also possible to mention the works in [12]-[13]. Some of them suggest heuristics of processing according to specific situations [14] or for identification of the viewed person [15]. Many other techniques for skeleton based action recognition have been proposed in recent years and their description is out of the scope of this paper. The interested reader can refer to [16] for a complete survey.

In this paper we adopted neural networks to process sensed 3D position of human skeleton joints to recognize some gestures that a person can perform to interact with a multimedia system. The neural network can be trained offline and, once trained, it processes only the 3D position of joints leading to very fast processing. The joints position were extracted with a Microsoft Kinect v2. RGBd image stream was not processed.

The paper is organized as follows: in Section II, we briefly introduce two popular architectures of neural networks and their advantages with respect to conventional machine learning approaches. In Section III, we describe the proposed action recognition approach and the pre-processing operations we performed on the sensed data. Some experimental results, comparing our approach with different network architectures and pre-processing strategies are reported in Section IV. Finally, Section V contains some conclusions and a discussion on future directions of the work.

II. NEURAL NETWORKS FOR TOUCHLESS MULTIMEDIA SYSTEMS INTERACTION

The conventional machine learning techniques have shown a set of drawbacks in the processing of raw data from Kinect-like sensors. The pattern recognition approaches, typically, require careful engineering and domain expertise to design feature extraction transforming data in discriminant and significant feature vectors [17].

On the other hand, deep-learning methods usually employ a set of non-linear modules that automatically extract a set of features from the input data and transfer them to the next module [17]. The weights of the layers involved in data processing are learned directly from data, enabling the discovery of intricate structures in high-dimensional data, regardless of their domain (science, business, etc.). Assuming that an adequate amount of training data is available, very complex functions can be learned combining these modules: the resulting networks are often very sensitive to minute details and insensitive to large irrelevant variations.

A. MLP Multilayer Perceptron

A Multi-Layer Perceptron (MLP) is a feedforward network that maps sets of input data onto a set of appropriate outputs; it consists of at least three layers - an input layer, a hidden layer, and an output layer - of fully connected nodes in a directed graph. Except for the input nodes, each node is a neuron (or processing element) with a nonlinear activation function - usually a sigmoid, or the hyperbolic tangent, chosen to model the bioelectrical behaviour of biological neurons in a natural brain. Learning occurs through backpropagation algorithm that modifies connections weights to minimize the difference between the actual network output and the expected result on training data.

B. LSTM

Long Short Term Memory networks (LSTM) have been designed by Hochreiter and Schmidhuber [18]. The key feature of LSTMs is the "cell state" that is propagated from a cell to another. State modifications are regulated by three structures called gates, composed out of a sigmoid neural net layer and a pointwise multiplication operation.

The first gate, called "forget gate layer", considers both the input x_t and the output from the previous step h_{t-1}, and returns values between 0 and 1, describing how much of each component of the old cell state C_{t-1} should be left unaltered: if the output is 0, no modification is made; if the output is one, the component is completely replaced.

New information to be stored in the state is processed afterward. The second sigmoid layer, called the input gate layer, decides which values will be updated. Next, a $tanh$ layer creates a vector of new candidate values, $\tilde{C}_t$, that could be added to the state.

$$f_t = \sigma(W_f \cdot [h_{t-1}, x_t] + b_f)$$
$$i_t = \sigma(W_i \cdot [h_{t-1}, x_t] + b_i)$$
$$\tilde{C}_t = \tanh(W_C \cdot [h_{t-1}, x_t] + b_c)$$
$$C_t = f_t * C_{t-1} + i_t * \tilde{C}_t$$

To perform a state update, C_{t-1} is first multiplied by the output of the forget gate f_t, and the result is added to the pointwise multiplication of the input gate output i_t and $\tilde{C}_t$.

$$o_t = \sigma(W_o \cdot [h_{t-1}, x_t] + b_o)$$

$$h_t = o_t * \tanh(C_t)$$

Finally, the output h_t can be generated. First, a sigmoid is applied, taking into account both h_{t-1} and x_t; its output is then multiplied by a constrained version of C_t, so that we only send to output the parts we are interested in.

III. ACTION DETECTION THROUGH CLASSIFICATION

To interact with a multimedia system, we assumed that the user performs an action and our system detect and classify the action that is mapped to some functions of the system. The set of actions that we want to detect and classify are the following *Hello with the right hand, Hello with the left hand, Stop with the right hand, Stop with the left hand, Come Here with the left hand, Come Here with the right hand, Pass right hand, Pass left hand.* At runtime, Kinect continuously acquire data and the classification system should detect actions triggering the corresponding function on the multimedia system The data acquired from Kinect consists of an RGBd dense image stream and a sequence of joint 3D positions. In our approach, we do not use RGBd stream. Nevertheless, we have to pre-process in some way, both spatially and temporally, the sequence of joint positions to let the neural networks coherently process the data.

Kinect estimates the 3D position of 25 joints however not all of them are necessary to recognize simple actions and unnecessary joints information can introduce noise in the system. The joints that have been selected as significant for the problem at hand are the following:

- Left Hand
- Left Wrist
- Left Elbow
- Left Shoulder
- Right Shoulder
- Right Elbow
- Right Wrist
- Right Hand
- Lower Spine
- Middle Spine
- Neck
- Head

Two examples of the acquisition of depth image and skeleton points are shown in Figure 1. On the left, there is the segmented silhouette while on the right are plot the corresponding points. Kinect cameras can acquire data up to 30 fps but, since we consider that human actions useful to control a multimedia system are quite slow and we don't need a very dense classification of the actions being performed, we down-sampled the data to 2 Hz. Experiments confirmed that this frequency is adequate to capture human actions. We need also to define the duration of the time window to use to capture information and associate the label. In fact, to increase robustness and reduce false positive we consider an action as a sequence of joint positions and not as a single instant snapshot. The simplest, and in many cases adequate, approach consists of defining a fixed time window that contains the development of a typical action. This size is a matter of experience and it depends on the data and on the task. In our case, we considered multiple duration of the time window containing the action and run several experiments on our dataset to understand how to make a reasonable choice. The data in the time window is then used to analyze the occurring action.

To cope with the temporal nature of the problem a sliding window approach has been adopted. As time goes on a new sample is added to the sequence of samples to be classified and the oldest is discarded.

To implement the neural network architectures and perform the tests, we used Keras library [19]. Keras is a high-level Python neural networks library, capable of running on top of two of the most important libraries for numerical computation used for deep learning: TensorFlow [20] and Theano [21]. The use of higher level libraries, like Keras, allows developers and data scientists to rapidly produce and test prototypes, while relaying most implementation details to the chosen lower level library.

Details on the neural networks implementation and testing are given in the next section.

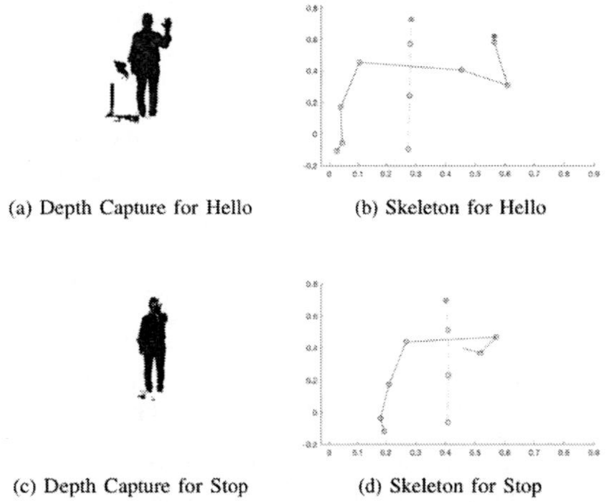

(a) Depth Capture for Hello (b) Skeleton for Hello

(c) Depth Capture for Stop (d) Skeleton for Stop

Figure 1. Example of acquisition of poses with depth image and the extracted skeleton position

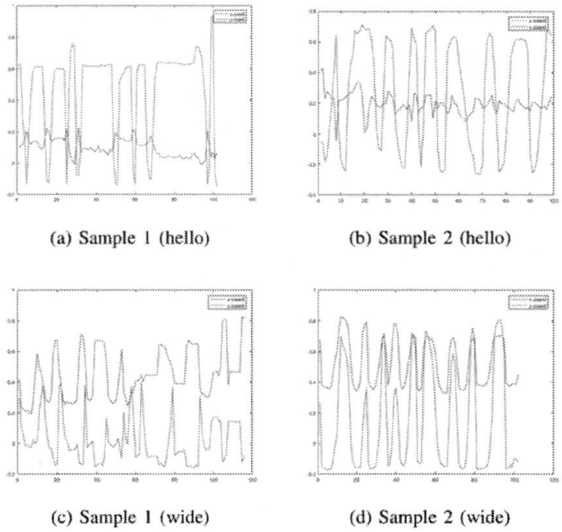

(a) Sample 1 (hello) (b) Sample 2 (hello)

(c) Sample 1 (wide) (d) Sample 2 (wide)

Figure 2. Plot of x,y coordinated of Left Hand while repeating the action *Hello*

IV. EXPERIMENTAL RESULTS

The dataset we used to demonstrate our approach is composed by a set of action samples. Each action sample is a matrix representing a single gesture made by a person. These samples were generated from CSV files created with Kinect for Windows SDK 2.0, containing 3D coordinates of the selected skeletal joint listed in previous section (a total of $12 \cdot 3 = 36$ columns).

The number of rows depends on the time interval used for recording. The CSV files were later imported in a Python script to down sample to 2 Hz and segment time window of different duration containing the actions. We also normalized the values in [-1, 1], because we are more interested in the differences between the frames and not the absolute value of the joints position. Some examples of the recordings are shown in Figure 2. The left plot is referred to a person, while on the right the plot is referred to a second person.

The experiments were conducted using different learning architecture. Different network topologies have been used during the training phase to evaluate whether the training process is stable with respect to different training settings. The dataset has been divided in two parts. Four fifths have been used for the training set while the remaining one fifth has been used as test set.

The results reported have been obtained restarting the training multiple times and varying the value of the batch size and averaging the obtained results. Restarting the training is equivalent to use multiple nets and compare their results after the training. Varying the batch size the number of samples that are processed before upgrading the weights of the net is changed. A larger value of the batch size can reduce the noise in the gradient descendent algorithm, that is the base of the backpropagation algorithm and converges quickly towards the minimum. On the other hand, a lower value of the batch size tends to generate a larger noise in the gradient descent algorithm and can help to escape from local minima.

The classification performance is evaluated comparing the label of the sample in the ground truth and the label chosen by the neural network. The value of the True Positive (TP) counts the number of samples that have been correctly classified. False Positive (FP) is the number of times a wrong label has been assigned to a sample. False Negative (FN) is the number of samples that have not been correctly classified. The values of True Negative (TN) is referred to the wrong labels that have not been assigned to a sample. For these experiments it has always been set to zero. The accuracy is then defined as:

$$Acc = \frac{TP + TN}{TP + TN + FP + FN}$$

Precision and recall are instead defined as:

$$Prec = \frac{TP}{TP + FP} \qquad Rec = \frac{TP}{TP + FN}$$

The harmonic mean of precision and recall is called F_1-score:

$$F_1 = 2 \times \frac{Prec \times Rec}{Prec + Rec}$$

The F1 metric can be calculated with different modalities. A modality is "micro" calculate the metric globally by counting the total true positives, false negatives and false positives. A "macro" modality calculates the metric for each label, and find their unweighted mean. This does not take label imbalance into account. The last is "weighted": the metric is calculated for each label, and find their average, weighted by support (the number of true instances for each label). This last modality takes into account the label imbalance; it can result in an F-score that is not between precision and recall.

Once defined the performance metrics, we ran several experiments to understand the behaviour of two neural network architecture, MLP and LSTM, on the problem at hand. The first experiment involved an MLP network. Figure 3 shows the values of precision, recall, accuracy and F1 parameters varying the number of hidden layers in the network. The performance does not have an increasing tendency with the number of layers. An increased number of layers does not imply a better performance. It seems that a reduced number of layers provides a better performance. A reason for this trend could be related to the relatively small number of examples used for the training. The values of accuracy, precision and recall are quite similar for two, three or four layers. The precision drops for four layers. Furthermore, the weighted F1 shows a better value for two layers. Changing the duration of the time window used to represent each action did not affected significantly the performance of the network.

A comparison between the MLP and a network with Long Short Term Memory has been carried on. A first LSTM network with two layers has been created with a layer of one hundred units and a full connected layer with nine out units. A second net with three layers has been tested adding an intermediate LSTM layer with forty units. A further network with four layers, formed adding a layer with seventy units between the first and the second layers has also been tested. The three networks correspond in the horizontal axis to the values 2, 3 and 4.

In the case of LSTM networks, we noticed a significant variation of performance depending on the duration of the time window used to represent the actions. Figure 4 shows the performance for network trained with samples having a time span equal to 2.5 sec. The values are very high both for precision and recall. The averaged value of F1 confirms this trend. Increasing the time span of the samples to be classified performance degraded abruptly. The result for samples with a time span of 5 secs are shown in Figure 5. In this case the results are clearly worse than in the previous case. The best F1 measure is 0.49 when the number of layers is equal to 2. An increased number of layers does not help the performance and in some case, both precision and recall are very low. Considering a larger time span (7.5 sec) results are slightly better (see Figure 6). A higher number of layers helps to increase the performance although the obtained results are still worse than the case when a shorter time span to represent actions is used.

According to our experiments, the best solution consists of considering a time span of 2.5 sec and an LSTM network. The LSTM network showed the best performance also with a not too deep network obtaining a F1 score of 0.904. Although an increased number of layers provides a better result probably the architecture with only two layers is already adequate for home and consumer practical applications of gesture controlled multimedia systems.

V. CONCLUSIONS

A pre-processing scheme and a few deep neural architectures have been tested for the detection of a set of simple actions to be used in multimedia systems control and interaction. Based on the experiments on an internal dataset both deep neural networks performed well. Most of the samples obtained from the Kinect camera were correctly classified. However, the experiments showed that the LSTM network, even with a very small number of layers, performs better than the considered MLP network. Moreover, the results in terms of accuracy suggest that this simple approach can be usefully

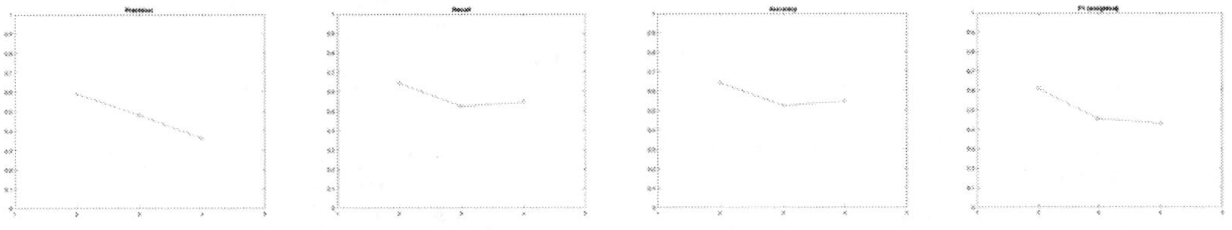

(a) Precision (b) Recall (c) Accuracy (d) F_1 weighted

Figure 3. Comparison of the performances of MLP net vs the number of network layers

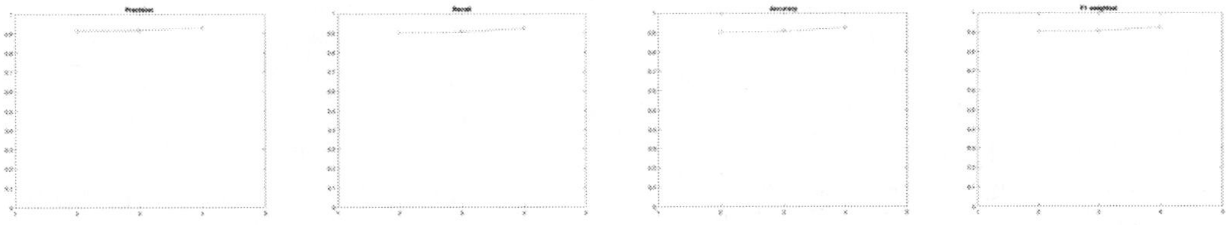

(a) Precision (b) Recall (c) Accuracy (d) F_1 weighted

Figure 4. Comparison of the performances vs number layers of LSTM network with time frame 2.5 sec

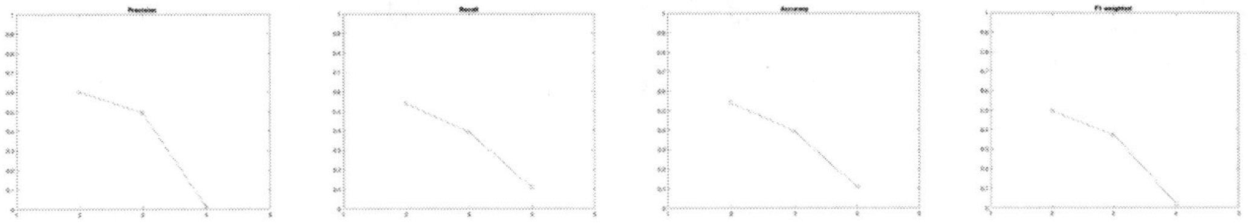

(a) Precision (b) Recall (c) Accuracy (d) F_1 weighted

Figure 5. Comparison of the performances vs number layers of LSTM network with time frame 5.0 sec

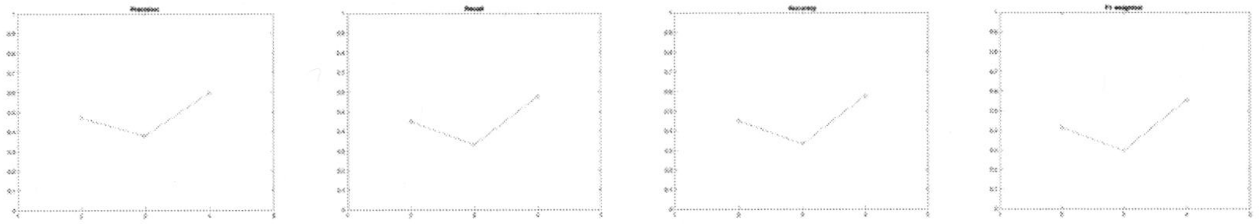

(a) Precision (b) Recall (c) Accuracy (d) F_1 weighted

Figure 6. Comparison of the performances vs number layers of LSTM network with time frame 7.5 sec

adopted to interpret user intention and control a multimedia system.

In the future, we plan to extend our experiments to more challenging datasets and compare the results obtained processing Kinect sensed skeleton data with results obtained with approaches based on standard RGB cameras. In fact, even tough results with Kinect-like cameras are very promising, it is still not clear if similar performance can be obtained with traditional cameras.

A study on the set of actions a user is more likely to learn and perform (without embarrassment) to control the system and the best mapping of these actions to functions of the system is also on the way.

VI. ACKNOWLEDGMENT

This work has been partially funded by project AMICO (ARS01_00900; CUP B46G18000390005) inside the PON "*Ricerca e Innovazione*" 2014-2020 of the Italian Ministry of

Education, University and Research (MIUR).

REFERENCES

[1] Z. Zhang, "Microsoft kinect sensor and its effect," IEEE multimedia, vol. 19, no. 2, 2012, pp. 4–10.

[2] H.-m. J. Hsu, "The potential of kinect in education," International Journal of Information and Education Technology, vol. 1, no. 5, 2011, pp. 365–370.

[3] M. Maidi and M. Preda, "Interactive media control using natural interaction-based kinect," in Acoustics, Speech and Signal Processing (ICASSP), International Conference on. IEEE, 2013, pp. 1812–1815.

[4] F.-S. Hsu and W.-Y. Lin, "A multimedia presentation system using a 3d gesture interface in museums," Multimedia tools and applications, vol. 69, no. 1, 2014, pp. 53–77.

[5] S. Sorce et al., "A touchless gestural system for extended information access within a campus," in SIGUCCS, International Conference on. ACM, 2017, pp. 37–43.

[6] S. Rhio, Herriyandi, L. Tri Fennia, and S. Edy, "Kinectation (kinect for presentation): Control presentation with interactive board and record presentation with live capture tools," Journal of Physics: Conf. Series, vol. 801, no. 012053, 2017, pp. 1–6.

[7] J.-Q. Liu, T. Tateyama, Y. Iwamoto, and Y.-W. Chen, "Kinect-based real-time gesture recognition using deep convolutional neural networks for touchless visualization of hepatic anatomical models in surgery," in International Conference on Intelligent Interactive Multimedia Systems and Services, 2018, pp. 223–229.

[8] J. C. Castillo et al., "A multi-modal approach for activity classification and fall detection," International Journal of Systems Science, vol. 45, no. 4, 2014, pp. 810–824.

[9] N. C. Krishnan and D. J. Cook, "Activity recognition on streaming sensor data," Pervasive and Mobile Computing, vol. 10, Part B, 2014, pp. 138 – 154.

[10] S. Saha, B. Ganguly, and A. Konar, "Gesture matching based improved human-computer interaction using microsofts kinect sensor," in Microelectronics, Computing and Communications (MicroCom), 2016 International Conference on. IEEE, 2016, pp. 1–6.

[11] L. Lo Presti, M. La Cascia, S. Sclaroff, and O. Camps, "Hankelet-based dynamical systems modeling for 3d action recognition," Image and Vision Computing, vol. 44, no. 1, 2015, pp. 29–43.

[12] P. Barros, G. I. Parisi, D. Jirak, and S. Wermter, "Real-time gesture recognition using a humanoid robot with a deep neural architecture," in Humanoid Robots (Humanoids), 2014 14th IEEE-RAS International Conference on. IEEE, 2014, pp. 646–651.

[13] E. Cipolla, I. Infantino, U. Maniscalco, G. Pilato, and F. Vella, "Indoor actions classification through long short term memory neural networks," in International Conference on Image Analysis and Processing. Springer, 2017, pp. 435–444.

[14] S. Loth, K. Jettka, M. Giuliani, and J. P. de Ruiter, "Ghost-in-the-machine reveals human social signals for human–robot interaction," Frontiers in psychology, vol. 6, no. 1641, 2015, pp. 1–20.

[15] F. Vella, I. Infantino, and G. Scardino, "Person identification through entropy oriented mean shift clustering of human gaze patterns," Multimedia Tools and Applications, vol. 76, no. 2, 2017, pp. 2289–2313.

[16] L. Lo Presti and M. La Cascia, "3d skeleton-based human action classification: a survey," Pattern Recognition, vol. 53, 2016, pp. 130–147.

[17] Y. LeCun, Y. Bengio, and G. Hinton, "Deep learning," Nature, vol. 521, no. 7553, 2015, pp. 436–444.

[18] S. Hochreiter and J. Schmidhuber, "Long short-term memory," Neural computation, vol. 9, no. 8, 1997, pp. 1735–1780.

[19] F. Chollet, "keras," https://github.com/fchollet/keras, 2015, [retrieved: january, 2019].

[20] M. Abadi et al., "TensorFlow: Large-scale machine learning on heterogeneous systems," 2015, [retrieved: january, 2019]. [Online]. Available: http://tensorflow.org/

[21] Theano Development Team, "Theano: A Python framework for fast computation of mathematical expressions," arXiv e-prints, vol. abs/1605.02688, May 2016, [retrieved: january, 2019]. [Online]. Available: http://arxiv.org/abs/1605.02688

Modular Testbed for KPI Monitoring in Omnidirectional Video Streaming Scenarios

Mario Montagud[1,2], Einar Meyerson[1], Isaac Fraile[1], Sergi Fernández[1]
[1]i2CAT Foundation, Media Internet Unit
[2]Universitat de València, Departament d'Informàtica
[1]Barcelona (Spain); [2]València (Spain)
e-mails: {mario.montagud, einar.meyerson, isaac.fraile, sergi.fernandez}@i2cat.net

Abstract—**The streaming of high quality and omnidirectional videos in Over-the-top (OTT) environments still faces many challenges. The research community is devoting efforts on devising optimized solutions for a variety of key aspects, such as encoding efficiency, Field-of-View (FoV) based streaming, adaptive quality switching, use of network assisted elements, etc. All these initiatives share a common denominator: it is essential to monitor relevant Quality of Service (QoS) and Quality of Experience (QoE) related metrics to better understand what are the limitations, propose appropriate solutions and corroborate the obtained performance. In this context, this paper presents a modular testbed to monitor and register Key Performance Indicators (KPIs) in (omnidirectional) video streaming scenarios, making use of the increasingly adopted Dynamic Adaptive Streaming over HTTP (DASH) technology. The paper describes the different components of the testbed and provides examples of the KPI metrics that can be collected by using it. Different application contexts where the testbed can provide valuable benefits are also discussed.**

Keywords-360° video; Dynamic Streaming over HTTP (DASH); Quality of Experience (QoE); Quality of Service (QoS).

I. INTRODUCTION

The relevance of media streaming services in the current society is beyond doubt. In the last years, the research community has been devoting efforts on overcoming a variety of existing challenges, especially when considering Over-the-Top (OTT) environments, novel (high quality) media formats and heterogeneous consumption devices. Herein, HTTP Adaptive Streaming (HAS) pull-based solutions have become dominant, due to their multiple advantages compared to traditional push-based solutions [1], such as: ubiquity, scalability and cost-efficiency. Different vendors/companies have devised their own HAS solution. Examples are HTTP Live Streaming (HLS) by Apple, HTTP Dynamic Streaming (HDS) by Adobe, and Microsoft Smooth Streaming. In order to increase the chances of worldwide deployment and maximize inter-operability, an international standardized HAS solution was proposed by Moving Picture Experts Group (MPEG) / International Organization for Standardization / International Electrotechnical Commission (ISO/IEC), called MPEG Dynamic Adaptive Streaming over HTTP (DASH) [2] [3]. Since then, DASH has been adopted by many other related standards, like Hybrid Broadcast Broadband TV (HbbTV) [4], and by many popular video streaming services.

Even though the DASH specification addresses many key aspects to provide successful and efficient streaming services, such as content preparation, delivery and signaling (briefly reviewed in Section II), many others are left open for implementers and/or service providers, but also play a key role. This in particular applies for streaming of omnidirectional (aka 360°) videos, which is more challenging than traditional video streaming in terms of bandwidth and resources consumption [5]. In this context, many open challenges for which the research community is proposing advanced solutions can be highlighted, such as:

- Encoding efficiency (e.g., [5]).
- Bandwidth optimization (e.g., [6]).
- Field-of-View (FoV) based streaming (e.g., [7]).
- Delay minimization (e.g., [8]).
- Hybrid synchronized streaming (e.g., [9]).
- Dynamic quality switching strategies (e.g., [10]).
- Use of network assisted elements (e.g., [11]).

All these research initiatives share a common denominator: it is essential to monitor relevant Quality of Service (QoS) and Quality of Experience (QoE) metrics to better understand what are the limitations, propose appropriate solutions and corroborate the obtained performance (probably in comparison with benchmarking or alternative solutions). With this premise in mind, this paper presents a modular and extensible testbed to monitor and register Key Performance Indicators (KPIs) in (omnidirectional) video streaming scenarios, making use of DASH. The testbed includes server-side components for testing with different encoding, representation and segmentation strategies for 360° videos [5], and for signaling and publishing them. Most interestingly, it includes extensions to an ad-hoc 360° video player, built on top of *dash.js*, to continuously monitor and register KPIs. Dash.js [12] is a reference JavaScript client implementation for DASH, which includes an Application Program Interface (API) to obtain relevant statistics regarding the incoming audio and video streams. The presented testbed periodically collects these statistics and other related ones, and registers them via a (remote) HTTP communication with a lightweight database for their posterior analysis.

The rest of the paper is organized as follows. Section II provides some background information and reviews other relevant platforms or testbeds for QoS/QoE evaluation in video streaming scenarios. Section III describes the presented testbed and details the KPI metrics that can be collected by using it. Different application contexts where the testbed can provide valuable benefits are also discussed. Section IV provides examples of results in a simple evaluation scenario. Finally, Section V concludes the paper, and provides some ideas for future work.

II. BACKGROUND & RELATED WORK

A. *Background Information*

The basic idea of HAS solutions, including DASH, consists of generating multiple versions (aka representations) of the media content (e.g., in different resolutions or bitrates), and divide each of these versions into a sequence of segments (aka chunks) of a short duration (e.g., from 1 to 10s). Each segment can be decoded and consumed independently of the others. In addition, an index or manifest file, called Media Presentation Description (MPD) in DASH, is created, containing the required metadata to describe the relationships between the segments, representations, and maybe between different available media assets. Both the generated contents and metadata files are stored in a conventional web server. Based on these resources, each client, by means of HTTP requests, will firstly download the manifest file and, after that, will dynamically decide which segment (of which representation) to download at each moment, based on the information contained in the manifest file and on the network (e.g., available bandwidth…) and/or end-system conditions/resources (e.g., buffer level, screen resolution, CPU load…). This process, illustrated in Figure 1, contributes to ensuring the adaptability and continuity of the media playout process.

In addition, when referring to 360º videos services, the streaming of the whole sphere in a high resolution results in an efficient approach in terms of usage of both bandwidth and computational resources. It is due to the fact that, at any moment, users do not watch the whole 360º area, but only a proportion of it, e.g. determined by the FoV of the consumption device in use (around 100º in typical Head Mounted Displays or HMDs). This has prompted the appearance of spatial segmentation strategies, which consist of dividing the 360º video in tiles (i.e., in a matrix of rows and columns), and selectively delivering them based on the current users' viewing direction [5].

The streaming of 360º videos using DASH is currently a hot research topic in order to minimize latency and bandwidth consumption, and to maximize the perceived quality based on the available resources, while enabling freedom to smoothly explore around the 360º area.

B. *Related Work*

As mentioned, many research efforts are being devoted on overcoming existing challenges for successfully delivering high quality media over non-managed OTT network environments. This is in particular true when streaming 360º video, and when making use of heterogeneous consumption devices, with dissimilar capabilities and/or resources. Due to this, the availability of a proper testbed to be able to collect and analyze relevant QoS and QoE related metrics becomes essential.

Previous works have presented related contributions in this context. The work in [13] presents a toolset for QoS evaluation of video streaming services, when using Real Time Protocol (RTP) and RTP Control Protocol (RTCP) [14] in simulated environments, using Network Simulator 2 (NS-2). That toolset is based on generating (text-based) traces of video files, feeding them into NS-2, and measuring network-level QoS metrics (such as throughput, delay, jitter or loss rate) for specific scenarios. In addition, based on the QoS statistics, reception video traces can be generated, from which an estimation of the received video can be reconstructed and played out. This also allows the measurement of the visual quality of the incoming video streams, by employing the most common objective quality metrics (like Peak Signal-to-Noise Ratio or PSNR) or subjective metrics (like Mean Opinion Score or MOS). However, that toolset is focused for its application for traditional video streaming, when using push-based RTP/RTCP protocols, in simulated environments. The work in [15] presents an emulation platform for evaluating traditional video streaming performance over Long Term Evolution (LTE) environments, by making use of NS-3, providing support for both RTP/RTCP and DASH. The advantage compared to [13] is that the use of NS-3 allows transmitting the actual video files and not traces of them, as in NS-2. However, that work is mainly focused on evaluating throughput and mobility aspects. The work in [16] presents an end-to-end DASH platform, including components for the encoding, segmentation and storage of the media contents at the server side, and for their delivery and adaptive consumption at the client side. Interestingly, that platform includes a newly developed DASH client, which includes a module to monitor KPIs and taking them into account for deciding the most proper quality for each DASH segment to be downloaded in each iteration. These KPIs include the available bandwidth, buffer fullness level, and other specific characteristics and status of the consumption device in use (like the battery level, screen resolution, and CPU load).

Acknowledging the relevance of these previous works, they do not provide support for 360º videos, do not include any database for registering and analyzing the collected statistics for multiple sessions, and they require the installation of specific applications for the clients. In the presented testbed, the player is web-based, so only a browser and Internet connectivity are required to make use of it.

III. TESTBED FOR KPI MONITORING IN DASH STREAMING

This section describes the different components of the presented testbed for KPI monitoring in omnidirectional video streaming scenarios, making use of DASH (Figure 1).

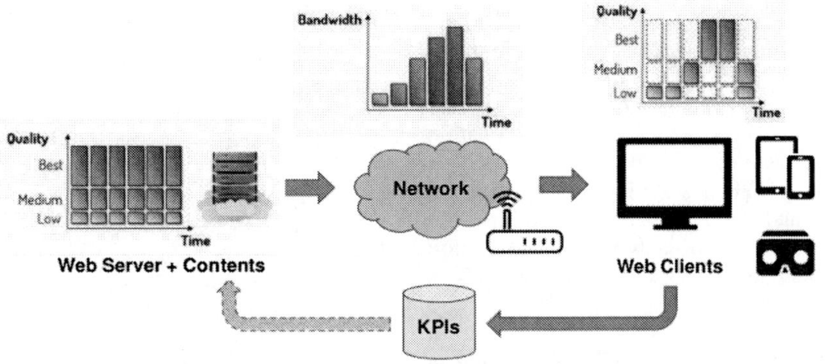

Figure 1. Overview of the testbed for KPI monitoring in (omnidirectional) video streaming services using DASH.

A. *Content Preparation and Publication*

The testbed includes different components and modules to convert input video files, whatever their format, in DASH, and to generate the related metadata. This includes processes for multi-quality encoding, conversion between Equirectangular and CubeMap Projection formats for 360° videos, generation of tiles, and segmentation of contents, with the desired configuration. This also includes the generation of the MPD for each video, and the generation / update of JSON / XML files listing and describing the available videos, respectively. Finally, all generated video and metadata files are stored on a Publication Server, which is basically an HTTP server (e.g., Apache).

More details about such processes can be found in [5][15].

B. *Content Consumption*

The video player has been developed by relying on web-based components, such as *dash.js* and *three.js* [17]. It includes the proper functionalities to select the desired contents from the Publication Server and to parse the JSON files to interpret the required metadata about such contents. If a 360° video with traditional Equirectangular Projection format is selected, the MPD can be directly processed. If a 360° video with traditional CubeMap Projection format and tiling strategies is selected, the player has to additionally process an XML file that describes the available tiles (number, distribution and qualities) [5]. In the latter case, the different tiles are retrieved as independent videos, so the player includes quality switching and inter-media synchronization mechanisms for optimizing the bandwidth consumption and perceiving the multiple meshes/videos as a single one, respectively [5].

C. *Registration of KPIs*

As mentioned, *dash.js* provides an API that allows obtaining statistics about certain KPIs. This API is used during the streaming session to get many of these KPIs, in addition to other related ones that are calculated by using the information from these KPIs, together with newly developed methods.

Although it is possible to register the gathered statistics within the memory of the web browser and/or in local files for each session, a Node.js [18] server with a MongoDB [19] database has been developed in order to register these KPIs, by making use of an HTTP-based communication protocol. This provides a better performance and stability of the player, getting persistence of the gathered statistics, and eliminates the need for having control on the consumption device on which the player has been run to retrieve the statistics. In addition, this allows gathering statistics from distributed and large-scale sessions, and enables higher flexibility for their analysis (e.g., by applying clustering or correlation strategies).

The frequency of measurement and registration of the KPIs (and thus of the communication with the database) can be configured in the player. In particular, the following KPIs are measured and registered in the presented testbed:

1) Objective / QoS-related KPIs:

- *Video Startup Latency*: Delay since the play button is clicked until the video is actually watched.
- *Evolution of Latency*: Periodic measurement of the end-to-end delay during the streaming session. *Jitter* can be also calculated as the variation of the delay.
- *Throughput*: Effective bandwidth during the session.
- Video Quality: The representation or quality index selected for each DASH segment during the session. Based on this KPI, the *Average Video Quality*, as well as the *Number, Frequency and Magnitude of Quality Switches* can be also calculated.
- *Video Stalls*: The evolution of both the playout time and the absolute time (e.g., Network Time Protocol or NTP based timestamps) can be periodically monitored. If they do not advance in accordance, and no playout control commands have been executed, it can be a sign of the occurrence of video stalls or a non-natural evolution of the playout process. This measurement determines how smooth / uninterrupted the playout is during the media session.
- *Buffer Fullness Level*: Occupancy of the playout buffer during the session (e.g., in percentages or in time units). If playout stalls happen, it can be due to buffer underflow / overflow situations. This information can be also used to select the most appropriate quality for the segments to be downloaded in order to avoid, or recover from, the undesirable underflow / overflow situations.

- *Asynchrony*: By comparing the playout and absolute times, the asynchrony (i.e., playout time difference) between media elements played out within the same device (i.e., local inter-media synchronization) and across devices (i.e., inter-device or inter-destination synchronization) can be calculated.
- *Viewing Direction*: When watching 360º videos, the current latitude and longitude angles referred to the center of the FoV can be measured. This information can be more accurate if eye-tracking functionality is available.
- *Duration of the session*: Amount of time since a video is selected and the session for this video is terminated. It can be shorter than the duration of the video if the session is terminated before the end of the video or seek forward commands have been executed, but also can can be longer if pause or seek backwards commands have been executed.

2) Subjective / QoE-related KPIs: In the presented testbed, the received audio and video files can actually be played out. Therefore, having knowledge about the obtained objective KPIs is important to better understand the allowable thresholds and ranges that can be tolerated by users, and result in satisfactory QoE levels, as well as to correlate QoS and QoE metrics. Next, key QoE related aspects are highlighted:

- *Video Startup & End-to-End Latency*: To what extent delays are tolerable by users.
- *Video stalls / pixelation / visual anomalies*: To what extent these effects are tolerable by users.
- *Overall Media Quality*: To what extent the overall media (audio / video) quality is tolerable by users, and the adopted quality switching algorithm can impact the perceived QoE (e.g., abrupt transitions can be noticeable and even annoying to users).
- *Synchronization levels*: To what extent inter-media and inter-device synchronization skews impact the perceived QoE. The impact of playout adjustments to achieve synchronization also apply in this context.
- *Smooth 360º Exploration*: To what extent the transitions between FoVs within the whole 360º area are perceived as smooth / instantaneous to users, and the perceived video quality in such transitions are perceived as acceptable. This KPI metric is relevant when using tiling / FoV-based streaming solutions, which will allow minimizing latency and bandwidth consumption compared to traditional solutions based on streaming the whole 360º area.

All these aspects can be evaluated by conducting subjective tests, making use of questionnaires, including MOS metrics or likert scales as evaluation metrics. Then, the obtained results from the subjective evaluations can be correlated with the measured objective results (e.g., when having used specific configurations and/or having forced specific conditions).

All these metrics can be extended in future release by making use of the *dash.js* API or even extending.

D. *Application Contexts*

The presented testbed has been developed to obtain valuable statistics and a deeper understanding about the performance in a variety of 360º video streaming scenarios, in which specific technical challenges are being addressed:

1) Minimization of Bandwidth and Delays

Achieving low latency is a big challenge in HAS. It is mainly due to the multi-quality encoding and segmentation processes, to the individual pull-based HTTP requests using the Transmission Control Protocol (TCP), and to the buffering strategies used at the client side.

One possible solution to overcome the delay is downloading the initial video segments in a low quality in order to start the playout as soon as possible, thus minimizing the startup delay. Another potential option is making use of HTTP/2 with *k-push* mechanism in order to get *k* video segments through a simple HTTP GET request. This avoids sending multiple independent requests, which would result in higher delays and traffic overhead. In this context, having an accurate knowledge about the magnitudes of delays and jitter becomes very valuable to set the sizes and thresholds of the playout buffer, in order to minimize latency while guaranteeing continuous playout.

Likewise, the adoption of appropriate quality switching strategies also has an impact on the perceived quality and on the experienced delays (higher quality segments require higher bandwidth and larger delays to be downloaded). Having an accurate knowledge about the available bandwidth, network delays, and other end-system's related metrics (like CPU load, buffer fullness level, number of active clients / services…) can also contribute to a more adequate media quality selection.

2) Smooth Exploration of the whole area in 360º video.

As mentioned, the streaming of the whole sphere in high quality in 360º video results in high processing load and bandwidth consumption. It also becomes inefficient, as the users can only watch a small region of the 360º area, determined by their FoV, at any time. In this context, the design and adoption of advanced encoding techniques, representation formats, spatial segmentation (i.e. tiling) strategies, and adaptive quality switching algorithms, can be proposed to maximize the quality for the current FoV, while reducing latency, bandwidth consumption and processing load [5]. However, these issues involve a key challenge, which is to guarantee a free and smooth exploration of the whole 360º area, without perceiving video stalls and abrupt video quality switches.

3) Hybrid Synchronized Multi-Screen Scenarios

It is possible to enrich conventional TV services by augmenting the traditional contents provided on the main TV with additional 360º videos to be played out on companion devices (e.g., smartphones, tablets, HMD…) [9]. This provides more personalized and immersive experiences. In such a case, it is essential to provide a synchronized playout across all involved devices, regardless of the media modality being consumed and the (broadband or broadcast) technology through which the contents are delivered.

IV. Test Scenario and Results

This section provides examples of results in a simple scenario to demonstrate the capabilities of the testbed.

A. Test Scenario

The test scenario consisted of an HTTP server (Apache) to host the player resources and media assets located at Network A, and a PC, smartphone (Samsung Galaxy S8) and HMDs (Oculus Go and Gear VR with a Samsung Galaxy S8) as consumption devices, located at Network B (same city as Network A) and connected via WiFi. The KPI database was installed on the same PC as the web server at Network A. Different traditional and 360° videos were converted to DASH. In particular, the traditional videos were encoded in 5 qualities and the 360° videos were encoded in 10 qualities, all of them with segments of 3s. This evaluation scenario adheres to the topology represented in Figure 1.

B. Test Results

First, it was assessed whether the type of video and the number of available qualities have an impact on the startup delay. For this purpose, streaming tests with a traditional and a 360° video encoded in both a single high-quality and in multiple qualities were conducted. The mean startup delays for 5 repetitions of all these conditions were: 0.558ms (traditional multi-quality video); 0.571ms (traditional single quality video); 0.781ms (360° multi-quality video); and 1.15s (360° single quality video). The results are as expected, since 360° videos are more heavy than traditional videos, and the availability of multiple qualities allows selecting lower ones at the beginning of the session to reduce startup delays.

Figure 2 shows the duration of 32 sessions for one of the videos, for sessions longer than 4min. Note that the duration of some sessions is higher than the duration of the video, which is 625s. It is due to the fact that some viewers paused the video and/or watched repetitions of some scenes.

Figure 3 represents the evolution of the throughput for three video players in a multi-screen session. In relation to this, Figure 4 represents the evolution of the selected DASH quality for two video players, one having selected a traditional video (5 qualities) and the other one having selected a 360° video (10 qualities). Figure 5 represents the evolution of the playout buffer fullness level in a multi-screen session of two devices. It can be observed that the buffers become progressively filled up to reaching a target threshold (in this case, 60%) at the beginning of the session. Then, the buffer occupancy levels slightly fluctuated during the session, being the fluctuation highly determined by the duration of the DASH segments. Finally, it can be observed that the buffers became progressively empty at the end of the session, as no more DASH segments were downloaded when reaching the end of the video.

Figure 6 represents the evolution of the asynchrony between three video players in a multi-screen session, once having activated the inter-device synchronization solution from [9], and by selecting a synchronization manager as the reference. It can be seen that the asynchrony was kept very low and stable most of the times, and that sporadic asynchrony situations occurred, but they were rapidly corrected thanks to the developed solution.

Finally, the instantaneous viewing fields for each 360° video were also measured, by monitoring the latitude and longitude angle values of the center of the FoV, every 2s. As an example, the intensity map for a specific session is represented in Figure 7. This allows representing heatmaps of viewing directions for multiple videos and sessions.

V. Conclusions & Future Work

Having an accurate and detailed knowledge about QoS and QoE related metrics in streaming services becomes essential. This work has presented a modular and extensible testbed to monitor and register KPIs when streaming omnidirectional videos using DASH. The different components of the testbed have been described, and examples of the statistics that can be collected have been provided. As future work, the testbed will be used in the different discussed application contexts, under a variety of conditions. The extension of the gathered KPIs will be also explored. In addition, real-time representation modules and advanced analysis and clustering features will be provided. As an example, the gathered KPIs will be adapted to be able to represent and compare heatmaps of viewing directions, as provided by the tool presented in [20].

Acknowledgment

This work has been funded by European Union's H2020 program, under agreement n° 761974 (ImAc project).

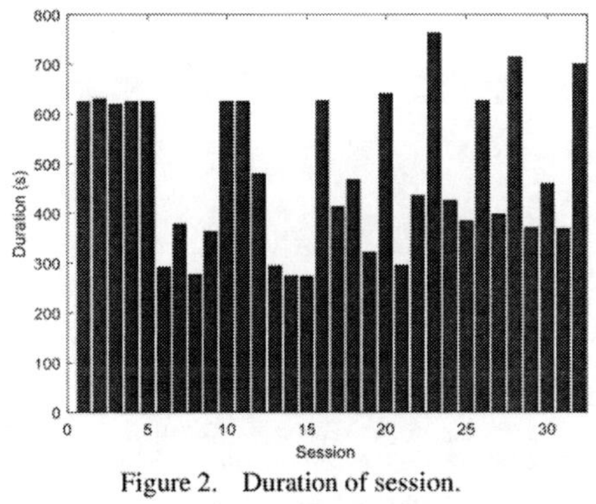

Figure 2. Duration of session.

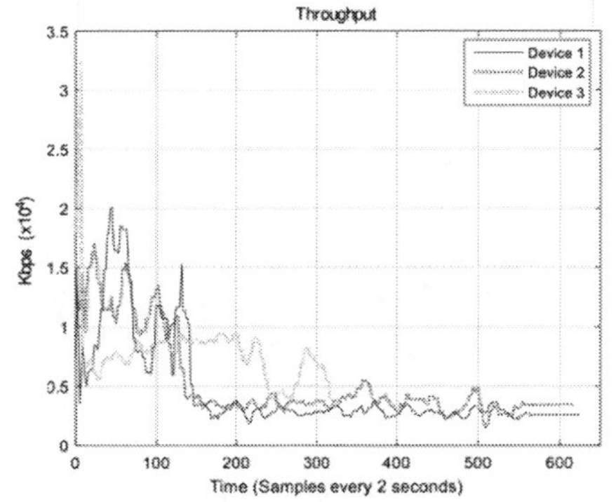

Figure 3. Evolution of throughput during the media session.

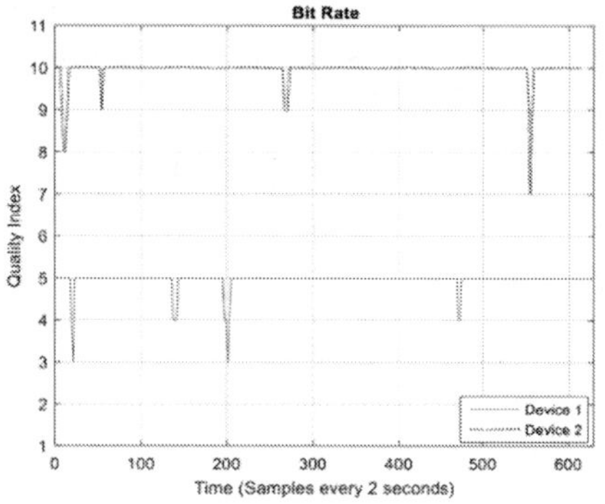

Figure 4. Evolution of the selected DASH quality.

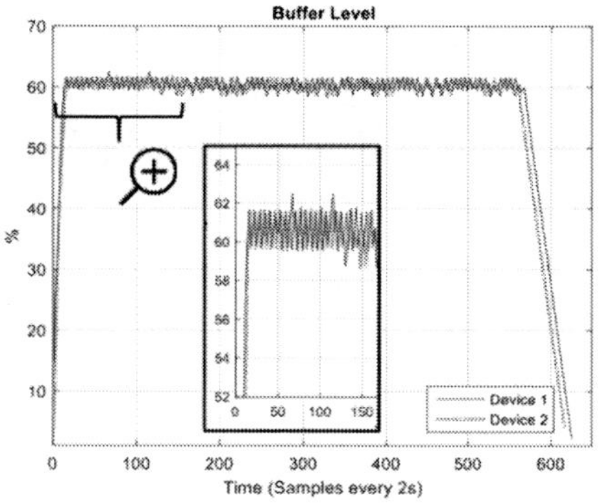

Figure 5. Evolution of the buffer fullness level.

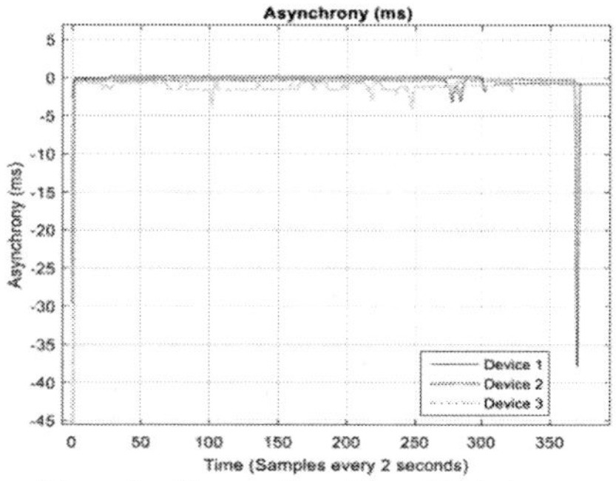

Figure 6. Playout Asynchrony Evolution.

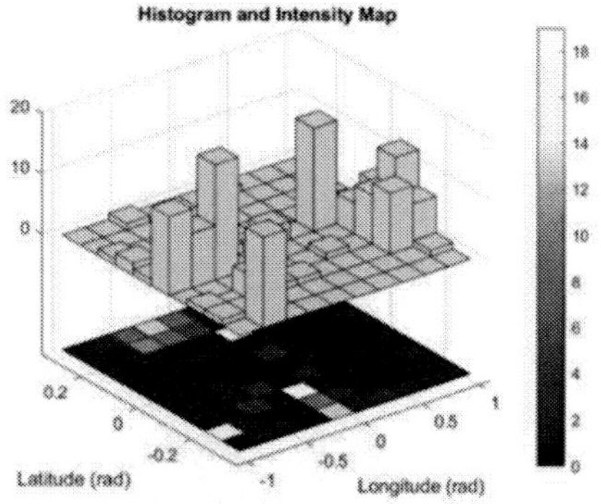

Figure 7. Intensity Map of Viewing Directions for a 360° Video.

REFERENCES

[1] A. Begen, T. Akgul, and M. Baugher, "Watching Video over the Web: Part 1: Streaming Protocols", IEEE Internet Computing, vol. 15, no. , pp. 54-63, 2010.

[2] T. Stockhammer, "Dynamic adaptive streaming over HTTP: standards and design principles", ACM MMSYS 2011, pp. 133-144 San Jose, CA (USA), February 2011.

[3] DASH: https://mpeg.chiariglione.org/standards/mpeg-dash Last Access: February 2019

[4] Hybrid Broadcast Broadband TV (HbbTV) standard specifications: https://www.hbbtv.org/resource-library/specifications/ Last Access: February 2019

[5] D. Gómez, J. A. Núñez, I. Fraile, M. Montagud, and S. Fernández, "TiCMP: A lightweight and efficient Tiled Cubemap projection strategy for Immersive Videos in Web-based players", ACM NOSSDAV'18, pp. 1-6, Amsterdam (The Netherlands), June 2018.

[6] M. Graff, C. Timmerer, and C. Mueller, "Towards Bandwidth Eficient Adaptive Streaming of Omnidirectional Video over HTTP", MMSYS'17, 261-271, Taipei (Taiwan), June 2017.

[7] X. Corbillon, G. Simon, A. Devlic, and J. Chakareski, "Viewport-adaptive navigable 360-degree video delivery", IEEE ICC 2017, pp. 1-7, Paris (France), 2017.

[8] S. Petrangeli, V. Swaminathan, M. Hosseini, and F. De Turck. "An HTTP/2-Based Adaptive Streaming Framework for 360° Virtual Reality Videos", ACM MM'17, Amsterdam (The Netherlands), 2017.

[9] J. A. Núñez, M. Montagud, I. Fraile, D. Gómez, and S. Fernández, "ImmersiaTV: an end-to-end toolset to enable customizable and immersive multi-screen TV experiences", Workshop on Virtual Reality, co-located with ACM TVX 2018, Seoul (South Korea), June 2018.

[10] A. Bentaleb, B. Taani, A.C. Begen, C. Timmerer, and R. Zimmermann, "A Survey on Bitrate Adaptation Schemes for Streaming Media over HTTP", IEEE Communications Surveys & Tutorials, pp., August 2018.

[11] E. Thomas, M. O. van Deventer, T. Stockhammer, A. C. Begen, and J. Famaey, "Enhancing MPEG DASH Performance via Server and Network Assistance", SMPTE Motion Imaging Journal, 126(1), pp. 22-27, February 2017.

[12] Dash.js: https://github.com/Dash-Industry-Forum/dash.js/wiki Last Access: February 2019

[13] F. Boronat, M. Montagud, and V. Vidal, "A More Realistic RTP/RTCP-Based Simulation Platform for Video Streaming QoS Evaluation", JMM, 7(1&2), 66-88, 2011.

[14] H. Schulzrinne, S. Casner, R. Frederick, and V. Jacobson, "RTP: a transport protocol for real-time applications", RFC 3550, July 2003.

[15] A. Fouda, et al., "Real-Time Video Streaming over NS3-based Emulated LTE Networks", International Journal of Electronics Communication and Computer Technology (IJECCT), 4(3), pp. 659-663, May 2014.

[16] D. Gómez, F. Boronat, M. Montagud, and C. Luzón, "End-to-End DASH Platform including a Network-based and Client-based Adaptive Quality Switching Module", ACM MMSYS 2016, Klagenfurt (Austria), May 2016.

[17] Three.js https://threejs.org/ Last Access: February 2019

[18] Node.js https://nodejs.org/en/ Last Access: February 2019

[19] MongoDB https://docs.mongodb.com/ Last Access: February 2019

[20] S. Rothe, T. Hoellerer, and H. Hussmann, "CVR-Analyzer: A Tool for Analyzing Cinematic Virtual Reality Viewing Patterns", ACM SUI'18, Berlin (Germany), October 2018